Understanding Interracial Unity

SAGE SERIES ON
RACE AND ETHNIC RELATIONS

Series Editor:
JOHN H. STANFIELD II
University of California at Davis

This series is designed for scholars working in creative theoretical areas related to race and ethnic relations. The series will publish books and collections of original articles that critically assess and expand upon race and ethnic relations issues from American and comparative points of view.

Understanding Interracial Unity

A Study of U.S. Race Relations

Richard W. Thomas

Sage Series on Race and Ethnic Relations

v o l u m e   1 6

SAGE Publications
International Educational and Professional Publisher
Thousand Oaks   London   New Delhi

For information address:

SAGE Publications, Inc.
2455 Teller Road
Thousand Oaks, California 91320
E-mail: order@sagepub.com

SAGE Publications Ltd.
6 Bonhill Street
London EC2A 4PU
United Kingdom

SAGE Publications India Pvt. Ltd.
M-32 Market
Greater Kailash I
New Delhi 110 048 India

Printed in the United States of America

Library of Congress Cataloging-in-Publication Data

Thomas, Richard Walter, 1939-
    Understanding interracial unity: A study of U.S. race relations / Richard W. Thomas.
        p.   cm.—(Sage series on race and ethnic relations; v. 16)
    Includes bibliographical references and index.
    ISBN 0-8039-4602-3.—ISBN 0-8039-4603-1 (pbk.)
    1. United States—Race relations.   I. Title.   II. Series.
E185.61.T464   1996
305.8'00973—dc20   95-41725

This book is printed on acid-free paper.

96   97   98   99   10   9   8   7   6   5   4   3   2   1

Sage Production Editor: Diana E. Axelsen
Sage Typesetter: Andrea D. Swanson

Contents

Series Editor's Introduction

The 1990s are becoming one of the most divisive racial eras in American history and, indeed, in the history of the world. In the midst of the symbolic and real events that characterize the racialized fissures in the American social terrain, we find few efforts to find ways to bring people together across racial lines in productive relationships, institutions, and communities. More than that, there are few models of such efforts, let alone empirical research on attempts to forge patterns of productive and functional multiethnic/racial experiences within social organizational frameworks. At best, the examples and the research we do have tended to be rooted in traditional liberal perspectives that, although well-intentioned, are of little assistance in finding effective ways to bring people together across racialized lines in the post Cold War era.

Before we launch such a new way of considering racial issues that explores common grounds and consensus building, rather than divisions and antagonism, there is need for a historical survey of models of people developing production and functional multiethnic/racial relationships, institutions, communities, and societies. This enlightening book by Richard Thomas helps to meet the need for a history of racial unity in the United States. It promises to be an opening shot in the development of a new subfield in racial and ethnic studies that attempts to explore and demonstrate ways to bring people together across racialized lines in order to build and maintain a just and pluralistic society and world.

JOHN H. STANFIELD II
Series Editor

Acknowledgments

This book has been inspired by years of interacting with people from all racial and cultural backgrounds who believe in interracial unity and cooperation and who practice it in their daily lives. I thank them for years of encouragement and support.

As always, my graduate students provided invaluable assistance to this project. They include Kimberly Andrews, Vibha Bhalla, Eric Ellison, and Charles Piotrowski. These young scholars not only assisted with research but shared valuable insights and ideas about the project.

My thanks to Fran Fowler, my secretary, who devoted long hours to the retyping and formatting of this book. She was one of my most valuable coworkers in completing this project. Thanks also to Marcia Eulenberg for editing the first draft portions of the manuscript and Lynn Anderson, who edited the entire final draft of the manuscript.

Dean Joe T. Darden of the Michigan State University Urban Affairs Programs was generous in providing graduate assistants for this project. I thank him for his continuous support.

June, my beloved wife, I thank for always encouraging me to develop my ideas concerning interracial unity and harmony. New World Associates, Inc., race relations workshops, and my associate, Jeanne Gazel, provided me with opportunities to share some of these ideas with a wider public.

I reserve my greatest thanks for the interracial fellowship of the Bahá'í community, where I first witnessed people of all racial and cultural backgrounds engaged in interracial unity and cooperation.

To the Bahá'ís of the United States
for their many years of faithful work
toward interracial unity

1

The "Other" History:
An Overview of Interracial Unity
and Cooperation in the United States

We have long since reached the point in the history of race relations in the United States at which we realize that race relations will not substantially improve unless a critical mass of concerned people from all racial backgrounds decides to dedicate their lives and resources not just to the management of periodic racial crises but also to the building of a multiracial society based on justice, interracial unity, harmony, and love. Nothing less will suffice. This is not new to countless people and organizations who, over the years, have worked unceasingly to achieve these objectives.

Even as the reader absorbs these words, thousands of people from a wide mix of racial, religious, cultural, and economic backgrounds are busy lighting their candles to dispel the darkness of racial hatred, conflict, and tension. A small stream of interracial workers has kept the torches burning to light the way through the twisting corridors of America's racial history. Unfortunately, the persistence and resilience of American racism have effectively kept these workers from influencing the masses of Americans. For example, few Americans are familiar with the history of the interracial struggle for racial justice and the role that struggle has played in the shaping of American race relations. Understandably, the history of racial oppression is better known to racial minorities and progressive whites who have had to study the history of racial oppression to better equip themselves to combat racism. However, few racial minorities and concerned whites are aware of the other side of American race relations—the interracial struggle for racial justice; cooperative efforts among blacks and whites for the social and economic advancement of African Americans; and the development of love, harmony, and fellowship within various religious communities. This is "the other tradition" of American race relations, the one that has the greatest potential to inspire good race relations in contemporary America. Understanding this tradition of American race relations and using its lessons can help us break out of the contemporary cycle of racial polarization and fragmentation and move into a cycle of racial unity and harmony.

The history of antiracism is a key component of the other tradition of American race relations. Herbert Aptheker (1975), in a seminal essay on the history of antiracism in the United States, mentioned the lack of research on this topic: "There is . . . almost no literature treating of the history of anti-racist thought in the United States. . . . A history of anti-racism, in any complete sense, would reflect opposition to racist attitudes and practices towards the Indians and Africans and the African-Americans" (pp. 16-18). Although this book is not a history of anti-racism, it includes significant strands of that history.

Many whites who were involved in movements in interracial unity and cooperation were not antiracists. In fact, some held racist views. Many of them became antiracists as a result of their interracial work, however. On the other hand, a number of whites with very little inter-racial experience were strong antiracists. In short, any history of inter-racial unity and cooperation in the United States must include a history of antiracism.

This book is based on the belief that the more we know about the history of interracial unity and cooperation, the better equipped we will be in our efforts to improve race relations in contemporary society. This history will play a vital role in transforming the racial perceptions of many blacks and whites who have lost faith in the possibility of improving race relations in the near future. Blacks will come to understand that throughout the history of white racial oppression, white allies fought alongside blacks in the struggle against racism. In that struggle, many bonds of genuine love and affection were created, thus transcending the racist history that constantly bore down on them. Young African Americans today, whether on college campuses or on inner-city streets, who have lost faith in Dr. Martin Luther King, Jr.'s dream of the "beloved community" of blacks and whites struggling together against racial oppression, might find in these pages convincing examples of how many blacks and whites struggled together for decades to overcome racial oppression.

In reading this history, whites will discover that, as pervasive as white oppression was, there were always bands, however small, of bold and courageous whites who chose to stand shoulder to shoulder with their black brothers and sisters in the struggle for racial justice and the advancement of African Americans. Many of these whites understood the historical connection between their participation in the interracial struggle and the spiritual transformation of American society. They could see that racial oppression prevented African Americans from joining in the "great American dream." Throughout the history of the interracial struggle for racial justice and the advancement of African Americans—from the antislavery struggle to the present interracial coalitions—progressive whites have made decisive moral choices that have placed them on the side of justice and moral decency. The present generation of whites needs to know this history so it will be motivated not by guilt but by a firm knowledge that it can, if it so chooses, claim its birthright and join the contemporary struggle for racial justice and interracial unity, harmony, and fellowship.

Another belief on which this book is based—a vision that drives it—is that the United States, as one of the first multiracial democracies in the modern world, has a major role to play in demonstrating to the world how a very diverse population can live, work, and play together, and by doing so can lift the entire society to new heights of human interaction. The world has been watching race relations in the United States for centuries. As a result of recent racial tensions and conflicts, the world has seen the worst side of our racial history. The other, less dramatic, side—the protracted interracial struggle for racial justice and the steady expansion of interracial harmony and fellowship in countless sectors of human interaction in workplaces and neighborhoods, spiritual communities, and friendships—goes largely unnoticed. (For some examples of this tradition, see Askew, 1979; Orenstein, 1979; Schofield & McGivern, 1979; Steele, 1979; Terkel, 1992.)

These positive interracial interactions hold the greatest promise, not just for better race relations in the United States but also for better human relations for the world. The United States is a human laboratory where we have been engaged in one of the greatest experiments in multiracial interaction in history. As the world continues to shrink into a neighborhood of increasing interdependency, where the quality of interaction will determine the quality of our lives, we must learn the lessons of unity, harmony, love, and fellowship or we will perish. The history of interracial unity, harmony, and cooperation in the United States can provide some valuable lessons on how to survive in this setting.

Accepting a positive approach to the present state of race relations will not be easy. Given the sad state of race relations in the United States, the reader would be justified in dismissing the history of interracial harmony as irrelevant. The heart of the issue is racism and racial polarization and fragmentation. How will this approach address the issues of black poverty, crime, and hopelessness? How will it address the still formidable racial barrier of white racism, which all too often places barriers in the path of racial minorities struggling to pull themselves out of poverty and misery? How will this approach bridge the widening gap between black central cities and white suburbs, these two "alien nations," that for at least a generation have lost touch with their common humanity? Given some of the views of the best and most experienced scholars in the field of contemporary race relations, it is hardly surprising that the average American of any color would have little faith in interracial unity and harmony.

In their national best-selling book, *Chain Reaction: The Impact of Race, Rights, and Taxes on American Politics,* Thomas Byrne Edsall and Mary D. Edsall (1992) point to a sad but true fact regarding contemporary race relations in the United States:

> Racial animosity can be found in community meetings, courtrooms, American Legion bars, political rallies, softball clubs, PTA sessions, public parks, and private gatherings across America. . . . On a daily level, a substantial number of whites view blacks as dangerous and as antagonistic to basic American values. . . . These whites do not distinguish between blacks of different social and economic classes. . . . A significant number of blacks— the most middle-class and successful among them—view whites as not only attempting to evade responsibility for the continuing consequences of slavery and discrimination, but as the entrenched wielders of power in a lopsided white-only system. (p. 285)

Other scholars have voiced similar views on the state of race relations. In his book, *Two Nations: Black and White, Separate, Hostile, Unequal,* Andrew Hacker (1992) writes,

A huge racial chasm remains, and there are few signs that the coming century will see it closed. A century and a quarter after slavery, white America continues to ask of its black citizens an extra patience and perseverance that whites have never required of themselves. So the question for white Americans is essentially moral: is it right to impose on members of an entire race a lesser start in life, and then to expect from them a degree of resolution that has never been demanded from your own race? (p. 219)

Douglas S. Massey and Nancy A. Denton (1993), in *American Apartheid: Segregation and the Making of the Underclass,* make a strong case for the role of residential segregation in the making of the black underclass. According to them,

The failure to end segregation will perpetuate a bitter dilemma that has long divided the nation. If segregation is permitted to continue, poverty will inevitably deepen and become more persistent within a large share of the black community, crime and drugs will become more firmly rooted, and social institutions will fragment further under the weight of deteriorating conditions. (p. 235)

These conditions will increase racial inequality, which will lead to white fear, which, in turn, will reinforce racial prejudices and result in an increase in white racial hostility toward blacks, "making the problems of racial justice and equal opportunity even more insoluble." Massey and Denton see the solution in dismantling the ghetto:

Unless we face up to the difficult task of dismantling the ghetto, the disastrous consequences of residential segregation will radiate outward to poison American society. Until we decide to end the long reign of American apartheid, we cannot hope to move forward as people and a nation. (p. 236)

Other scholars writing about the state of race relations acknowledge the same problems of racism, although differing somewhat on the solutions. John Hope Franklin (1993) states, "Without any pretense of originality or prescience, with less than a decade left in this century, I venture to state categorically that the problem of the twenty-first century will be the problem of the color line" (p. 5). This conclusion arises, Franklin argues, "from the fact that by any standard of measurement or evaluation, the problem has not been solved in the twentieth century, and this becomes part of the legacy and burden of the next century" (p. 5).

He suggests that the first thing that we should do is "to confront our past and see it for what it is. It is a past that is filled with some of the ugliest possible examples of racial brutality and degradation in human history. We need to recognize it for what it is and not explain it away, excuse it, or justify it" (p. 74). Having done this,

> We should then make a good-faith effort to turn our history around so that we can see it in front of us, so that we can avoid doing what we have done for so long. If we do that, whites will discover that African Americans possess the same humanity that other Americans possess, and African Americans will discover that white Americans are capable of the most sublime expressions of human conduct of which all human beings are capable. (pp. 74-75)

To reach a place where this is possible, Franklin advises, we will "need to do everything possible to emphasize the positive qualities that all of us have, qualities which we have never utilized to the fullest, but which we must utilize if we are to solve the problem of the color line in the twenty-first century" (p. 75).

Perhaps one reason why the majority of blacks and whites have not been able to emphasize and use their positive qualities is that they are not aware of the part of their shared history in which the best, the most courageous, and the most noble blacks and whites shared major portions of their lives in interracial struggles for racial justice. These black and white men and women who rode the antislavery circuits, hid slaves, marched together against racial discrimination, fought court battles, and built racially integrated labor unions and political coalitions represent the most "positive qualities" to be found in our history.

Cornel West (1994) provides an understanding of the burden of racism and the need for hope. In *Race Matters,* he explains that his aim is "to revitalize our public conversation about race, in light of our paralyzing pessimism and stultifying cynicism as a people" (p. 158). As a radical democrat, he believes, "that it is late—but maybe not too late—to confront and overcome the poverty and paranoia, the despair and distrust that haunt us" (p. 158). West recognizes that

> in these downbeat times, we need as much hope and courage as we do vision and analysis; we must accent the best of each other even as we point out the vicious effects of our racial divide. . . . We simply cannot enter the twenty-first century at each other's throats, even as we acknowledge the weighty forces of racism. (p. 159)

We have arrived at a

> crucial crossroad in the history of this nation—and we either hang together by combating these forces that divide and degrade us or we hang separately. Do we have the intelligence, humor, imagination, courage, tolerance, love, respect, and will to meet the challenge? Time will tell. None of us alone can save the nation or the world. But each of us can make a positive difference if we commit ourselves to do so. (p. 159)

All of the scholars just mentioned agree that racism continues to be a formidable problem in American society. Yet there is little consensus as to what should be done. Although they all agree that racism is still a major problem threatening to dog our tracks into the future, they do not refer to that part of our past that might offer us some answers. It is almost as if they believe that all the past and present can show us are the failures of policies, the lack of political will, or both. For example, Massey and Denton (1993) feel that all that is needed for their recommended policies is "political will." "Given the will to end segregation, the necessary funds and legislative measures will follow. But political will is precisely what has been lacking over the decades, and resistance to desegregation continues to be strong" (p. 234). How do we develop political will to address residential segregation in a racially polarized and fragmented society? Are there lessons we can learn from the history of interracial struggles or from countless examples of blacks and whites working out these problems in various settings at various times?

If there has ever been a need for understanding the best of our interracial history, it is now, when we are so sorely lacking bold and courageous examples of interracial unity and harmony in pursuit of racial justice. I see no other way out of the present racial crisis but to tap into this tradition and, armed with a belief in the organic unity of the human race, to go forth and fashion a movement for interracial unity and harmony. Without such a firm belief in interracial unity and harmony and a movement to carry it forth to millions of people of all racial backgrounds, crime and hopelessness will increase, the gap between black central cities and white suburbs will grow wider, and another generation of blacks and whites will move even farther away from their common humanity. We must learn from our common history of interracial unity and cooperation. We must seek to understand how and why blacks and whites choose to work together when they do.

This introduction would not be complete if the reader did not know the source of my inspiration for this book. I have always been interested in racial justice and the unity of racially and culturally diverse peoples. For over 30 years, I have been a member of the multiracial-multicultural Bahá'í community in the United States. As a young African American living in Detroit in the early 1960s, in the midst of racial confrontation and rising black separatism, I came across this community of racially and culturally diverse people who believe in the organic oneness of the human race and who take every opportunity to live this principle. They make mistakes, but because they are driven by the vision of interracial unity, harmony, love, and fellowship, they continue to struggle to unify people from diverse backgrounds. Throughout the 1960s, 1970s, 1980s, and into the 1990s, when racial polarization and fragmentation were driving blacks and whites apart, local Bahá'í communities around the country were holding racial unity picnics, rallies, and scores of other race-related activities. (For some examples of the interracial work of the Bahá'í community in the United States, see Thomas, 1993, pp. 113-177.)

As I found myself interacting with people from racially and culturally diverse backgrounds, I discovered how easy it was to get to know them and love them as members of the human family. For years, I participated in the process of community building, of sharing pain and joy and celebrating a common humanity with this spiritual family. Outside this multiracial-multicultural spiritual fellowship, however, there existed little sharing of community across racial and cultural lines. Most blacks and whites had little interest in building a shared community. Although in most cases blacks were much more willing than whites to build interracial communities, more and more blacks were rejecting any suggestion of the failed integration attempts of the 1960s. Only in the Bahá'í community could I find the hope and vision of interracial unity, harmony, and fellowship. As a result of these experiences in interracial community building, I learned that interracial unity—particularly between blacks and whites—is possible. For over three decades, I observed and participated in numerous Bahá'í interracial activities. The more I observed this process, the more I became convinced that interracial unity, harmony, and fellowship are possible throughout the United States if the right social and spiritual conditions are at work. All that is needed is a shared belief in the organic oneness of the human race and the will and determination to live out this belief in all aspects of one's life.

The Bahá'í community's focus on interracial unity has provided a range of opportunities for scholars and practitioners to discuss the importance of applying this approach to the racial crisis in the United States. In November 1990, the Association for Bahá'í Studies held a conference in Atlanta, Georgia, titled "Models of Racial Unity." The purpose of this conference was to explore models of racial unity rather than the traditional focus of racial crises and conflicts. The Bahá'í community in the United States for decades had been trying to model this approach, with varying degrees of success. The Bahá'ís have spent considerable time applying this approach to their own internal racial problems and are still in the process of doing so.

One of the first fruits of the conference was a joint project, "Models of Unity: Racial, Ethnic, and Religious," conducted in the spring of 1991 by the Human Relations Foundation of Chicago and the American National Spiritual Assembly. The purpose of this joint project was

> to find examples of efforts that have successfully brought different groups of people together in the greater Chicago area. Both organizations were concerned about the prominence of publicity about interracial violence, confrontation, and conflicts and were convinced that examples of interracial harmony, peaceful coexistence, and unity were common, yet less well known. (*Models of Unity,* 1992, p. 1)

The sponsors of the project took a bold first step in this fairly new direction by explicitly stating that "scholarship on interracial interaction has explored the conflicts in detail, but has done little to examine the roots of interracial unity" (p. 1).

In April 1992, several months after the publication of the joint project report, the National Spiritual Assembly of the Bahá'ís of the United States sponsored a Race Unity Conference at the Carter Presidential Center in Atlanta, Georgia. The purpose of the conference was stated thus:

> During the next few years the City of Atlanta will be the focus of efforts to transform its society and to alleviate social illnesses that affect the city and the entire nation. We believe that these efforts cannot succeed if the races are not united in common purpose and vision. The purpose of this conference is to explore specific actions which may be taken by different groups and institutions to establish racial unity as the foundation for the transformation of our society. (*Visions of Race Unity,* 1992)

My many years of involvement in these kinds of Bahá'í efforts to promote interracial unity is what motivated me to study and teach about interracial unity and cooperation. As a young professor at Michigan State University in the early 1970s, I began teaching race relations courses in which I shared my belief and interest in interracial unity with students. On numerous occasions, I have lectured on the need to study the history of interracial unity and cooperation alongside the history of racial oppression. In several publications, I have discussed both interracial conflict and cooperation as key aspects of race relations in the United States (Darden, Hill, Thomas, & Thomas, 1987; Thomas, 1987, 1993). Over the years, I have tried to teach race-related courses that focus both on the history of racial conflicts and on the history of interracial unity. Whenever possible, I have formed interracial research teams in my classes so that students from diverse backgrounds have the opportunity to learn the value of working with racially diverse people on common projects. Most of the research topics have focused on some aspect of the history of interracial unity and cooperation. Students have written on interracial cooperation within the antislavery movement; the labor movement; and the worlds of music, sports, and politics. This has been a very rewarding experience for students who have spent most of their lives in all-black or all-white environments only to realize, after they arrive at a Big Ten university, that the world is far more racially and culturally diverse than they had ever imagined. Whenever possible, I have tried to use my classroom to prepare students for life in an increasingly racially and culturally diverse global community. By teaching students about both racial oppression and the interracial struggle against racial injustice, I have been able to provide them with a knowledge of racial oppression and an understanding of how brave souls of both races worked to overcome it.

At present, I teach a core course in the Urban Affairs Programs at Michigan State University that focuses on race, poverty, and social policy. For several years, I have attempted to discuss these issues within the framework of the principle of the organic unity of the human race. When applied to the persistent problems of racism and poverty, this principle illuminates the basic cause of these problems as the lack of genuine unity and fellowship among racial groups. As simplistic as this may sound, this lack of unity and fellowship among suburban whites and inner-city blacks is contributing to the ever increasing racial polarization and fragmentation in present-day society. The lack of political will referred to by Massey and Denton (1993) is, at bottom, a lack of spiritual connectedness between blacks and whites. White suburbanites all too often see themselves as totally unconnected to the black segment of their humanity that sometimes lives just a few miles away in crime-ridden and violence-ridden ghettos. Few suburban whites feel any real connection to the misery of inner-city blacks. They delude themselves into believing that the world of black poverty, crime, and misery will not ultimately affect their lives. They believe that they are safe on their white suburban islands and that they are protected by a wide moat. White children reared on these suburban islands grow to maturity thinking that predominantly white suburbs are, or should be, the norm for the rest of society, that black inner cities are creations of black laziness, crime, and violence that must be kept at a safe distance by any means necessary. These are the white youth that I have encountered in classes for over 25 years, who come armed with racist beliefs of all kinds. These beliefs were given to them by parents who either fled the central cities during the turbulent 1960s or were themselves reared in suburban racial isolation.

These white youths must be taught that they are connected to their black inner-city counterparts, whether or not they want to be. They must understand that, in a world that is growing smaller and more interdependent each moment due to advanced technology and communications, no person, racial group, or nation can function as an island. Teaching white students about the history of the interracial struggle for racial justice and how that struggle contributed to the social, economic, political, cultural, and spiritual development of the larger society helps them appreciate the organic unity of the human race as applied to the present state of race relations. This history exposes them to the key role that whites played in improving race relations.

In addition, young whites need to be exposed to the white heroes and heroines of the interracial struggle for racial justice who dedicated their lives to the long struggle for human rights in the United States. They need to develop a deep appreciation of the motives of such whites as the Grimké sisters and how they felt about the racial oppression of blacks at a time when the vast majority of white Americans believed that slavery was a normal and justifiable condition for people of African descent. Why did these whites side with the black slaves against the white masters and the vast majority of their white peers? What motivated them? What was the source of their transformation?

Why was John Brown so fanatical in his determination to end slavery, even at the expense of his own life, the lives of friends, and the lives of members of his own family? Why did Thaddeus Stevens fight for the protection of the rights of blacks throughout most of his long political career? Why did the early white founders of the National Association for the Advancement of Black People (NAACP) bother to worry about the plight of a racial group that the majority of whites wanted to ignore? I could go on, but the point is this: These whites represented a spiritual elite within the larger white society that chose to take a stand for racial justice. In doing so, they challenged the racial mores of white society and forced it to confront its spiritual contradictions. In a way, these white heroes and heroines of the interracial struggle for racial justice saved the souls of all white Americans by challenging them to assume a more spiritual relationship with blacks. Centuries of white racial oppression of both African Americans and Native Americans, codified in law and embedded in custom, had eroded all sense of human fellowship. Only an interracial struggle for racial justice could begin the healing process necessary for achieving genuine racial unity and harmony among whites and people of color in the United States.

As the present generation of whites discovers the role that past progressive whites played in the interracial struggle for racial justice, I hope that they will emulate their progressive predecessors by joining in the present interracial struggle for racial justice, interracial unity, harmony, and fellowship. By doing so, this present generation of whites will be aligning themselves with one of the greatest social and spiritual movements of modern times—the one that has the greatest possibility of taking the United States and the world to a higher stage of human interaction.

Some African Americans find it difficult to see how the history of the African American struggle overlaps with the interracial struggle for racial justice and the advancement of African Americans. One of the most valuable insights African Americans can gain from the study of the history of interracial unity and cooperation is the role of whites in the struggle. This history can expose black youth to examples of courageous and self-sacrificing whites who dedicated their lives to combating racism and improving the social, economic, and political conditions of African Americans. At a time when we are shaking off the effects of two decades of resurgent white racism and when racial segregation and polarization between blacks and whites have reached record highs, African Americans need to know that there have always been whites willing to share the burden of opposing racism because they truly cared for African Americans as fellow human beings; and they need to know that there still are whites who carry on this proud tradition.

Black students also need to understand the history of interracial unity and cooperation and the history of the interracial struggle for racial justice and the advancement of blacks. The emergence of predominantly black central cities has created the same isolation that characterizes predominantly white suburbs. This isolation breeds more disconnectedness between suburban whites and inner city blacks. Few inner-city blacks see any relevance in appeals for racial unity. Understandably, their concerns are for more jobs, better housing, and less crime and violence. The harsh realities of their lives are such that they cannot afford the time and energy to explore the benefits that they would derive from applying the principle of interracial unity and cooperation to their conditions. Yet, without interracial unity and cooperation between white suburbs and black cities, the massive resources needed to address these conditions will not be forthcoming.

Because there is no other choice but to seek interracial unity, I have attempted to teach black and white students how to apply the principle of the organic oneness of the human race to racially polarized and fragmented communities. The most effective way to begin this process is to familiarize students with the history of the interracial struggle for racial justice.

The present generation of black and white leaders might benefit from this book. Blacks and whites are probably more alienated from each other than at any other time in the recent history of race relations. There has been a widening gap between traditional allies in the interracial struggle for racial justice, such as African American and Jewish leaders. Sensitive issues such as affirmative action have blinded these traditional allies to the crucial lessons of interracial problem solving found in the rich history of the interracial struggle for racial justice.

To be certain, during each period of history, there have been significant conflicts over issues on which African American and Jewish leaders failed to agree, but in many cases, the leaders were able to transcend certain differences because they shared a common vision. This common vision has been eroded by powerful forces of racial polarization and fragmentation. Far too many African American and Jewish leaders have retreated to their tribal zones for an illusory respite from the inescapable necessity of working together for the common goal of interracial unity.

The retreat of these leaders to their tribal zones reinforces racial polarization and fragmentation in the larger society by weakening the forces of interracial unity and harmony. Both African American and Jewish leaders have a responsibility to educate their communities about the role that African American and Jewish leaders have played in the interracial struggle for racial justice and the advancement of African

Americans. Both African American and Jewish leaders must tap into the lessons of this struggle so they can assist each other in improving the present state of race relations.

African American leaders must educate the black masses to understand how their present and future social, economic, and political conditions are organically linked to those of other racial and ethnic groups in the larger society. These leaders must introduce the principle of the organic unity of the human race into the ongoing discussion of the present state of the black community so that the black community can see its connectedness to other racial groups. The more the black community can appreciate its organic relationship with other racial and cultural groups and how such a relationship can enhance its growth and development, the more the black community will appreciate the necessity of participating in biracial and multiracial-multicultural coalitions. Jewish as well as non-Jewish white leaders who are interested in addressing the present state of race relations must work much harder to overcome the effects of the last two decades of racial polarization and fragmentation. They will have to raise the consciousness of their communities by exposing them to the historical roles that certain whites have played in the interracial struggle for racial justice. These leaders must introduce their young people to those bold and courageous whites who dedicated their lives to this struggle so that they in turn will be inspired to join in the contemporary movement for interracial justice, unity, and harmony.

I hope that this book will help both African American and white leaders appreciate the historical benefits of interracial unity and cooperation by pointing out how, historically, blacks and whites accomplished far more in the struggle against racism by working together for racial justice and the advancement of African Americans than they could have achieved separately. This should not be interpreted to mean that the African American community could not have fought these battles by itself. Rather, it means that, without white allies at critical stages of the protracted struggles against racism, the struggle would have been far more difficult and the larger society would have been deprived of much needed models of interracial unity and cooperation.

Many contemporary African American leaders are losing faith in interracial coalitions as a viable means of combating racism and eliminating black poverty. Therefore, it is important that they study historical examples of interracial coalitions that addressed these problems with varying degrees of success. For example, contemporary African American leaders can learn from the strategies and methods employed by blacks and whites in the antislavery movement, the NAACP, the National Urban League, the Labor Movement, the Democratic Party, and the civil rights movement. These movements and organizations can offer African American leaders invaluable lessons for framing the next stage of the interracial struggle for racial justice and the advancement of African Americans. African American leaders can learn to avoid the mistakes of the past in working across racial lines; they can inspire others with the visions that have kept them moving forward against incredible obstacles. At a time when racial polarization is widening the perceptual and ideological chasm between many black and white leaders, historical examples of interracial cooperation between black and white leaders are crucial to renew faith in the present struggle.

Many contemporary progressive white leaders are also becoming disillusioned with the present state of race relations; they do not know where to stand on the many complex racial issues of the day, such as affirmative action. With the steady attacks on white racial liberalism from some black leaders and conservative and neoconservative white leaders, progressive white leaders often find it difficult to take a solid position on key racial issues. Much of this difficulty stems from progressive white leaders' lack of moral vision on key issues of racial justice. They either have forgotten or never knew the history of those bold and courageous whites who seldom wavered in their moral position on the key racial issues of their day. Present-day progressive white leaders must become familiar with the heroic white figures of the past and walk boldly in their steps. They can do this by joining in the interracial movement for racial justice, interracial unity, and cooperation.

As more white and black leaders become familiar with the tradition of interracial unity and cooperation, they will gain the courage to reach out in genuine love and fellowship across the racial chasm that divides them and their communities. Much depends on the ability of blacks and whites of this generation to heal the racial wounds inflicted on present-day society by decades of white racism and black bitterness. Blacks and whites can accomplish this task only if they have before them examples of courageous black and white souls who walked arm in arm over the decades to combat racism and build a just multiracial society. There is an urgent need to train leaders from all racial and ethnic communities in the art of community building across racial, ethnic, and cultural boundaries. We can begin this task by exposing the current generation of young leaders to the history of black-white cooperation.

There is yet another purpose for this book. For far too long, the field of race relations has been dominated by studies that focus on the worst aspects of race relations in the United States. Much of this focus has been dictated by the urgent need to show the negative effects of racism on racial minorities. Research interest in racism has contributed to the struggle against racism. As a result of a widespread interest in the field of race relations in the United States, racial studies has become one of the most developed fields within the social sciences and the humanities. This field is driven, however, by "racial problems" rather than a vision of what race relations could be like in the future. Few visionaries are in the field of race relations. Instead, endless lines of racial doomsayers specialize in uncovering layers of racial conflicts, tensions, and hatred. Scholars and race relations "experts" compete on a wide range of racial issues. We wait in vain for visionaries who can lift our sights to the mountaintop spoken of by Dr. Martin Luther King, Jr. Without such visionaries, race relations in the United States can only get worse. Few contemporary scholars have the vision to match their studies. They can inform us, as they have done for decades. The problem of race relations in the United States is not due to a lack of scholarly research and publication but rather to a lack of a powerful vision and spiritual force that will radically improve the present state of race relations.

One final purpose of this book remains to be stated. I am not just an academic; I am also a long-time consultant in the field of race relations. It has been in my role as a consultant that I have been able to appreciate the connection between knowledge and practice. For years, I have used the history of race relations to help clients understand specific racial problems. In fact, this book was written in large part to highlight some of the history of interracial unity and cooperation so that I could better apply the lessons of the past to the problems of the present to create a more racially just and unified society in the future. In one sense, this book is a brief guide to the history of interracial unity and cooperation in the hope that the reader will find it useful in working to improve the present state of race relations.

ORGANIZATION OF THIS BOOK

The book is organized around five major themes that have proven useful in teaching race-related topics on campus and in conducting race relations workshops in the larger community. It is not designed to be a comprehensive historical study of interracial unity and cooperation. Rather, it is designed to encourage readers to examine more carefully the valuable lessons to be learned from the blacks and whites who have worked together over the centuries.

Chapter 2 is a general survey of interracial unity from the colonial times to the present. The main purpose of this chapter is to expose the reader to examples of blacks and whites working together in various historical settings. Chapter 3 examines how certain modes of interracial cooperation have maintained white racism or other aspects of the traditional racial status quo.

Chapter 4 examines how the rising expectations and demands of blacks have affected two major modes of interracial cooperation. Interracial unity and cooperation are developmental, not static, and the rising expectations and demands of blacks are, more often than not, major developmental stages of modes of interracial cooperation.

Chapters 5 and 6 examine the role of whites in the interracial struggle for racial justice and the advancement of African Americans in the 19th and 20th centuries. Chapter 5 examines the roles of four outstanding whites during the 19th century who dedicated much of their lives to the struggle against racism and the advancement of African Americans. Chapter 6 presents profiles of dedicated whites who carried the white abolitionist legacy well into the 20th century. These chapters were written for the express purpose of providing white role models to the present generation of whites so that it will have the opportunity to make a moral choice: to perpetuate racial injustice by ignoring it or to encourage racial justice by supporting it. These chapters can also be helpful to blacks who have lost faith in whites in the interracial struggle for racial justice and the advancement of African Americans.

Chapter 7 is an attempt to connect the history of interracial unity and cooperation with the present state of race relations. I hope that this chapter will help the reader see the significance of applying to specific racial problems some of the lessons learned from this brief history of interracial unity and cooperation.

2

Interracial Unity From
Colonial Times to the Present

THE COLONIAL AND
REVOLUTIONARY PERIODS

In 17th-century Northampton, Virginia, free Africans and English were interacting with "one another on terms of relative equality for two generations," which led two historians to remark that "the possibility of a genuinely multiracial society became a reality during the years before Bacon's Rebellion in 1676" (Breen & Innes, 1980, p. 5). By the end of the 17th century and the emergence of the slave codes of 1705, all hopes of such a multiracial society were doomed. The codes marked the period in which "the tragic fate of Virginia's black population was finally sealed" (p. 5). The preceding decades do have much to teach us about the lost possibilities of achieving a multiracial society based on interracial unity, cooperation, and harmony. Understanding the "other tradition" in American relations should begin with understanding these lost possibilities, because they suggest that had slavery not been such a powerful and pervasive force in the shaping of the early history of the United States, the other tradition might have prevailed.

It is necessary to be cautious in putting forth this theory of race. An attempt to understand a historical string of interesting circumstances might prevent people from falling into the trap of reading the state of modern-day race relations into the situations of the past. Breen and Innes (1980) provide such examples in their discussion of 17th-century court decisions on interracial gangs of runaway laborers that they consider to be cases of "highly instructive interracial cooperation" (p. 29). These cases of black and white laborers running away together are perhaps some of the first examples of the other tradition of race relations. Explaining this early form of black-white cooperation, Breen and Innes make this point:

> The need for cooperation increased once the group set out on its journey. The laborers had lived in the colony only a short time, and their knowledge of the winds and currents was consequently limited. The irresponsibility of any man placed the lives of all in jeopardy. The importance of strong personal ties would not have been reduced if these runaways had taken to the woods, where Indians waited to capture or kill the fugitives. Moreover, if the workers did not husband their provisions well, they could starve. Despite these formidable obstacles, blacks and whites persisted in running away together. (pp. 29-30)

These joint black-white escapes worried the House of Burgesses, which in 1661 attempted to stop them by enacting legislation that stated that if any English servant ran away with a black, the former would have to serve " 'for the time of the said negroes absence as they are to do for their own' " (Breen & Innes, 1980, p. 30). The legislation did not work, and "the possibility of large-scale interracial cooperation continued to worry the leaders of Virginia" (p. 30). Ten years later, leaders' worries over interracial cooperation of runaways were increased by their abortive attempts to recapture a group of fugitive slaves who, they feared, might be joined by other blacks, whites, and Indians. Furthermore, as Breen and Innes argue,

> For every group of mixed runaways who came before the courts there were doubtless many more poor whites and blacks who cooperated in smaller, less daring ways on the plantation. . . . These forms of interaction did not mean that white servants . . . necessarily regarded Negroes as their equals, nor for that matter, that Emanuel [black] thought any better of Miller [white] because he was white. (p. 30)

Interracial cooperation during this period on Virginia's eastern shore was not limited to racially mixed runaways. Blacks and whites interacted in a variety of ways that belie present views of race relations. For example, free blacks had daily contact with "non-gentry whites, small planters and indentured servants. Members of the two races exchanged land, traded livestock, worked for each other, sued one another, and socialized together. On this level, blacks and whites dealt with each other essentially as equals" (Breen & Innes, 1980, p. 104). Clearly, race was not as important as economic status, which "seems to have been the key element in determining the structure of these relations" (p. 104). This particularly unique interracial climate explains why in 1674 a Northampton court "did not hesitate to place a white infant in the home of a free black, even though that action meant the child would be under the care of and authority of black parents until it reached the age of twenty-four" (p. 104). Although this unique racial climate would change by the end of the 17th century, it is instructive as a historical backdrop for examining the other tradition of race relations.

The American Revolutionary War provided the impetus for another key development of the other tradition of American race relations. By the beginning of the war, more than a century of slavery had all but destroyed the possibility of creating a genuine multiracial society characterized by racial equality, cooperation, and harmony. The proverbial die had been cast. The tradition of white racial dominance was firmly in place. Yet the other tradition was slowly emerging to challenge the more powerful tradition of racial dominance. The moral contradictions of the war and the military needs of the Continental Army contributed to the growth and credibility of the tradition of racial cooperation, unity, and harmony.

The Quakers played a leading role in raising the consciousness of the revolutionary generation concerning slavery and prejudice against blacks. But it was the threat of the British mobilization and arming of slaves that forced Americans, perhaps begrudgingly, to integrate their forces to resist the British forces (see Jordan, 1969, pp. 271-276; Quarles, 1961, pp. 51-58).

American wars would come to play a crucial role in creating conditions conducive to or dependent on black-white cooperation. The American Revolutionary War was the first example. The vast majority of blacks fought alongside whites in the Continental Army. One of the most memorable scenes of black-white cooperation during the Revolutionary War is John Trumbull's painting of Lieutenant Thomas Grosvernor and his servant, Peter Salem, fighting together at the Battle of Bunker Hill. Salem participated in several battles where he won distinction and was introduced to George Washington " 'as the soldier who killed British Major Pitcairne at Bunker Hill' " (Nash, 1990, p. 185).

The participation of blacks on the side of the American revolutionaries contributed to the growth and development of the antislavery movement that became the historical cornerstone for interracial cooperation and the other tradition of race relations during the 19th century. Most blacks who fought in the war won their freedom. The war also prompted a groundswell of antislavery feelings related to the moral contradiction of holding slaves while professing to wage a war for freedom and liberty. As historian Benjamin Quarles (1961) points out,

> Since the war had been fought in the name of liberty, many Americans were led to reflect seriously upon the impropriety of holding men in bondage. The feeling that slavery was inconsistent with the ideals of the war cropped out in many quarters, becoming manifest in the attitude of prominent national figures, in the formation of abolitionist societies, in the concern for Negroes displayed by religious sects, and in the antislavery activities of state and federal governments. (p. 185)

This period of self-scrutiny forced white Americans to reflect on more than the obvious moral contradictions surrounding professed beliefs and actual deeds. It forced them to reflect on their views and feelings about the humanity of black people. By the end of the Revolutionary Era, blacks and whites, slave and free, had experienced more than a century and a half of varied interaction, some hostile, some intimate. The Revolutionary War had forged unprecedented interracial bonds of friendship, as future wars would. But the growing strength of slavery, with its attendant formidable racist ideological rationale, constituted a challenge to such bonds. The other tradition of race relations could not have been sustained by the brief good feelings and guilt of the revolutionary generation. In the minds of most of this generation, interracial cooperation between blacks and whites was merely a means to an end, that end being the liberty and future well-being of a newly emerging white nation. As Jordan (1969) says, "For the post-revolutionary generation of white Americans, the most pressing political problem was the formation of a viable nation union" (p. 315). If the other tradition was to survive, it would have to rely on the antislavery movement.

THE ANTISLAVERY MOVEMENT

The antislavery movement provided the first relatively large-scale opportunity for the development of black-white cooperation and antiracism. For all of its failures, flaws, and shortcomings in relation to many of its grand ideals, the antislavery movement was the seedbed that produced some of the first examples of blacks and whites working together.

The early abolitionist movement between the colonial period and the founding of the first meeting of the American Anti-Slavery Society in December 1833 in Philadelphia failed on two basic counts: It was moderate and conciliatory, and no blacks or women held membership in its organizations (Quarles, 1969). As Quarles points out, however, "the early abolitionist movement was by no means barren of accomplishment. It had rescued hundreds of Negroes illegally held in bondage . . . [and] showed an interest in the free Negro, particularly in his education" (p. 12).

One such abolitionist society, the New York Anti-Slavery Society, focused its primary attention on supporting and maintaining schools for free African Americans. The African Free School was among the society's greatest work, and New York abolitionists took great pride in it. This school produced the most celebrated African American artist of the 19th century, Ira Aldridge, "who played Othello at the Royal Theatre in London before he reached thirty and was the rage of Europe for a quarter of a century" (Quarles, 1969, p. 13). The abolitionists in Pennsylvania also contributed to the educational development of African Americans when the state failed to do so. In 1802, the state provided public schools for whites. Yet no public school existed for blacks until 1820, when abolitionists donated a building in response to state officials who claimed that they could not educate blacks because they lacked funds for a facility.

These early abolitionists contributed to the social and economic well-being of free blacks in their communities. And, no doubt, there were many cases of genuine interracial cooperation in the educational projects these abolitionists established on behalf of free blacks—a type of interracial relationship I will explore in a later chapter. It was not these early white abolitionists who laid the foundation for the genuine black-white cooperation that would come to characterize the other tradition of race relations, however.

The antislavery movement that emerged in the early 1830s became the seedbed for the type of interracial unity and cooperation that would characterize the other tradition of race relations. Quarles (1969) argues,

Thus did abolitionism take on a new character, a direct confrontation—not a flank attack—on slavery. Impelled by a sense of urgency hitherto missing, these new spokesmen [and women] insisted that the nation face up to the question. Believing that they best served their countrymen by rebuking them for their faults, they were determined to rivet public attention on an issue most people would have preferred to ignore. (p. 14)

This more radical antislavery movement produced more radical white allies, such as William L. Garrison, the Grimké sisters, and John Brown. These and other white abolitionists did not just work on behalf of blacks but worked with them, drew support from them, and interacted with them as friends and allies, not simply as wards. There were still problems at this stage of black-white cooperation, but the problems were a developmental phase of a new and more balanced interracial relationship rather than the unbalanced, paternalistic interracial relationship that characterized the earlier abolitionists' relationship to free blacks.

The establishment of the American Anti-Slavery Society in 1833 paved the way for this new development in interracial cooperation. But the radically changing racial climate that forged this new stage included the publication in 1829 of Walker's appeal to slaves to rise and the 1831 Nat Turner Rebellion. Black-white cooperation during this time was tested to the limit, but it survived.

No sooner had William Lloyd Garrison "launched his antislavery offensive" in 1831 than "Negro abolitionists responded with warm enthusiasm" (Litwack, 1965, p. 137). Writing to Garrison in March 1831, James Forten, a rising black star in the abolitionist movement, commended his white comrade for the effect his radical stand on slavery was exerting on black youth. It " 'has roused up a Spirit in our young People that had been slumbering for years' " (p. 137). In the early years of this new, more radical phase of the antislavery movement and black-white cooperation in that movement, Garrison personified the new, more radical role of whites.

The first indication of this more balanced role in interracial cooperation occurred when Garrison reversed his stand on African colonization, which many blacks opposed.[1] Garrison soon became one of the most beloved white abolitionists within the black community. J. McCune Smith, a black doctor and abolitionist, reflecting on the love affair between Garrison and blacks, commented that it was " 'hard to tell which loved the other the most—Mr. Garrison the colored people, or the colored people Mr. Garrison' " (Quarles, 1969, p. 18). As he traveled from city to city, Garrison's talks on antislavery were geared to the concerns of his black listeners. Sensitive to many free blacks' opposition to colonization, he relentlessly attacked this project, "doing much to dislodge it from the abolitionist movement" (p. 19).

Garrison's ardent support for the antislavery cause, particularly his attacks on African colonization, provided early impetus for some of the strongest bonds of interracial cooperation. As Quarles (1969) points out, "The Negro response to this 'Daniel come to judgment' was immediate and full" (p. 19). This response was demonstrated in the manner in which blacks supported Garrison's newspaper, *The Liberator.* It was in this reciprocal relationship that one sees the development of the first fruits of the other tradition expressed as interracial cooperation.

From the very beginning, blacks supported Garrison's newspaper. Even before the first edition appeared, black abolitionist James Forten sent payment for 27 subscriptions, which "enabled Garrison and his publishing associate, Isaac Knapp, to buy the necessary ream of paper" (Quarles, 1969, p. 20). Garrison later mentioned that he doubted whether *The Liberator* would have come into being had Forten not provided assistance at that crucial time. Several weeks later, Forten sent $20 for more subscriptions. Black support made the crucial difference for *The Liberator* during its first 3 formative years. In 1834 whites represented only one fourth of the 2,300 subscribers (Quarles, 1969). Black agents for *The Liberator* made up another vital link in the interracial cooperative chain between Garrison and the black community.

Another product of the interracial cooperation between Garrison and the black community was his trip abroad in spring 1833. The purpose of the trip was to spread the new gospel of freedom, raise money for a black manual labor college, and attack the fund-raising drive of Elliot Cresson of the American Colonization Society. These efforts could not have been undertaken without interracial cooperation, because Garrison had no money and few among his black supporters at the time had the clout and influence of a white radical abolitionist such as Garrison. Black individuals and organizations took up a collection to send Garrison on this mission. The Colored Female Religious and Moral Society of Salem sent presents and a group of black youth, the Juvenile Garrison Independent Society, presented Garrison with a silver medal just before he set sail.

The black support within this cooperative relationship extended to England. After 4 months in England, Garrison had no money to return to the United States. He was rescued by Nathaniel Paul, a black Baptist clergyman on a fund-raising trip in the British Isles on behalf of the Wilberforce settlement in Canada. Paul lent Garrison $200 to return home. In a letter to fellow abolitionist Lewis Tappan, Garrison told how Paul's assistance kept him from begging to obtain funds to return home. After his return to Boston, his black friends held a public reception for Garrison at Marlboro Chapel (Quarles, 1969).

As a radical white abolitionist, Garrison often put his life on the line for the antislavery cause. This role bonded him to blacks. In turn, blacks not only supported his projects, such as his newspaper and his trip abroad, but they also provided him with protection while at home. "Negroes sought to protect Garrison from bodily harm." Quarles (1969) writes, "Fearing that he might be waylaid by enemies, they followed him late at night wherever he walked the three miles from his office to his Roxbury home, Freedom Cottage" (p. 21). Garrison, who believed in nonresistance, was unaware of these unsolicited protectors "armed with their cudgels to protect him" (p. 21).

During this early period, Garrison was to many blacks the premier white ally and friend in the struggle against slavery and racial prejudice. He and his black coworkers contributed to the development of a new stage of interracial cooperation. As his work in the antislavery movement continued, blacks showered him with appreciation. Some blacks named their sons after him; for example, David Walker's son was christened Edward Garrison Walker. Black organizations in Boston and New York "bore the name of Garrison in their titles" and the famous black painter, Robert Douglas, Jr., "completed a lithographic portrait of Garrison, copies of which sold for 50 cents to further the cause" (Quarles, 1969, p. 22).

Garrison was not the perfect ally. He had many shortcomings and would, like many white abolitionists of his time, run afoul of major black leaders of the time. But "whatever the catalogue of his shortcomings, his unswerving championship of human rights marked him a providential figure in an age when the forces of slavery and antislavery met head-on in America" (Quarles, 1969, p. 22).

If Garrison could be considered one of the main pillars of the other tradition of race relations during this phase of the antislavery period, Frederick Douglass was most certainly another one. During the period in which they worked together as black and white brothers and coworkers under the banner of the Massachusetts Anti-Slavery Society, traveling together; sharing platforms; breaking bread; and sharing the burdens of wear, tear, and physical abuse and verbal ridicule, the relationship of these two men was one of the most impressive examples of interracial cooperation during the antislavery movement. Even after their final and tragic split in 1851, their earlier years of working together continued to contribute to the creation of bonds of interracial cooperation.

Frederick Douglass was the architect of his own destiny, as well as one of the chief architects of interracial cooperation within the antislavery movement. By the early 1840s, he had become the "prize exhibit" of the Massachusetts Anti-Slavery Society, presenting public lectures on his experiences as a slave. The society hired him as a lecturer, and in that role he contributed to its credibility not only as an antislavery organization but also to its credibility as an organization in which blacks could participate (Quarles, 1968).

Douglass came on the antislavery scene at a time when the movement was in the process of being transformed from one dominated by well-meaning but paternalistic whites who believed in moral suasion, gradualism, and segregation within their organizations, to one in which blacks were not only accepted but played a key role. This "new spirit of abolitionism" found "its widest expression in the formation of the American Anti-Slavery Society at Philadelphia on December 4, 1833" (Quarles, 1969, p. 23). According to Quarles, "No public gathering of abolitionists was more memorable than this three-day organizational meeting at Adelphi Hall" (p. 23). Blacks played major roles at this organizational meeting and in the organizational meetings of the affiliates of this new parent society. The new national antislavery organization provided a vehicle for increased interracial cooperation between blacks and whites. Several weeks after the formation of the American Anti-Slavery Society, the Female Anti-Slavery Society was born. Lucretia Mott was its guiding spirit. Four African American women were among those who signed the society's charter. Of these women, Sarah M. Douglass was the most widely known. The others were Harriet Purvis, Sarah Forten, and Margaretta Forten. Sarah M. Douglass and two white abolitionist sisters, Sarah and Angelina Grimké, also contributed to the establishment of the other tradition by the genuineness and quality of their interracial friendship and cooperation (Quarles, 1969).

This was the state of interracial cooperation within the circles in which Douglass found himself by the 1840s. He was fortunate to join the movement at this stage of its interracial development, because it provided him with an unprecedented opportunity to contribute to this evolving tradition and to carry on its legacy.

In his role as the society's prize exhibit, Douglass joined an interracial band of abolitionists who traveled and lectured together, presenting one of the few examples of interracial cooperation seen by most Americans.

This circle included John Collins, the general agent of the Massachusetts Anti-Slavery Society (who convinced the organization to hire Douglass as lecturer); William Lloyd Garrison; Samuel J. May, the famous black abolitionist; Charles Lenoz Remond, born free and the first black lecturer against slavery; Parker Pillsbury, a former Congregational pastor who had left his church for the antislavery cause; and Wendell Phillips (Quarles, 1968).

Notwithstanding his later differences with the Garrisonians, triggered in part by his decision to start his own newspaper against the advice of Garrison,[2] Douglass's work as an abolitionist helped weave the fabric of interracial cooperation within the movement. He continued to work within interracial circles even when tensions between some black and white abolitionists were increasing over blacks' "more frequent demands for ideological and political independence" (Litwack, 1965, p. 143).

Douglass was a devoted supporter of the women's movement, which expanded and strengthened the networks of interracial cooperation. Because of the great unpopularity of the women's movement in certain circles, many feminists linked their struggle to the antislavery movement "in order to get before a reform-conscious abolitionist gathering and present a public airing of women's grievances" (Quarles, 1968, pp. 131-135). Black leaders, on the other hand, saw the benefit of allying themselves with these militant women, some of whom, like the Grimké sisters, ranked with the best of the male antislavery workers and far surpassed them in certain areas of antislavery activities. This alliance, which at times had its problems, nonetheless increased and enhanced interracial cooperation. Douglass was exposed to women's active involvement in the antislavery movement early in his career as an abolitionist, which influenced his pioneering linkages with the women's movement. At the first convention for equal rights for women, held in Seneca Falls, New York, Douglass was the only man among 37 present who supported the then very radical suffrage resolution. He spoke at the first national women's rights convention held in Worcester, Massachusetts, in October 1850. The motto of the convention reflected the growing relationship between the antislavery and women's rights movements: "Equality before the law without distinction of sex or color." In addition, one of the convention's resolutions "expressed concerns over the plight of the slave woman" (Quarles, 1968, pp. 134-135).

Douglass continued to weave a fabric of cooperation between the two reform movements that, by its very nature, nurtured interracial cooperation. He attended women's state and national conventions and published announcements of women's rights meetings in his newspaper. In fact, on one occasion, which may reflect a common practice, Susan B. Anthony told a friend to refer to Douglass's paper for such announcements. Douglass also persuaded the Negro conventions he attended to place themselves on record "as opposing discrimination on account of sex" (Quarles, 1968, p. 136). At a Philadelphia convention of blacks in 1848, which Douglass helped organize, an invitation was extended to black and white women to join in the deliberations (Quarles, 1968).

As important as Douglass's role was in developing the network of interracial cooperation by forging linkages between the antislavery and women's movements, the black and white women in these movements contributed as much or more to this enterprise. These women played a major role in confronting a primary barrier between black and white abolitionists—racial prejudice within the antislavery movement. As Gerda Lerner (1963) points out,

> By and large, the antislavery women showed a greater awareness of the implications of prejudice than their contemporaries: their meetings were integrated; they braved mobs frequently and developed the tactic of "non-violent resistance" by walking out of a mob, arm-in-arm, one Negro woman and one white; they gave their Negro members a chance to take leadership positions. (p. 285)

Few white men contributed as much as the Grimké sisters did to the struggle against slavery and racial prejudice and for interracial friendship. These two women, daughters of one of the most famous planters in South Carolina, gave up their lives of luxury, went North, and became abolitionists. Soon they became disillusioned with the racial prejudices within the Society of the Friends in Philadelphia and began protesting by sitting at the "Negro Bench." During this period, the sisters were becoming close friends of the Douglass family, a black family that attended Quaker meetings. Increasingly upset by the racial prejudices of the Quakers, Angelina Grimké wrote and asked Sarah Forten to supply her with examples of racial prejudice and the colonization movement. This interracial cooperative effort to combat racism within the Quaker religious community is probably the reason why, in early 1839, British Quaker friend Elizabeth Pease requested the Grimké sisters to supply her with any information they might have demonstrating racial discrimination within the Quaker community so that the British Quakers could " 'bring pressure to bear to end such practices' "

(Lerner, 1963, p. 284). Sarah Grimké wrote to Sarah Douglass and asked her to provide her with some examples " 'of how her mother, cousins and she had been treated by white Quakers in particular social settings, such as funerals and the infamous Negro Bench' " (p. 284).

After receiving the information from Douglass, Sarah Grimké wrote a 40-page letter to Pease in which she incorporated the black women's information on racism. In April 1839, segments of this letter, without names, were published in England in a pamphlet titled "Society of Friends: Their Views of the Anti-Slavery Question and Treatment of the People of Color" (Lerner, 1963). The publication of this pamphlet was an example of international interracial cooperation among black and white antislavery women. It also marked a stage in the development of antiracism within the abolitionist movement.

Both Grimké sisters were ousted by the Quakers, ostensibly because of Angelina's marriage out of the faith and the attendance of her sister at the wedding. But it was clear that the Quakers had problems with the radicalism of the Grimkés (Lerner, 1963).

The Grimkés' deep friendship with Sarah Douglass and Sarah Forten (daughter of James Forten) formed the basis of their unique style of interracial cooperation. The close friendship between Sarah Grimké and Sarah Douglass is one of the best examples not only of interracial cooperation during this period but also of interracial friendship, love, and fellowship. I will return to this relationship in a later chapter.

The underground railroad, the network of people and places through which escaped slaves traveled on their long, arduous, and dangerous trek northward, was another key example of interracial cooperation during the pre-Civil War period. The real underground railroad was different from the myth or legend in which fugitive slaves tended to be passive victims waiting to be rescued by benevolent Quakers, reflecting a form of paternalistic interracial cooperation. The real underground railroad involved a form of interracial cooperation in which blacks played a major role.

For example, free black leaders, such as William Still, Frederick Douglass, and Harriet Purvis, worked with white abolitionists on vigilance committees to help fugitive slaves move North. William Still of Philadelphia was one of the most famous black leaders to direct an interracial vigilance committee in this work (Gara, 1967). Although interracial cooperation may have been overshadowed by the larger-than-life figure of Levi Coffin of Newport, Indiana, who became a legend in the history of the underground railroad for his more than two decades of openly assisting fugitive slaves, even his great accomplishments would have been impossible without black participation along the way.[3]

The relationship between the most famous fugitive slave woman, Harriet Tubman, and the well-known Quaker, Thomas Garrett of Wilmington, Delaware, is perhaps the most impressive example of interracial cooperation within the history of the underground railroad. Although Tubman received help from many whites, Garrett probably played the most important role. Garrett's home was the most important station on Tubman's route. According to Conrad (1969), "Garrett was the outstanding champion of the Negro in the state of Delaware" (p. 58), and in the course of his career he aided about 2,700 fugitives in their flight toward the North. He admired nobody more than Harriet Tubman, whose caravans he constantly sheltered.

Tubman was sheltered by both blacks and whites. Sometimes she and her fugitives found shelter with Susan B. Anthony or with the family of Frederick Douglass. White ship captains also assisted in this drama of interracial cooperation. According to Conrad (1969), "Harriet Tubman more and more saw the scene in the Douglass view, of utilizing all allies, of advancing step by step, by large and small measures" (p. 88). The network of interracial cooperation developed by black and white abolitionists increased the circles of such allies. For example, Tubman's friendship with William H. Steward, "whose home in Auburn, New York, housed her fugitive broods" (p. 88) was a by-product of this network of interracial cooperation.

This same network brought together the interracial band of John Brown, Harriet Tubman, Frederick Douglass, and a host of others. John Brown had several meetings with black abolitionists before his abortive attempt at Harper's Ferry in October 1859. One could say that John Brown's interracial band, some of whom died at Harper's Ferry and others who were executed, represented the highest stage of interracial cooperation in the struggle for racial justice during the pre-Civil War era. Brown himself represented that small but devout group of whites who were willing to sacrifice everything, including their lives, for the freedom of their black brethren (Franklin, 1993; Oates, 1984).[4]

The next stage of interracial cooperation, built in large part on the long tradition of interracial cooperation within the antislavery movement, was the recruitment of black soldiers to fight in the Union forces and the resulting transformation of the racial attitudes of many white officers who commanded black units. Many of these white officers held the same racial beliefs as their fellow whites in the larger society. But after sharing the horrors of war with their black comrades in arms, many white officers experienced deep and dramatic transformations in their attitudes toward blacks. As one historian explains, "From the standpoint of the white officers, they entered positions of command with a wide array of preconceptions about blacks, based predominantly on readings and gossip and strikingly similar to those held by southerners" (Glatthaar, 1990, p. 98). Interracial cooperation within the context of war altered many of these preconceptions. It was "through actual service alongside black troops [that] many of them were able to shed much of their prejudice" (p. 98).

This wartime interracial cooperation was also dependent on black troops' perception of white officers' commitment to racial justice. Interracial cooperation between black troops and white officers would have been impossible without such a commitment. "As long as these white officers maintained their commitment to the eradication of slavery and the uplifting of the black race, they retained the respect and cooperation of their men" (Glatthaar, 1990, p. 98).

Despite the resurgence of white racism after the Civil War, this legacy of interracial cooperation between black troops and their white officers continued to exert influence on the eradication of racism. Several former white officers continued the struggle for racial justice. One of the best examples of this was Dr. Burt G. Wilder, who had been an assistant surgeon with black troops during the war. Wilder became "one of the most distinguished scientists in the United States, professor of neurology and zoology at Cornell Medical College, and his area of expertise was the study of the brain. Thus he was admirably suited to challenge racists on the basis of personal and scientific knowledge" (Glatthaar, 1990, p. 259). Undoubtedly, Wilder's interracial experience and his exposure to black-white cooperation during the war had much influence on his later decision to "battle racism by emphasizing the physical similarities of blacks and whites" (p. 259).

POST-CIVIL WAR PERIOD
TO THE TURN OF THE CENTURY

Interracial cooperation during the antislavery period played a significant role in the growth and development of the other tradition of American race relations. Notwithstanding their flaws, shortcomings, and ideological conflicts, black and white abolitionists represented the first instance of large-scale and long-term interracial cooperation in U.S. race relations. They established the foundation for interracial cooperation in the struggle for racial justice and helped shape and inspire future movements involving interracial cooperation.

The period from the end of the Civil War to the turn of the century witnessed another struggle between the two traditions of race relations. The tradition of interracial unity and cooperation was represented by social and political forces dedicated to the healing of a social order long divided by slavery and racism, whereas the tradition of white racial control, partially destroyed by the abolition of Southern slavery, was represented by a host of political, economic, and social forces, in the South and the North, dedicated to the perpetuation of white racial control of the recently freed Southern black laborers. This was the historical arena in which the two traditions battled for the soul of America. This battle would determine the nature and future role of interracial cooperation in the shaping and healing of race relations in the United States. (For a brief survey of these conflicting forces, see Franklin & Moss, 1988, pp. 201-223.)

The forces for interracial cooperation and racial justice during this period were best represented by former abolitionists and radical Republicans, such as Thaddeus Stevens, who opposed the forces of white racial dominance represented by President Andrew Johnson and a host of ex-Confederate veterans. The radical Republicans won for a while because of the political importance of Southern black votes to the growth and maintenance of Republican political power in the South. For a brief period, interracial cooperation characterized some of the reconstructed Southern state governments, as black and white legislators worked together to enact progressive state laws that would benefit both blacks and whites. For example, black lawmakers in North Carolina played a key role in the establishment of the first public school system in that state (Franklin & Moss, 1988).

Despite the great odds operating against those who represented the tradition of interracial cooperation for the healing of their racially fragmented society, strong black and white voices were heard above the howls of skeptics. Many such skeptics, steeped in the tradition of white racial dominance and control, found it difficult to accept the state constitutional conventions in which blacks and whites would participate imposed by the Reconstruction Act. Yet, the brief experiment in interracial democracy in pre-Civil War Southern political history had demonstrated, however faintly, the possibility of interracial cooperation. The *Charleston Daily News* was so impressed by the black delegation to the state convention that it commented:

> "Beyond all question, the best men in the convention are the colored members. Considering the influences under which they were called together, and their imperfect acquaintance with parliamentary law, they have displayed, for the most part, remarkable moderation and dignity." (Franklin & Moss, 1988, p. 217)

This dignity and moderation, complemented by what one historian described as the typical "magnanimity of the Negro" during this period, were reflected in a speech presented by delegate Beverly Nash to the interracial delegates at the constitutional convention of South Carolina:

> "I believe, my friends and fellow-citizens, we are not prepared for this suffrage. But we can learn. Give a man tools and let him commence to use them, and in time he will learn a trade. So it is with voting. We may not understand it at the start, but in time we will learn to do our duty. . . . We recognize the Southern white man as the true friend of the black man. . . . In these public affairs we must unite with our white fellow-citizens. They tell us that they have been disenfranchised, yet we tell the North that we will never let the halls of Congress be silent until we remove that disability." (Franklin & Moss, 1988, p. 217)

In the praise of black delegates by a Southern white newspaper and in the magnanimity of a black delegate were the seeds of racial healing that required faithful nurturing.

C. Vann Woodward's (1974) classic study of Jim Crow opens a window into this period of racial transition. Northern and foreign observers, such as Colonel Thomas Wentworth Higginson (who conspired with John Brown prior to Harper's Ferry and commanded black troops during the Civil War) and Sir George Campbell ("a member of Parliament [who] traveled over a large part of the South, with race relations as the focus of his interest") (Woodward, p. 17), testified to the climate of racial tolerance. Higginson went South with the "eyes of a tolerably suspicious abolitionist." According to Woodward, Higginson had "expected to be confronted by contemptuous or abusive treatment of Negroes." Instead, when Higginson compared

> the tolerance and acceptance of the Negro in the South on trains and street cars, at the polls, in the courts and legislatures, in the police force and the

militia with attitudes in his native New England, [he] decided that the South came off rather better in the comparison. (pp. 16-17)

Sir George Campbell was equally "impressed with the freedom of association between whites and blacks, with the frequency and intimacy of personal contact, and with the extent of Negro participation in political affairs" (Woodward, 1974, pp. 17-18). Woodward writes that Campbell was particularly surprised with and commented on the "equality with which Negroes shared public facilities." Campbell commented that

"the humblest black rides with the proudest whites on terms of perfect equality, and without the smallest symptom of malice or dislike on either side. I was, I confess, surprised to see how completely this is the case; even an English Radical is a little taken aback at first." (pp. 16-17)

Although in many cases whites in Columbia avoided sitting with blacks in lecture halls or theaters " 'if the halls be not crowded,' " blacks in Columbia in 1877 were "freely admitted to the theatre . . . and to other exhibitions, lectures . . . [and were] served at the bars, soda water fountains, and ice-cream saloons, but not generally elsewhere" (Woodward, 1974, p. 18). An October 13, 1886, editorial in the *Richmond Dispatch* offers another glimpse of the possibilities for racial healing— what Woodward calls "forgotten alternatives"—that existed during this period:

"Our State Constitution requires all State officers in their oath of office to declare that they 'recognize and accept the civil and political equality of all men.' We repeat that nobody here objects to sitting in political conventions with negroes. Nobody here objects to serving on juries with negroes. No lawyer objects to practicing law in court where negro lawyers practice. . . . Colored men are allowed to introduce bills into the Virginia Legislature; and in both branches of this body negroes are allowed to sit, as they have the right to sit." (Woodward, 1974, p. 19)

Some black observers during this period also noticed the racial tolerance and relatively peaceful coexistence of blacks and whites in some areas. In 1885, T. McCants Steward, a black newspaperman and corresponding editor of the *New York Freeman,* returned South after 10 years and found that conditions had changed tremendously. He wrote, " 'I think the whites of the South are really less afraid to [have] contact with colored people than the whites of the North' " (Woodward, 1974, p. 21). Woodward points out that for some time the majority of the saloons served blacks and whites at the same bar and, although restaurants used separate tables, they served blacks and whites in the same room.

During this period, when neither the South nor the North had yet decided to heal their sectional wounds at the expense of leaving the nation's racial wounds open to bleed long into the future, some opportunities to heal America's racially fragmented society remained. A few national trade unions attempted to heal the racial wounds within their ranks.

At the end of the 1860s, about 32 national unions existed but most of them excluded blacks. They could not avoid the questions of what to do about the recently emancipated Southern blacks, however. During its 1866 national convention, the National Labor Congress appointed a committee to look into the "Negro problem." The congress recognized that if it did not join with blacks in opposing capitalism, capitalists would use blacks as "an engine against" the congress. The chairman of the Negro Labor Committee reported to the convention that " 'the time when such cooperation should take effect we leave to the decision and wisdom of the next Congress . . . believing that such enlightened action will be developed as to resound to the best interest of all concerned' " (Block, 1958, p. 12).

Unfortunately, the Negro question was dropped and black union membership was "left to the discretion of individual unions," many of which either completely excluded blacks or thought of them only with regard to "mechanical labor" rather than as competent craftsmen (Block, 1958, p. 13). Rather than working to build interracial cooperation, individual national unions chose racial exclusion, which contributed to decades of racial conflict.[5]

It was left to the Knights of Labor, organized in 1869, to carry on the tradition of cooperative race relations and to contribute to the healing process by opening its membership to black workers. The belief in worker solidarity summed up the philosophy of the Knights of Labor. As one historian explains, "With the organization of men and women, Negro and white, foreign-born and native-born, with no practice of religious or political discrimination, the Knights of Labor became more than a labor union, but a popular movement" (Kessler, 1952, pp. 248-249).

This "popular movement" demonstrated that black and white workers could join hands against the employers determined to exploit both races

and to use them against each other. Despite its demise after the Haymar-
ket riots in 1886, the Knights of Labor was the one union during this
period that stood "as the outstanding vehicle of Negro-White unity"
(Kessler, 1952, p. 276).

Several times during the 1880s and 1890s, black and white farmers
experimented with various degrees of interracial cooperation. As the result
of pressing economic times, Southern farmers organized a radical movement. By the end of the 1880s, the Southern Farmers' Alliance had set up
branches throughout the South. They did not accept blacks but recognized
the need for a separate black agrarian organization. As a result, black
farmers organized themselves into the Colored Farmers' National Alliance
and Cooperative Union. Before long, this organization experienced rapid
growth. Five years after its founding, its membership exceeded 1 million.
For a while, there was some interracial cooperation under a national
organization. The agendas conflicted, however, when the Colored Farmers'
Alliance threatened to call a general strike of black cotton pickers, and the
white president of the National Farmers' Alliance argued against it on the
grounds that blacks were trying to improve their condition at the expense
of whites. The white president said he would rather see white farmers leave
their cotton in the field than pay black cotton pickers 50 cents a pound to
pick it (Franklin & Moss, 1988).

Interracial cooperation between black and white farmers reached a
high point during the early years of the Populist Party, when Tom
Watson, a radical leader from Georgia, began a brief flirtation with
biracial political cooperation. According to Woodward (1974), "the
Populist experiment in interracial harmony, precarious at best and
handicapped from the start by suspicion and prejudice, was another
casualty of the political crisis of the nineties" (p. 63). But "while the
movement was at the peak of zeal the two races had surprised each other
and astonished their opponents by the harmony they achieved and the
good will with which they cooperated" (p. 63).

Interracial cooperation between black and white Populists failed for
a number of reasons, among them the inability of the white Populists to
overcome their legacy of racism when their political opponents used
racism to divide them from black Populists. "When it became apparent
that their opponents would stop at nothing to divide them . . . and would
steal the Negro vote anyway, the biracial partnership of Populism began
to dissolve in frustration and bitterness" (Woodward, 1974, p. 63). As
blacks became "apathetic and ceased political activity altogether," some
white Populists understood that their black comrades were victims of,

rather than the cause of, the downfall of the Party (p. 63). The majority, however, reverted to traditional racist rationalization. As Woodward points out, for these white Populists, "it came much easier to blame the Negro for their defeat, to make him the scapegoat, and to vent upon him the pent-up accumulation of bitterness against the legitimate offenders who had escaped their wrath" (p. 63).[6]

The fusion of the early Populist and leftover Republican state organizations created some degree of biracial cooperation that led to black political empowerment in several Southern states, with North Carolina being one of the best examples. But by 1896, as the agrarian movement, with its legacy of attempted interracial cooperation, groaned on its death bed, Southern white politicians decided that white political unity was more important than an interracial political cooperation that tended to split whites off into various interracial combinations.

> When it became evident that white factions would compete with one another for the Negro vote, and thus frequently give the Negro the balance of power, it was time for the complete disenfranchisement of the Negro, the Fifteenth Amendment of the United States Constitution to the contrary notwithstanding. (Franklin & Moss, 1988, pp. 234-235)

If interracial cooperation could survive at all in the South, it would not do so within the area of politics. It would have to seek out a new channel in the twisted racial terrain of the Southern white landscape.

The only channel through which interracial cooperation could find expression was the accommodationist mode that would come to be associated with the rise of Booker T. Washington. It was the only approach that did not frighten the racially paranoid white South bent on maintaining control of blacks. Black and white America got a glimpse of this new form of interracial cooperation in 1895 (the same year that Frederick Douglass, the architect of an earlier and more radical form of interracial cooperation, died). During Washington's famous Atlanta speech, in which he said, "In all things that are purely social we can be as separate as the fingers, yet one as the hand in all things essential to mutual progress," Washington was accommodating the racial status quo, unlike Douglass, who never accommodated the racial status quo of his day (Harlan, 1972a, p. 75). Given the racially oppressive conditions for blacks at the time, Washington had little choice.[7]

Washington became the personification of a new and—to many whites in both the South and the North—more realistic approach to America's

racial problems. His accommodationist approach enabled him to gener-
ate support from whites throughout the country for the Tuskegee Institute. One example of how Washington used this approach occurred
during the early years in the town of Tuskegee, when he needed white
support for the school:

> I noted that just in proportion as we made the white people feel that the
> institution was a part of the life of the community, and that, while we
> wanted to make friends in Boston, . . . we also wanted to make white friends
> in Tuskegee, and that we wanted to make the school of real service to all
> the people, their attitude toward the school became favorable. (Harlan,
> 1972a, p. 288)

Before long, the school became the basis for local interracial cooperation. On one occasion when word got out that the school was
planning a new building, a Southern white man who owned a local
sawmill offered to provide the school with all the lumber it needed, with
only Washington's word for guarantee that payment would be made as
soon as the school had the money. Washington writes,

> I told the man that at the time we did not have in our hands one dollar of
> the money needed. Notwithstanding this, he insisted on being allowed to
> put the lumber on the grounds. After we had secured some portion of the
> money we permitted him to do this. (Harlan, 1972a, p. 289)

Black people also played a role in this interracial project. Washington
writes about an "old antebellum coloured man" who had no money to
give to the school but brought one of his two fine hogs to donate toward
the erection of the new building (p. 290).

Washington's accommodationist mode of interracial cooperation became the strategic foundation of his philosophy of vocational education,
which attracted Southern and Northern whites. It maintained white
supremacy in the South and it provided Northern whites who were
"weary of racial and sectional conflicts . . . a formula for peace in the
South with the establishment of a satisfactory economic and social
equilibrium between the races" (Franklin & Moss, 1988, p. 247).

Realizing the limitations of his accommodationist mode as an approach for combating racial discrimination, Washington secretly supported various efforts against racial discrimination (Meier, 1970). The
accommodationist mode, however, was the means by which Washington

became the most powerful black leader of his day. His interracial connections included major white philanthropists who sought his advice as to which black institutions should receive financial assistance. As a result, Washington's power and influence were felt throughout the black community. On more than a few occasions, he abused his power to quiet and control his critics. This abuse contributed in part to the rise of a more radical mode of interracial cooperation, the National Association for the Advancement of Colored People (NAACP) (Meier, 1970).

TURN OF THE CENTURY
TO THE GREAT DEPRESSION

Antiblack violence in the South and North during the early years of the 20th century raised questions about the usefulness of Booker T. Washington's accommodationist mode of interracial cooperation. Antiblack rioting in the North was particularly disturbing to some whites who had supported Washington and who would later join the more radical mode of interracial cooperation represented by the NAACP (Boskin, 1976; Meier, 1954). An antiblack riot in Springfield, Illinois, in August 1908, in which a white mob lynched two blacks, destroyed some black businesses, drove blacks from their homes, and forced the governor to call out the militia, shocked many whites (Crouthamel, 1976; Franklin & Moss, 1988). The writer William English Walling was among those whites who could not remain silent. Walling visited the scene of the riot and gathered material for an article titled "Race War in the North" that appeared in the *Independent*. Walling not only describes the atrocities of the riots but draws on the legacy of the abolitionist movement, particularly its antiracist elements:

> "Either the spirit of the abolitionists, of Lincoln and of Lovejoy, must be revived and we must come to treat the Negro on a plane of absolute political and social equality, or [racists like] Vardaman and Tillman will soon have transferred the Race War to the North." (Franklin & Moss, 1988, p. 287)

Then Walling throws out the challenge that gave birth to a more radical form of interracial cooperation on behalf of racial justice for black Americans: " 'Yet who realizes the seriousness of the situation and what large and powerful of citizens is ready to come to their aid?' " (p. 287).

Walling's challenge was answered by several influential whites. Among them was Mary White Ovington, a wealthy New Yorker and social worker who had made a study of racial problems. After reading Walling's article, she discussed it with Walling and Henry Moskowitz, a Jewish social worker. Among these three, Ovington had by far the most experience and firsthand knowledge of the effect of racism on blacks.[8] These three decided to schedule a conference for Lincoln's birthday in 1909 to move forward on Walling's challenge. The announcement was written by Oswald Garrison Villard, the grandson of William Lloyd Garrison: " 'We call upon all believers in democracy to join in a National conference for the discussion of present evils, the voicing of protests, and the renewal of the struggle for civil and political liberty' " (Hughes, 1962, p. 18).

The young black radicals of the Niagara Movement[9] were invited to participate in the conference. Most accepted. Yet some black radicals, such as Monroe Trotter, refused to attend. Trotter's refusal was based on his mistrust of white motives, which was understandable given the checkered history of interracial cooperation. The conference did attract an impressive array of blacks and whites, including judges, social workers, educators, publicists, professors, and bishops. They made plans for the establishment of a permanent organization that came to be known as the National Association for the Advancement of Colored People. A program of action was laid out and agreed on. The newly formed organization dedicated itself to the abolition of "all forced segregation, equal education for Negro and white children, the complete enfranchisement of the Negro, and the enforcement of the Fourteenth and Fifteenth Amendments" (Franklin & Moss, 1988, p. 288).

This radical mode of interracial cooperation was "denounced by most of the white philanthropists; and even some Negroes thought it unwise" (Franklin & Moss, 1988, p. 288). These two groups had grown used to the accommodationist mode of interracial cooperation institutionalized by Booker T. Washington, which was accepted as the only practical way in which blacks and whites could work for the benefit of each other. Unfortunately, this accommodationist mode had not been able to check the unrelenting wave of antiblack violence occurring in both the North and the South. Deepening racism had forced the need for a more radical mode of interracial cooperation devoted to combating racism in the best tradition of antiracism.

From the very beginning of the NAACP, one could see the important role that interracial cooperation would play in the long struggle for racial justice. When the formal organization was set up in 1910, however, W. E. B. Du Bois was the only black officer on the staff. The white officers were Moorfield Storey of Boston, president, and William E. Walling, chairman of the executive committee. One of the hardest-working and longest-serving whites on the NAACP staff was J. E. Spingarn, a distinguished professor of English at Columbia University. He was elected chairman of the board of directors in 1914 and remained with the NAACP until his death in 1939 (Ross, 1972).

The NAACP has come to represent the longest tradition of interracial cooperation and antiracism on behalf of the black community in American race relations. This mode of interracial cooperation was not spared some of the problems inherent in all modes of interracial cooperation. A major problem has been white paternalism, a topic I will discuss in Chapter 3.

Whereas the NAACP represented the radical legalistic-protest mode of interracial cooperation in pursuit of black advancement, another interracial organization pursued a more social and economic approach, similar to certain aspects of Booker T. Washington's black self-help approach. This organization, the National Urban League, was formed in 1911 from the merging of other organizations whose focus was the plight of urban blacks. These were the Committee for Improving Industrial Conditions of Negroes in New York and the National League for the Protection of Colored Women (NLPCW) (Weiss, 1974).

The NLPCW, founded by Frances A. Kellor, a white woman described by Weiss (1974) as "an archetypal reformer of the progressive tradition," already boasted an interracial board (p. 15). The other whites who belonged to this organization were philanthropist-reformer types "whose interest in racial problems stemmed from family and religious influence" (p. 19). These included people such as Elizabeth Walton, who was "a staunch Quaker . . . [and] a daughter of abolitionists," and Ruth Standish Baldwin, the widow of William H. Baldwin, Jr., president of the Long Island Railroad and an official of the Tuskegee Institute (p. 19). There were two black members, Eugene P. Roberts, a physician from New York, and Fred R. Moore, the organizer of the National Negro Business League, who would later assume the role of editor of the black newspaper, the *New York Age*.

Some of the same people who worked with the NLPCW were also active on the Committee for Improving the Industrial Condition of Negroes in New York (CIICN). This organization was particularly crucial in that it "prefigures the National Urban League both in the industrial support it attracted and in the industrial program it promoted" (Weiss, 1974, p. 20). William H. Baldwin, Jr., had come up with the idea of establishing an industrial organization to assist New York blacks that reflected the influence of Booker T. Washington. Much like Washington, Baldwin's philosophy of interracial cooperation saw industrial education for blacks as benefiting both blacks and the economy; in addition, "he saw it as a vehicle for expanding a common ground of interracial cooperation and understanding" (p. 38). According to this philosophy, "cooperation and common values . . . would hold out hope for peace between the races in America" (p. 35). The founders of the National Urban League had great faith in this approach:

> This faith in the power of interracial cooperation, in the importance of bringing together blacks and whites of good will in an effort beneficial to both races, would be cited time and time again by the leaders of the National Urban League as the distinctive fundamental principle of their organization. (p. 35)

In many ways, this philosophy of race relations was little more than a retread of Washington's accommodationist mode of interracial cooperation. In fact, some of the blacks who served on the CIICN were friends and allies of Washington. After her husband's death, Ruth Standish Baldwin represented the strain of "an enlightened conservative philosophy of racial reform, strongly influenced by Booker T. Washington" within the National Urban League (Weiss, 1974, p. 28).

Both the NAACP and the National Urban League would play key roles in the expansion and consolidation of interracial cooperation for decades to come, representing in their own ways different orientations within the other tradition. Their views of the state of race relations in the United States, however, as reflected in their respective magazines, differed greatly. As explained by Weiss (1974),

> The NAACP titled its magazine *Crisis,* thus summing up its view of the racial situation; the Urban League, by calling its publication *Opportunity,* expressed an optimism that "the Negro problem" could be eased substantially if only whites could be persuaded to give Negroes a chance. (p. 69)

The *Crisis,* which had a much larger circulation than did *Opportunity,* directed its appeal to the black community, whereas *Opportunity* directed its appeal to an interracial readership.[10] Although both organizations were committed to the principle of interracial cooperation, in May 1918 the Urban League adopted as one of its requirements for local affiliation, "the establishment of interracial executive boards" (p. 112).

The National Urban League's concern for interracial cooperation as a means for the social and economic uplifting of blacks was much more pronounced than that of the NAACP. For the league, interracial cooperation was key to the success of its work. In April 1921, President Warren G. Harding expressed his consideration for the league's emphasis on interracial cooperation in a letter to Eugene K. Jones, executive secretary of the National Urban League:

My dear Mr. Jones: The National Urban League has, as I understand its work, been particularly useful in its contributions toward the solution of the problems of races in the United States, because it has sought to secure the cooperation of leading people of both races in attacking these problems. (Harding, 1923, p. 259)

The president reminded Jones that in his recent message to Congress he had stated that

this represents the only procedure by which we can hope for the fullest and most desirable results. The race problem is one that concerns all of us and which we must all join in handling. I shall hope for, and be confident of, your hearty cooperation in every effort in this direction. (p. 259)

Acknowledging the fact that "interracial cooperation had been known . . . on a limited scale prior to the organization of the League," a November 1935 *Opportunity* editorial claims, "But the Urban League, it may be said, has transformed this idea from mere academic formula into vigorous reality. And therein lies the hope of a better America and a better world" ("Editorials," 1935).

The NAACP and the Urban League continued to work within the tradition of their different modes of interracial cooperation for decades, each in its own way contributing to the growth and development of the other tradition.

In the wake of the racial tensions following World War I, another interracial organization emerged, the Commission on Interracial Cooperation (CIC). Organized in 1919, it was the major and "most extensive liberal civil rights organization in the South" (Stanfield, 1987, p. 2). Its goal was "to quench, if possible, the fires of racial antagonism which were flaming at the time with deadly menace in all sections of the country" (Franklin & Moss, 1988, p. 319). The CIC centered its work primarily in the South and reflected the hopes and aims of a minority of Southern white liberals who were forced by tradition to work within some aspects of the racial status quo. Yet according to one scholar,

> The establishment of the Commission on Interracial Cooperation . . . was an important landmark for southern liberalism. The existence of these white Southerners who questioned, disagreed with, and spoke out against traditional Southern mores suggests that some Southerners envisioned alternatives to the prevailing early twentieth-century "Southern lynch-law." (Pilkington, 1985, p. 56)

The CIC strategy for change was not to confront the hard-core system of Southern racial segregation but to "humanize and soften the Southern system of segregation by rallying the better element of white Southern society to forward-looking social programs for blacks" (Pilkington, 1985, p. 56). The acceptance of black members who were "free to voice complaints" meant that they were altering the racial status quo of Jim Crow, even though that may not have been their intention (p. 56). The interracial composition of the CIC represented, in part, some traditional modes of the accommodationist interracialism of Booker T. Washington, which Pilkington describes as a "post-1919 triangular alliance of Southern whites, Northern philanthropists and foundations, [and] conservative blacks of the Tuskegee school" (p. 57).

The CIC was a Southern white-dominated organization established by Will Alexander and John J. Eagan. Alexander was a dissatisfied Methodist minister who felt the church had failed to bring blacks and whites together. Eagan was a religious Atlanta millionaire whose social work as an assistant to the secretary of the Navy during World War I had exposed him to the problems of blacks and some possible solutions to postwar race relations. These two, along with other whites, formed the core of the CIC. Working with carefully selected conservative blacks and avoiding at all cost radical blacks, such as those associated with the NAACP, the CIC set about its program of education in race relations (Pilkington, 1985).

The CIC's major program of racial relations involved the establishment of local interracial committees throughout hundreds of Southern counties. But the CIC failed to live up to its "professed goal of creating truly biracial committees" (Pilkington, 1985, p. 71). Most of these committees were either white or black, with occasional joint white and black membership for "conference and cooperation." In addition, white and black secretaries responsible for forming these committees received different wages, with whites receiving from one half to two thirds more than blacks. Notwithstanding these obvious shortcomings, the CIC impressed such scholars of race relations as Gunnar Myrdal, who in 1944 pointed out that making " 'interracial work socially respectable in the conservative South' " (Pilkington, 1985, p. 80) was one of the CIC's most important long-term results.

Although the organizations described earlier represented the three major large-scale organizational efforts of interracial cooperation during this period, there were smaller, yet no less significant, efforts occurring throughout the country. The American Inter-Racial Association was established in 1927. It explained its purpose as being "dedicated to the task of encouraging inter-racial contacts, organizing interracial groups, and creating an inter-racial press." Significantly, the association saw its interracial press as being different from interracial magazines, such as *Opportunity* and *Crisis,* which, it said, tended to focus on the "cause of the Negro rather than the cause of interracial relations" (Calverton, 1927, p. 23).

The American Bahá'í community was one of the most progressive religious communities in the field of interracial cooperation during this period. The Bahá'í teachings on racial unity and cooperation emanate from the wealth of teachings by Bahá'u'lláh (1817-1892), the prophet-founder of the Bahá'í Faith, on the unity of the human race. The principle of unity stands at the very heart of Bahá'u'lláh's revelation and Bahá'í community life:

O CHILDREN OF MEN! Know ye not why We created you all from the same dust? That no one should exalt himself over the other. Ponder at all times in your hearts how ye were created. Since We have created you all from one same substance it is incumbent on you to be even as one soul, to walk with the same feet, eat with the same mouth, and dwell in the same land, that from your inmost being, by your deeds and actions, the signs of oneness and the essence of detachment may be made manifest. Such is My counsel to you, O concourse of light! Heed ye this counsel that ye may obtain the fruit of holiness from the tree of wondrous glory. (Bahá'u'lláh, 1976, p. 20)

The early American Bahá'í community consisted of predominately white Americans who were just beginning to understand the tremendous social and historical significance of the Bahá'í teachings on racial unity. It would take them many decades to understand fully and to apply these teachings to their community life. 'Abdu'l-Bahá, the son of the prophet-founder of the Bahá'í faith, visited North America in 1912 and lectured on and demonstrated the Bahá'í teachings on racial unity and love (" 'Abdu'l-Bahá," 1982; Ward, 1979).

A year earlier, 'Abdu'l-Bahá had sent a message to the 1911 University Races Congress in London in which he explained the importance of the diversity of the human family and compared humankind to a flower garden adorned with different colors and shapes that " 'enhance the loveliness of each other' " (Spiller, 1970). In 1912, 'Abdu'l-Bahá spoke at Howard University in Washington, DC. According to a companion who kept diaries of 'Abdu'l-Bahá's Western tours and lectures, wherever 'Abdu'l-Bahá witnessed racial diversity, he was compelled to call attention to it. During 'Abdu'l-Bahá's talk at Howard University, this companion reports, " 'here, as elsewhere, when both white and colored people were present, 'Abdu'l-Bahá seemed happiest' " (Ward, 1979, p. 40).

As he looked over the racially mixed audience at Howard, 'Abdu'l-Bahá remarked, "Today I am most happy, for I see here a gathering of the servants of God. I see white and black sitting together" (" 'Abdu'l-Bahá," 1982, p. 44). After two talks, 'Abdu'l-Bahá was visibly tired as he prepared for a third talk. He was not planning to talk long. But here again, when he saw blacks and whites in the audience, he became inspired: " 'A meeting such as this seems like a beautiful cluster of precious jewels—pearls, rubies, diamonds, sapphires. It is [a] source of joy and delight' " (Balyuzi, 1972, pp. 181-182). 'Abdu'l-Bahá then elaborated on the theme of racial unity to an audience that probably had never heard such high praise for a gathering that many white Americans would have frowned on and just as many black Americans would have avoided. "Whatever is conducive to the unity of the world of mankind is most acceptable and praiseworthy. . . . Therefore, in the world of humanity it is wise and seemly that all the individual members should manifest unity and affinity" (" 'Abdu'l-Bahá," 1982, p. 56). Returning to his use of positive racial images woven into the new language of racial unity and fellowship, he painted a picture for his audience: "In the clustered jewels of the races may the blacks be as sapphires and rubies and the whites as diamonds and pearls. The composite beauty of humanity will be witnessed in their unity and blending" (pp. 56-57). To another racially mixed audience, 'Abdu'l-Bahá commented, "As I stand here tonight and look upon this assembly, I am reminded curiously of a beautiful bouquet of violets gathered together in varying colors, dark and light" (p. 49).

Realizing the depth of American racism from his conversations and correspondences with black and white American Bahá'ís years before he visited the United States, 'Abdu'l-Bahá did not miss any opportunity to demonstrate to all Americans, black and white, young and old, the Bahá'í approach to the racial problems in the United States. While visiting the Bowery Mission area in New York, some poor boys visited 'Abdu'l-Bahá in his room. As the boys filed into the room 'Abdu'l-Bahá greeted each one. The last boy to enter the room was a very dark African American. Because he was the only black boy in the group, he may have felt that 'Abdu'l-Bahá would not accept him. But as an observer reports,

When 'Abdu'l-Bahá saw him His face lighted up with a heavenly smile. He raised His hand with a gesture of princely welcome and exclaimed in a loud voice so that none could fail to hear; that here was a black rose.

The room fell into instant silence. The black face became illumined with a happiness and love hardly of this world. The other boys looked at him with new eyes. I venture to say that he had been called a black—many things, but never before a black rose. (Ives, 1976, p. 65)

As in his talks to racially mixed audiences, 'Abdu'l-Bahá compared beautifully diverse flowers and jewels to an equally beautiful mixture of people, particularly black and white, and by doing so transformed the traditional racist color symbolism and imagery into the symbolism and imagery of racial unity. 'Abdu'l-Bahá presented black and white Americans with new eyes and a new spiritual language with which to visualize and achieve a spiritual fellowship. By calling on black and white Americans to see themselves in a new light, as different colored flowers and jewels complementing each other, 'Abdu'l-Bahá enabled them to counter and transcend the racist cultural tendencies so ingrained in the American national character.

While in the United States, 'Abdu'l-Bahá's every act seemed to be calculated to demonstrate the Bahá'í teachings on the importance of love and unity between all members of the human race, especially blacks and whites. He used every opportunity to demonstrate how Bahá'ís should treat racial minorities. One such opportunity came during a luncheon held in his honor in Washington, DC. The luncheon had been arranged by two Bahá'ís, Ali-Kuli Khan, the Persian chargé d'affaires, and Florence Breed Khan, his wife. Some of the guests were members of Washington's social and political elite. Before the luncheon, 'Abdu'l-Bahá sent for Louis Gregory, a well-known black Bahá'í. The two chatted for a while, and 'Abdu'l-Bahá invited Louis Gregory to the luncheon. The assembled guests were no doubt surprised not only by 'Abdu'l-Bahá's inviting a black person to a white upper-class social affair but even more by the affection and love shown by 'Abdu'l-Bahá for Gregory when he gave the latter the seat of honor on his right. A biographer of Louis Gregory writes of this event, "Gently yet unmistakably, 'Abdu'l-Bahá had assaulted the customs of a city that had been scandalized only a decade earlier by President Roosevelt's dinner invitation to Booker T. Washington" (Morrison, 1982, p. 53).

At the time of 'Abdu'l-Bahá's visit to the United States many blacks and whites did not accept interracial marriage. Many states outlawed the practice or did not recognize such unions. Yet 'Abdu'l-Bahá never wavered in his insistence that black Bahá'ís and white Bahá'ís should not only be unified but also should intermarry. In Palestine, he had discussed the matter of interracial marriage with several black and white Western Bahá'ís and explored the sexual myths and fears at the core of American racism. His solution was to encourage interracial marriage. As the supreme model of the Bahá'í teachings and principles, he brought together a black American Bahá'í, Louis Gregory, and an English Bahá'í, Louisa Mathew. It was the first black-white interracial marriage between Bahá'ís and became known as the marriage that was personally encouraged by 'Abdu'l-Bahá. This demonstration of Bahá'í teaching and principles proved difficult to accept for some Bahá'ís, who doubted that such a union could last in a segregated society, but the marriage lasted until their deaths close to four decades later. Throughout this period, the Gregorys became the ultimate American Bahá'í symbol of racial unity, love, and friendship (Morrison, 1982).

Historians of American race relations in the early 20th century will one day examine the influence of 'Abdu'l-Bahá's 1912 visit to the United States on certain aspects of American race relations, as well as the effect of Bahá'í-initiated race amity conferences on the history of race relations. 'Abdu'l-Bahá warned American Bahá'ís that bloodshed would occur if America did not solve the racial crisis.

Years later, from his home in Palestine, 'Abdu'l-Bahá initiated a plan to address the racial crisis in America. He laid out a plan to organize

a series of large, well-publicized interracial meetings, conducted not to protest any specific grievance or to seek improvement of the lot of American blacks in some particular way, but to proclaim the oneness of mankind and to promote "racial amity" between black and white Americans. (Morrison, 1982, p. 132)

The first of these conferences took place in 1921 in Washington, DC. Decades later, race amity or race unity conferences would become the hallmark of the American Bahá'í community's contribution to American race relations.

THE GREAT DEPRESSION TO THE EVE OF THE CIVIL RIGHTS MOVEMENT

The seeds of various forms of interracial cooperation planted during the first two decades of the 20th century began to sprout during the 1930s, assisted by the social, political, and economic upheavals and transformations of that decade. A college interracial movement began in the early 1930s. As one observer reported in 1934,

It seems a fair estimate to predict that there will be some forty-five to fifty colleges and universities, from among the one hundred-fifty such institutions . . . from Texas to Virginia, having student organizations studying the race problem and practicing interracial fellowship at least once during the school year of 1934-1935. (Clayton, 1934, p. 267)

The Southern college interracial movement was "carried on all but exclusively by the YMCA and the YWCA as a part, though an integral part, of their student program" (Clayton, 1934, p. 267).

In 1934, New York Catholics established a Catholic Inter-Racial Council. This would prove to be vital in addressing the racial prejudices of many European ethnic groups who were Catholics and who would be playing a key role in uniting with blacks during the unionization movement during the late 1930s, as well as in the interracial political coalition that would put the Democrats in power.

The social and economic upheavals of the 1930s created the conditions for radical interracial cooperation between blacks and whites. An example of this cooperation is found in the American Communist Party (CP), which represented the most radical form of interracial cooperation in the 1930s. The CP was critical of other interracial organizations, such as the NAACP, the National Urban League, and the Commission on

Interracial Cooperation (Record, 1971). This more extreme radical form of interracial cooperation was a challenge to the less radical interracial organizations and no doubt forced them to take more militant stands against racism.

The radical interracialism fermented by the CP in part influenced the policies of the Congress of Industrial Unions. According to Philip Foner (1981), John L. Lewis, president of the Congress of Industrial Organizations (CIO), "knowingly hired members of the Communist Party to work as organizers, primarily because of their special interest in the unity of black and white labor and their achievement of such unity in the unions set up by the TUUL [Trade Union Unity League]" (p. 216). Through the organizing efforts of key CIO unions, the CP pushed for nondiscrimination. "The Party was aware that in the CIO it had a very effective instrument for organizing Negro workers and realizing the much-desired Negro-white unity" (Foner, 1981, p. 145).

Although the coalition of interest groups, particularly of blacks and whites, that propelled the Democratic Party to victory in the early 1930s was not the most radical form of interracial cooperation, it did reflect the growing awareness among a new generation of Northern white Democrats that interracial politics was the wave of the future. The political modernization of Northern black ghettos forced many of these politicians to accept interracial political coalitions as the only way to maintain some degree of political power.[11]

By the early 1940s, several streams of interracial cooperation began to emerge in an ever-widening river of national racial consciousness. Nurtured by a long tradition of interracial cooperation, broken at times by relentless attacks on it by a much stronger tradition of racism, a vanguard of courageous interracialists continued to be driven by the vision of racial fellowship. The first stream of interracialists destined to contribute to the expansion of the other tradition was the Congress of Racial Equality (CORE), founded in Chicago in 1942 (Meier & Rudwick, 1975).

CORE was the prototypical interracial organization that expanded the national racial consciousness. The organization grew out of the American pacifist movement and, according to Meier and Rudwick (1975),

[its] foundations were laid at a time when growing segments of the white public, stimulated by the ideological concerns of the New Deal for America's dispossessed citizens and by the irony of fighting the racist Nazis while tolerating domestic racism, were gradually becoming more sensitive to the black man's plight. (p. 4)

At the same time,

> In the black community, as a result of the legal victories achieved by the NAACP during the 1930s, the encouragement of leading New Dealers like Eleanor Roosevelt, and the obvious contradictions between America's democratic war propaganda and the violation of democracy at home, a more militant mood was becoming widely evident. . . . In the radical vanguard of this slow shift in sentiment among blacks and whites were the founders of CORE. (p. 4)

The black and white founders of CORE were themselves products of the "Christian student movement of the 1930s . . . and members of the Christian pacifist Fellowship of Reconciliation (FOR)" (Meier & Rudwick, 1975, p. 4). Within that organization, a small band was part of a group dedicated to "applying Gandhian techniques of satyagraha, or nonviolent direct action, to the resolution of racial and industrial conflict in America" (p. 4). FOR's interest in race relations dated to World War I; in 1940, when A. J. Muste became chief executive, "the Fellowship moved beyond philosophical opposition to war to experimenting with nonviolent direct action for social justice in the United States" (p. 4). FOR organized "peace teams or cells." The team that was organized at the University of Chicago in October 1941 was "deeply interested in applying Gandhian principles to racial problems. From the activities of this race relations a cell of about a dozen members emerged the first CORE group, the Chicago Committee of Racial Equality" (p. 4).

James Farmer and George Houser, one black, the other white, were among the founders of CORE, along with Betty Fisher, also white, who was one of the most ardent white advocates of interracial cooperation. " 'One of our motivations,' " Fisher once proclaimed, " 'had been the determination that there should be a thoroughly interracial organization, . . . not another Negro group with a token membership of whites' " (Meier & Rudwick, 1975, p. 10). Much like earlier radical interracial organizations, such as the NAACP, which saw itself as a radical departure from the more accommodationist mode of interracial cooperation of Booker T. Washington, the founders of CORE were critical of the interracial approaches to racial injustice characterized by the NAACP and the National Urban League. They preferred a more direct approach. As Houser put it, racism " 'must be challenged directly, without violence or hatred, yet without compromise' " (Meier & Rudwick, 1975, pp. 5-6).

During the first year, Chicago's CORE exemplified the new, more radical interracial approach to achieving racial justice. Besides establishing a short-term male interracial cooperative called Fellowship House in January 1942 as a method of circumventing housing discrimination against blacks, it actively challenged the racially exclusionary policy of the White City Roller Rink and racial discrimination at the University of Chicago's hospital, medical school, and barbershop. The Chicago CORE's greatest efforts were directed toward racial discrimination in restaurants. Other CORE affiliates, such as those in New York and Denver, targeted other public accommodations, including theaters, hotels, and retail stores (Meier & Rudwick, 1975).

Restaurants that practiced racial discrimination were "a particularly popular object of attack" (Meier & Rudwick, 1975, pp. 26-27). They presented an opportunity to demonstrate to white owners and patrons that racism would not go unchallenged and that it would be challenged by an interracial group. Interracial challenges to racial discrimination in places of public accommodation undermined the sense of normalcy that far too many whites felt about racism. In addition, interracial challenges during a war against Nazism, with its virulent racism, forced many white Americans to confront their hypocrisy.

Although restaurants were popular objects of attack for CORE's interracial teams, they also attacked racially segregated housing and the Red Cross practice of segregating the plasma of black and white blood in blood banks (Meier & Rudwick, 1975).

The early CORE was made up of fairly well-educated blacks and whites from the middle class, with some blacks from the working class. Many CORE members were college students. There was a range of racial mixture within CORE affiliates, however, from predominantly black to predominantly white (Meier & Rudwick, 1975). Notwithstanding this range, CORE was dedicated to a radical mode of interracial cooperation. Often this approach put it into conflict with other modes of interracial cooperation, such as the NAACP and the Urban League, but these three interracial organizations were able to work together to achieve mutual goals, such as boycotting and employment campaigns. Yet CORE's greatest conflict seems to have been with such radical interracial organizations as the Social Workers Party, which some more moderate interracists accused of subversing their organizations.

The vision of an interracial nonviolent movement was uppermost in the minds of some of the early founders and influenced CORE's history and ideology for some time. By the fall of 1945, Houser, who had been promoting this vision, felt such a need for this kind of movement that he "circulated a . . . memorandum again urging the establishment of a year-long leadership training project in preparation for a 'mass non-violent interracial movement' " (Meier & Rudwick, 1975, p. 22).

Unfortunately, the time was not right for such a movement and Houser's vision died, not to be revived until the 1960s.

In 1947, CORE conducted the "Journey of Reconciliation," a "two-week interracial foray into the South" (Meier & Rudwick, 1975, p. 33). On advice, it was limited to the upper South: Virginia, North Carolina, and Kentucky. A group of blacks and whites rode the bus together to challenge racial segregation in Southern transportation. Although this action did not lead to the desegregation of Southern transportation, according to one CORE official this interracial journey was " 'perhaps the most unique and outstanding understanding CORE has ever made' " (p. 33). Meier and Rudwick argue that

> it functioned as a dramatic high point, a source of inspiration to CORE for years to come . . . [and] fourteen years later it served as the model for the famous Freedom Ride of 1961, which projected CORE into the forefront of the Civil Rights movement. (p. 38)

The Highlander Folk School, founded in 1932 by Myles Horton, a white male from Tennessee, and Septima Clark, director of workshops from St. Johns Island, South Carolina, was another example of how the forces of interracial cooperation influenced race relations in America during this period. Although interracial cooperation and desegregation were not the priority they would later become, Highlander was destined to play a major role in training and preparing leaders for the interracial movements for racial justice that would emerge in the 1950s and 1960s (Hughes, 1985).

Highlander began as an integrated institution and laid a foundation for interracial cooperation and racial justice several decades before its engagement in the civil rights movement. Its first announcement in 1932 stated that it was open to both blacks and whites. Blacks began to attend as students in 1944, although they had been invited as speakers since the school's start. Sociologist Charles Johnson from Fisk University was one of the first black lecturers at the school. Highlander in turn produced a filmstrip for the Race Relations Department at Fisk (Langston, 1993).

At a time when many other institutions compromised on the issue of racism, Highlander refused to budge from its explicit policy on racial justice, particularly as it related to integrated meetings. In its early role as a worker education institution during the period when many unions unabashedly practiced racial exclusion of blacks, in 1940 the school "informed all unions it served that the school would no longer hold worker education programs for unions that discriminated against blacks" (Langston, 1993, p. 152). Highlander did not even back down for the powerful United Auto Workers Union (UAW), which "after refusing for four years . . . finally accepted an invitation to attend an integrated workshop" (p. 152). As a result of the school's firm stand on racially integrated meetings, 40 black and white UAW members attended, which led to other unions following their example. In 1949, during a campaign meeting at the school to reelect UAW President Walter Reuther, only white members were invited, but a black UAW member came anyway. The school staff interrupted the union gathering and gave it the ultimatum to integrate "or leave before the next meal." The all-white gathering decided to stay and conduct a racially integrated meeting. Predictably, this bold stand on racial justice was "viewed by Southern society as Communist-inspired and immoral" (p. 152).

The Southern Conference for Human Welfare (SCHW), founded in 1938 in Birmingham, Alabama, by Southern black and white liberals, was another attempt at addressing racial injustice that would evolve into a mode of interracial cooperation. The SCHW was, in fact, Southern liberals' response to a report of the region's economic health put out by the National Emergency Council (NEC) established by President Franklin D. Roosevelt. The NEC report described the South as the nation's number one economic problem, pointing out that the region had the potential of becoming the richest region but was hampered by institutional deficiencies, which included the racial plight of blacks. In short, the "Roosevelt administration and the NEC linked southern poverty and racism in an unprecedented way, but having presented a negative comment on the South, left southerners to search for their own solutions" (Reed, 1991, p. xx).

Black and white Southern liberals responded to the NEC report by setting up SCHW in 1938 and the Southern Conference Educational Fund (SCEF) in 1946 to achieve tax-exempt status and to increase SCHW's work in race relations. The leading spirit of this new movement of interracial cooperation in the South was a Southern white woman, Louise O. Charlton, who was at the time a U.S. commissioner in Birmingham. SCHW's primary role, in light of both the NEC report and the advice of a generation of Southern white liberals, was to "help southern whites to understand that to remove limitations on its black citizens was to ensure the region greater prosperity" (Reed, 1991, p. xx).

SCHW recommended several radical racial reforms that challenged the racial status quo of the South, as well as some racial views held by President Roosevelt, Congress, and the average Southern citizen. SCHW pointed to very specific aspects of the racial status quo that had to change for the region to prosper. Among these were the unequal facilities of black and white school children, unequal salaries of black and white teachers, and unequal incomes of black and white farmers. These were examples "of the inequity and wastefulness of a racially segregated society. Races that could not reap equal benefits for their labor could not live together harmoniously" (Reed, 1991, p. xxi).

From 1938 to 1948, SCHW focused most of its attention on working for the repeal of the poll tax by instituting, through its Civil Rights Committee, a National Committee to Abolish the Poll Tax (NCAPT). NCAPT became the vanguard of a 10-year campaign to abolish this institutional form of voter restriction by elevating a regional issue to a national issue. According to NCAPT, the poll tax effectively disenfranchised 11 million American citizens—7 million whites and 4 million blacks in seven Southern states. This form of publicity played a key role in NCAPT's educational work. Because of a number of problems, including financial instability and the resistance of Southern racists, NCAPT was not able to continue its struggle into the 1950s, but it paved the way for the defeat of the poll tax that came in 1964 with the adoption of the Twenty-Fourth Amendment to the Constitution (Reed, 1991).

In 1948, the SCHW board decided to terminate SCHW's operation and pass the torch to the Southern Conference Educational Fund (SCEF) "to carry on the public campaign to convert the heretofore unconvinced white supremacist" (Reed, 1991, p. xxi). This decision paved the way for SCEF to continue the work it had been doing since 1946 in pushing for integrated education, whereas SCHW was concentrating its energy in the political arena. During the 1950s and 1960s, SCEF played a key role in the racial integration of schools, particularly in higher education. It also played a part in other areas of the civil rights movement, such as voter registration drives (Reed, 1991, p. xxi).

The interracial composition of the SCHW and SCEF qualified them as two of the major interracial organizations in the nation between 1938 and 1950. Although the members tended to be well-educated black and white Southern liberals, they represented an impressive web of interracial cooperation. Among the black members were Frederick Patterson, president of Tuskegee Institute; John P. Davis, National Negro Congress; Charles S. Johnson, sociologist and president of Fisk University;

Roscoe Dunjee, editor of the *Black Dispatch* of Oklahoma City; Charlotte Hawkins Brown, founder and president of North Carolina's Palmer Memorial Institute; Mary McLeod Bethune, founder and president of Bethune-Cookman College (Bethune was a member of the executive boards of SCHW and SCEF for over a decade); A. Philip Randolph, president of the Brotherhood of Sleeping Car Porters; Benjamin Mays, president of Morehouse College; and Dr. Martin L. King, Jr. During the 1950s and 1960s, the number of blacks among SCEF's officers increased and the organization selected several black presidents during the latter decade. The white members included Frank Graham, president of the University of North Carolina; Barry Bingham, owner and publisher of the Louisville *Courier-Journal;* Governor Carl Bailey; Lucy Randolph Mason; H. L. Mitchell, executive of the Southern Tenant Union; and James Dombrowski, executive secretary for SCHW in 1942 (Reed, 1991).

This interracial group did its best to hold the high ground against racial segregation until the emergence of the civil rights movement. During the 1950s, SCEF's struggles against racial segregation and discrimination exposed it to Southern politicians who used red-baiting tactics against the organization (Reed, 1991). Yet SCEF survived long enough to sustain the tradition of interracial cooperation in pursuit of racial justice. As the result of SCEF's work, the South and the nation were brought farther along the road to racial justice.

Some other vital developments both influenced and were themselves influenced by the radical changes occurring in American race relations during the 1940s. Interracial cooperation was becoming acceptable in wider and wider circles. This is not to say that white racism and interracial conflicts were being driven from the field. Rather, the forces of interracial cooperation were gathering strength and credibility among many sectors of society. Certain institutional changes and policies during the 1940s contributed to a more favorable environment for the growth of interracial cooperation. For example, the growth of the black-labor alliance within the CIO during the 1930s was one of the more powerful examples of the interracial cooperation that played a key role in combating racism in the unions and the workplace. Although forced by A. Philip Randoph's threat to march on Washington, President Roosevelt's 1941 Executive Order banning racial discrimination in war industries contributed to a changing racial climate conducive to interracial cooperation. The integration of major league baseball in 1947 and the desegregation of the U.S. Armed Forces in 1948 both signaled significant changes in the racial status quo, paving the way for the gradual acceptance of racial integration and, by extension, interracial cooperation, among the general public (Franklin & Moss, 1988; Nalty, 1986; Tygiel, 1984).

In addition to institutional changes in the racial status quo, various impressive and far-reaching local institutional experiments in interracial cooperation were widening the influence of the other tradition. The Church for the Fellowship of all People in San Francisco, one of the first interracial churches of its kind, was a beacon of interracial fellowship during the 1940s. Under the leadership of Howard Thurman, the famous black minister, philosopher, and educator, the Fellowship Church put into practice the vision of interracial cooperation at its finest. The basis of membership in part said, " 'I desire to share in the spiritual growth and ethical awareness of men and women of varied national, cultural, racial, and creedal heritage united in a religious fellowship' " (Thurman, 1979, p. 143).

THE CIVIL RIGHTS ERA TO THE PRESENT

By the start of the civil rights era in the mid-1950s, interracial cooperation had emerged as a formidable tradition within American race relations. A web of interracial cooperation crisscrossed a vast array of organizations cemented by interpersonal relations across race, class, and gender boundaries. Decades of interracial cooperation were beginning to bear fruit. The 1954 landmark Supreme Court decision, *Brown v. Topeka,* was the victorious result of a network of interracial cooperation, including the efforts of Esther Brown, a Jewish housewife who, after seeing the conditions of the schools that her maid's children had to attend, joined with the Topeka NAACP to fight segregated education. The local interracial effort laid the groundwork for the combined efforts of Robert Carter and Jack Greenberg, one black, the other white, of the NAACP Legal Defense Fund, who were sent to prepare the case. Interracial cooperation again proved crucial in fulfilling the NAACP's need for expert witnesses to prove that segregation was harmful to black children. Esther Brown persuaded the Topeka Jewish Community to assist lawyers from New York in locating expert witnesses, who in turn located Midwestern professors to work on the *Brown* case. (I will discuss this case in greater depth in Chapter 6.)

The best example of how interracial cooperation contributed to the Brown decision was the financial support given to Kenneth Clark, an

African American psychologist, by the American Jewish Committee to prepare and deliver a paper on segregation and black children in 1950 at the White House Conference on Children. Clark's work and his testimony based on it was key in convincing the Supreme Court to abolish racial segregation in education. At the behest of the NAACP chief lawyer, Thurgood Marshall, 35 of the leading social scientists in the United States endorsed Clark's work and testimony. These included Jerome Bruner, Gordon Allport, Samuel Stouffer, Otto Klineberg, Robert Merton, Paul Lazarsfeld, Hadley Cantril, M. Brewster Smith, Arnold Rose, and Alfred McClung Lee from such leading educational institutions as Harvard, Columbia, Princeton, and Vassar (Kaufman, 1988).[12]

The triumph of interracial cooperation in the *Brown* decision cannot be overestimated in its historical importance to the credibility of the other tradition of American race relations. The nation and the world were impressed with the array of blacks and whites both in the NAACP and among the expert witnesses who, in their combined intellectual strength, gave meaning to the vision.

The civil rights era, at least from about 1954 to 1964, witnessed both a widening of interracial cooperation and the highest stage of interracial development among certain organizations, often described as "the beloved community." This was accompanied by the threat of a greater black challenge to interracial cooperation as an ideology and strategy of racial change. In less than a decade, the other tradition moved from the bliss of interracial unity and fellowship in certain instances to profound interracial tension and confusion in other instances.

The Student Nonviolent Coordinating Committee (SNCC) is one of the best examples of both the successes and the failures of interracial cooperation during this period. Whites had been involved in the SNCC since its founding in 1960 and had played key roles in its organization. The SNCC came to represent the essence of the beloved community. Many Northern white students experienced interracial interaction for the first time through the SNCC. Freedom Summer Project in the summer of 1964 contributed much to interracial interaction during the civil rights era. But by 1964, interracial tension was beginning to take its toll on the interracialists within the organization. Whites in the SNCC were criticized by some black members for taking over leadership positions because of their advantage in certain skills. As the civil rights era gave way to the Black Power era, these interracial tensions within the SNCC grew worse until, by the fall of 1966, "only a handful of white activists remained on SNCC's staff," driven out in large part by the black separatists within the organization (Carson, 1981; McAdam, 1988).

CORE's interracialism suffered the same fate. Notwithstanding CORE's impressive history of interracial cooperation, the increasing radicalization of black members could not be stopped. As early as the summer of 1963, the demand was growing for more black leadership in the organization. As more black cries were raised restricting white participation in CORE and whites "confused and sometimes bitter, [began] to withdraw in the face of quiet snubs, open attacks, and a constriction of their participation," (Meier & Rudwick, 1975, p. 393), CORE's long tradition of interracial cooperation began to come to an end.

A host of social, political, and economic forces led to the decline of the once dynamic interracial movement and an increase in racial polarization and fragmentation in large metropolitan areas. The Black Power Movement, black urban rebellions, white flight from the central cities to the suburbs, white resentment of remedial efforts on behalf of racial minorities, resurgent white racism in politics and community life, and the expanding black underclass have all occupied center stage in race relations during these years (Allen, 1969, pp. 21-127; Boskin, 1976; Franklin & Moss, 1988, pp. 458-483; Massey & Denton, 1993, pp. 115-185; Wiebe, 1979).

The state of race relations reached such depths of despair and alienation that many blacks and whites lost all hope of ever achieving an interracial society based on justice, love, and harmony. In 1985, Robert McCabe, president of Detroit Renaissance, commented on how suburban whites felt about the predominantly black central city: " 'I'd find people who had this tremendous sense of pride because they haven't been in downtown Detroit in 15 years and don't intend to go' " (McGill, 1985, p. 7a). Black leaders in Detroit, such as Superintendent of Schools Arthur Jefferson, understood this brand of suburban racism:

"[Race] is an issue that prevents us from moving forward on many fronts. In education, we have some of the finest technical facilities in Southeastern Michigan. How come there isn't more collaborative effort with surrounding communities? I suggest to you that if the coloration were different in this city and more compatible with the demographics and ethnic and racial majority in the suburban communities, there would be efforts." (p. 7a)

Even in the depths of racial despair and alienation and amid increasing racial polarization and fragmentation, interracial movements continued.

In 1967 in Detroit, out of the ashes of the worst urban disorder in the nation's history, an interracial-interfaith group formed to build bridges and heal wounds. Before the riot was 24 hours old, this group set up an Interfaith Emergency Center. Its membership included representatives of the local Council of Churches, the Archdiocese, the Jewish Community Council, and the black Interdenominational Ministerial Alliance. The churches and synagogues were used as distribution centers to meet the medical and food needs of the affected populations (see Gordon, 1971). Among the most impressive interracial organizations that grew out of the 1967 riots and are still functioning today are New Detroit, Inc. and Focus Hope. Both organizations played key roles in building interracial bridges during the postriot period and stand as proof that interracial movements can overcome interracial despair and alienation (New Detroit, 1990; Thomas, 1987).

As a city that suffered two of the most devastating race riots in U.S. history between 1943 and 1967, it is a wonder that Detroit has made so many efforts to heal itself of racial polarization and fragmentation. That it has done so is a tribute to its faith in interracial unity, cooperation, and harmony.

The interracial efforts that occurred in the post-1967 black urban rebellion in Detroit were part of a healing process in American race relations. Notwithstanding the trend of racial polarization and fragmentation that has plagued metropolitan areas throughout the nation, a small but determined army of people from all racial backgrounds is working to continue the tradition of interracial unity and cooperation. There are countless examples of religious and secular organizations reaching out across racial, religious, ethnic, and class barriers to build what Dr. Martin Luther King, Jr. described as "the beloved community."

One such religious community that has steadily kept its "eye on the prize" of interracial unity and cooperation is the Bahá'í community. During the most turbulent periods of racial conflicts, tensions, and suburban-central city polarizations, the Bahá'í have continued their commitment to antiracism and interracial unity and cooperation. Throughout the United States, local Bahá'í communities, encouraged by their national and international legislative bodies, have been in the forefront of the movement for interracial unity and cooperation. Their national governing body has issued statements condemning racism and encouraging Bahá'ís in local communities to support interracial unity and cooperation (see Thomas, 1993, chap. 8). The Bahá'ís, therefore, offer one of many examples of how the other tradition of American race relations is a potent force for improving race relations in the United States.

CONCLUSION

This brief historical survey of interracial unity and cooperation should demonstrate that we should learn to appreciate another tradition of race relations. Not that we should stop paying attention to the tradition of racism that is still a plague on all our houses. As we continue antiracism struggles, however, we must at the same time build Dr. Martin Luther King, Jr.'s beloved community. To build that community, we must be well-grounded in the tradition of interracial unity and cooperation in which community was first conceived. We must teach ourselves and our children about the brave men and women of all races who, while fighting against racism, were also building a community based on loving fellowship as a model for the world to emulate.

To do this, we must draw meaning from the history of interracial unity and cooperation. We must learn to see through all the horrors of slavery and racism to those fragile, short-lived, but nonetheless crucial bonds of interracial unity. Beginning in the colonial period and continuing into the present, blacks and whites have woven bonds of fellowship and community. The antislavery movement played a key role in this process by providing the first relatively large-scale opportunity for the development of black-white cooperation and antiracism. This movement was the seedbed that produced the first examples of blacks and whites working together. Other examples followed soon after.

The Civil War provided another opportunity for blacks and whites to engage in a process of racial unity and cooperation. Black enlisted men and white officers in the Union Army, working against a backdrop of racism, managed to forge an interracial bond that contributed yet another example of the other tradition. For a brief moment, blacks and whites worked together in the Southern reconstructed state governments. Although the cooperation did not last, it did demonstrate that under the right opportunities, blacks and whites in the South could work together in a biracial democracy.

In the 1880s and 1890s, the forces of interracial cooperation found expression in the Knights of Labor and the Southern Populist Movement. The Knights demonstrated that black and white workers could come together under the right conditions. Interracial cooperation between black and white farmers reached a high point during the early years of the Populist Party. This was the period of Tom Watson's brief flirtation with biracial political cooperation; but in the end, he and other white Populists chose the timeworn path of white supremacy.

By the era of Booker T. Washington, white supremacy in the South allowed only an accommodationist mode of interracial cooperation to thrive; this mode did not frighten the racially paranoid white South bent on maintaining control of blacks. Washington did what he could within this accommodationist mode of interracial cooperation.

Several new modes of interracial cooperation emerged between the turn of the century and the Great Depression; each one had its own particular approach. The NAACP drew on the abolitionist tradition; it was one of the most radical modes of interracial cooperation during this period, which focused attention on promoting racial justice for African Americans. This approach was diametrically opposed to the accommodationist approach of Booker T. Washington.

The NAACP mode of interracial cooperation became the most effective mode in challenging and dismantling the structure of legal racial discrimination; but, just as Washington's accommodationist mode did not address racial equality, the NAACP's mode of interracial cooperation did not address the social and economic problems of Southern black migrants in Northern industrial cities. Another mode of interracial cooperation was needed to address these problems.

The National Urban League met this need by focusing its interracial cooperation on the plight of urban blacks. In this sense, it shared many of the same beliefs of the Washington school of social uplift.

The racial tensions following World War I gave rise to the CIC, which soon became the key liberal civil rights organization in the South. Its goal was "to quench, if possible, the fires of racial antagonism which were flaming at the time with deadly menace in all sections of the country" (Franklin & Moss, 1988, p. 319). Working primarily in the South, the CIC reflected the hopes and aims of a minority of Southern white liberals who were forced by tradition to work within the racial status quo. As a result, they tended to be paternalistic. Within the limited social space allotted to them, however, they managed to do some good.

During this period the American Bahá'í community was one of the most progressive religious communities in the field of interracial cooperation. In the 1920s, it initiated a series of race amity conferences to foster interracial unity between blacks and whites. The Bahá'í community's interracial work has contributed greatly to the tradition of interracial unity and harmony.

Other interracial organizations emerged during the period from the Great Depression to the eve of the civil rights movement. Among these were the Southern Conference for Human Welfare, the Southern college interracial movement, the Catholic Inter-Racial Council, the American Communist Party, CORE, and the Highlander Folk School. These organizations contributed to the growing network of interracial cooperation throughout the country and would soon constitute a unique subculture. Each one of these organizations contributed to the growth and development of the tradition of interracial cooperation. They also created a climax for the acceptance and support of the civil rights movement during the 1960s.

Interracial cooperation from the 1950s to the late 1960s reached a high and low point. Interracial cooperation played a major role in the legal victories that culminated in the *Brown* decision. Blacks and Jews, in particular, cooperated in winning that decision. Black and white students in SNNC took interracial cooperation to a new level. But by the late 1960s, a host of factors combined to strike at the roots of a long tradition of interracial cooperation. The Black Power Movement, black urban rebellions, white flight from the central cities, and white backlash against black gains all contributed to the decline in interracial cooperation.

In the midst of this decline in interracial cooperation, a few brave souls and organizations stood firm. Such people and organizations as Father Cunningham and Focus Hope of Detroit and Bahá'í communities throughout the country continued working for racial healing. They refused to give up their faith in interracial unity and cooperation. They still believe in the legacy left by an army of black and white warriors to redeem this land by healing it of racism with the forces of justice and love.

NOTES

1. The American Colonization Society was founded in 1817 to colonize free blacks in Africa. The idea of colonizing free blacks was proposed by whites as early as 1714. After the Revolutionary War, Samuel Hopkins and Reverend Ezra Stiles explored the same possibility for getting rid of free blacks. In 1777, Thomas Jefferson headed a Virginia legislative committee that came up with a plan to emancipate and deport blacks gradually. By 1832, more than a dozen legislatures had given official approval to the society (see

Franklin & Moss, 1988, p. 155). (For free blacks' rejection of colonization, see Mehlinger, 1916.)

2. For an understanding of the development of the conflict between Douglass and Garrison, see Quarles (1938, pp. 1, 44-54).

3. For Coffin's role in the underground railroad, see Gara (1967, pp. 4-6); for the role of fugitive slaves in this network, see Gara (1967, chap. 3).

4. For a black perspective on John Brown's interaction with blacks, see Du Bois (1962, pp. 248-254).

5. For examples of the long history of racial conflicts within the labor movement, see Foner (1981).

6. For a more detailed treatment of the racial issues affecting Tom Watson and the Populists and a critique of some of Woodward's views concerning Watson and the Populists, see Crowe (1970).

7. For examples of the oppressive and brutal ways in which Southern blacks were treated during this period, see Williamson (1986, pp. 96-140) and Franklin and Moss (1988, pp. 235-238).

8. According to Langston Hughes's (1962) study of the NAACP, "The idea of the NAACP really began with a letter written by Mary White Ovington" (p. 18).

9. A group of young black radicals under the leadership of W. E. B. Du Bois met in Niagara Falls, Canada, in June 1905 to draw up a "platform for aggressive action" that included "freedom of speech and criticism, manhood suffrage, the abolition of all distinctions based on race, the recognition of the basic principles of human brotherhood, and respect for the working person" (Franklin & Moss, 1988, p. 286). They were attacked as radicals, but they persisted and reconvened at Harper's Ferry the next year, where they drew up another radical document. After several more meetings at historic abolitionist sites, such as Oberlin, Ohio, and Faneuil Hall in Boston, they ceased meeting (see Du Bois, 1988, pp. 236-253; Franklin & Moss, 1988, pp. 286-287).

10. For examples of some of the articles published in *Opportunity* addressing interracial cooperation during the early decades of the league's work, see Bond (1923), Brown (1933), Foster (1929), Jones (1926), Lasker (1925), and Steele (1929).

11. For an example of how Northern white politicians used interracial cooperation to maintain power, see Bunche (1973, p. 587).

12. For more information on the use of the Clark data, see Davis and Clark (1992, pp. 156-158).

3

Maintaining the Racial Status Quo

The history of interracial cooperation in the United States and other multiracial societies reveals certain patterns of majority group resistance to changes in the racial status quo. In most instances of interracial cooperation, certain aspects of the racial status quo appear to have remained unchanged. This is not unusual in stratified societies in which cooperation between majority and minority groups takes place within prescribed power relationships that remain largely inviolate or unchallenged throughout the process of majority-minority cooperation. Interracial cooperation between blacks and whites in the United States, however, has challenged and changed many core aspects of the racial status quo while reinforcing or maintaining other aspects. For example, interracial cooperation in the antislavery movement challenged slavery as the dominant mode of white racial oppression of blacks, simultaneously maintaining certain aspects of the power relations within the racial status quo, such as the paternalistic roles of white abolitionists. This same pattern has operated in other cases of interracial cooperation between blacks and whites in the United States.

What explains this tendency among certain whites within movements based on interracial cooperation to maintain certain aspects of the racial status quo? Why do we see this tendency within movements particularly concerned with reducing racial conflicts and uplifting African Americans?

The tendency of certain whites to maintain certain power-related aspects of the racial status quo, even while involved in interracial cooperation, is linked to the white-skin privilege that has historically bestowed on whites a wide array of material and emotional rewards. This system of white-skin privilege was an obvious by-product of the institutionalization of white racial dominance in the United States, beginning in the colonial period. Notwithstanding the class distinctions among whites, whites all shared some aspects of the system of white-skin privilege. Some whites rejected the most extreme forms of white-skin privilege because they conflicted with some basic beliefs and values. The early Quakers who opposed slavery were among this group. But although, to their credit, they were willing to give up this extreme case of white-skin privilege, many were not able or willing to give up the social advantage of being white. Many among the Society of Friends held to their racial prejudices, not because they were mean or evil people but because they lived in a system that rewarded whites for being white. Although cooperating with blacks in challenging the admittedly worst aspect of white-skin privilege—slavery—they chose to maintain other aspects of the racial status quo.

In response to the second question, studying the tendency to maintain certain aspects of the racial status quo is vital to research on interracial cooperation, because interracial cooperation is the highest and most progressive form of race relations in any biracial or multiracial society. The degree to which a biracial or multiracial society is able to foster genuine and equitable forms of interracial cooperation represents the degree to which it has achieved interracial health. Racial justice is a prerequisite for genuine interracial cooperation. But racial justice and genuine interracial cooperation are unattainable if whites who participate in interracial cooperation maintain certain power-related aspects of the racial status quo. White-skin privilege can be removed as a barrier to interracial cooperation only by conscious and ever-vigilant antiracism efforts. Antiracism keeps the focus on the need to challenge all aspects of white-skin privilege. This chapter focused on selected historical examples of this pattern of maintaining certain aspects of the racial status quo within modes of interracial cooperation.

WHITE RACIAL PREJUDICE
AND PATERNALISM

As white America went about building a white nation and fashioning an ideological rationale to justify dominance over Native and African peoples, in what I have described as the "other tradition" of race relations, a growing segment reached out to embrace the humanity of African slaves within their midst. This process took many forms and experienced many emotional gyrations as these exceptional white Americans struggled to plant and nurture the seeds of interracial cooperation. Other white Americans, notably the founding fathers, were primarily concerned with building and consolidating a white nation. To this latter group, interracial cooperation was a means to an end, that end being the growth and protection of America as a white nation.

The first example of interracial cooperation as a means of maintaining white racial dominance occurred during the American Revolutionary War when, after some reluctance, General George Washington and Congress agreed to allow blacks to bear arms alongside whites in defending the country. There can be no doubt that interracial cooperation between black and white soldiers contributed to the success of the American Revolutionary War. But this interracial cooperation was a military necessity for protecting one white nation from another, both of whom used blacks in their armed forces to serve their objectives of dominance (Quarles, 1961).

Notwithstanding the great contribution that the antislavery movement made to the development of interracial cooperation, this movement exhibited what would come to be recognized as classic symptoms of unequal power relations within interracial movements. In addition, there were the persistent problems of racial prejudice and paternalism among some white abolitionists. These problems were related to the maintenance of selected aspects of racial dominance based on the sense of white-skin privilege. To gain a more in-depth appreciation of the complex racial dynamics at work during this stage of interracial cooperation, one must reflect on the discussion in the previous chapter.

In the discussion of interracial cooperation during the start of the militant phase of the antislavery movement, beginning with the emergence of Garrison and his newspaper, *The Liberator,* I mentioned how appreciative blacks were of Garrison's efforts on their behalf. Litwack (1965) characterizes this stage of white-black cooperation as appearing "to be an auspicious beginning of effective interracial cooperation for mutual gain." He also points out, however, that "the attempted coalition, though not unproductive, was to reveal to the abolitionists—white and black—fundamental differences in assumptions, goals and emphasis" (p. 137).

Historical hindsight grounded in trial and error and a long tradition of race relations research enables contemporary scholars to understand some of the problems that plagued black-white cooperation during this stage of the antislavery movement. Given the oppressive racial climate in the country, especially after the Nat Turner insurrection, blacks welcomed all the white allies they could get. The best white allies were those such as Garrison who "forcefully challenged the colonizationists, the doctrine of racial inferiority and antislavery which did not include as an objective the elevation of the free Negro" (Litwack, 1965, p. 138). These white allies, however, brought their racial cultural baggage into the relationship, including aspects of the racial status quo. Some black abolitionists, such as Sarah Forten of Philadelphia, understood the problems facing white abolitionists who allied themselves with blacks, challenging, in part, major aspects of the racial status quo. Forten once related a story of a white abolitionist friend who remarked to her that when she, as a white, walked with a black, " 'the darker the night, the better Abolitionist was I.' " Forten was willing to forgive this type of racist behavior because she felt that many white abolitionists were being forced to make " 'great sacrifice to public sentiment' " (Litwack, 1965, p. 140).

Other black abolitionists were not as understanding or forgiving of white abolitionists' racist conduct. Rev. Theodore S. Wright expected white abolitionists to live up to the highest moral standards. Speaking before the convention of the New York State Anti-Slavery Society in Utica on September 20, 1837, Wright made it clear that there could be no maintenance of any aspects of the racial status quo within the interracial antislavery movement:

> "Three years ago, when a man professed to be an abolitionist, we knew where he was. He was an individual who recognized the identity of the human family. . . . Unless men come out and take their stand on the principle of recognizing man as man, I tremble for the ark. . . . The identity of the human family, the principle of recognizing all men as brethren—that is the doctrine, that is the point which touches the quick of the community." (Aptheker, 1967, pp. 171-172)

Wright explained to the gathering just how this principle related to the abolitionist movement:

> "It is an easy thing to ask about the vileness of slavery at the South, but to call the dark man a brother, heartily to embrace the doctrine advanced in the second article of the constitution, to treat all men according to their moral worth, to treat the man of color in all circumstances as a man and brother—this is the test." (Aptheker, 1967, p. 172)

Wright then made an interesting suggestion as to how abolitionists could apply this principle to their work:

> "Every man who comes into this society ought to be catechized. It should be ascertained whether he looks upon man as man, all of one blood and one family. A healthful atmosphere must be created in which the slave may live when rescued from the horrors of slavery." (p. 172)

Wright's expectation of white abolitionists challenged them to move beyond their commitment to rescuing slaves to accepting them as members of the human family. Such a challenge went far beyond what many white abolitionists felt compelled to do. If white abolitionists were required to be "catechized" as to whether they looked on "man as man, all of one blood and one family," their commitment to blacks as fellow human beings would not stop at the point of freeing blacks from slavery but would continue until the freed slave was uplifted as a fellow human being. Not many white abolitionists were prepared to go that far in challenging the racial status quo, however. Wright suspected some white abolitionists of forming constitutions of antislavery societies so that " 'they will be popular.' " He remarked,

> "I have seen constitutions of abolition societies, where nothing was said about the improvement of the man of color! They have overlooked the great sin of prejudice. They have passed by this foul monster, which is at once the parent and offspring of slavery." (Aptheker, 1967, p. 172)

Wright penetrated the problem of the antislavery movement as a mode of interracial cooperation when he pointed to "the great sin of prejudice . . . at once the parent and offspring of slavery." This great sin was grounded in white America's sense of racial superiority. To be white in the America of the 1830s was to be part of the racial ruling class. Although white abolitionists objected to white persons holding black slaves, rarely did they object to the privilege that white skin provided them. If compassion for slaves extended to the uplifting of free blacks—perhaps to the level of whites—such privilege would eventually vanish. This was the full implication of Wright's admonishment to the gathering—that every person who joined the society should be catechized so that he or she would see that all persons were of one blood and one family.

Whereas Sarah Forten would forgive white abolitionists for their breach of this principle because they were being forced to "make great sacrifices to public sentiment," Wright counseled white abolitionists who failed to live up to the high moral principle of racial justice and equality to be consistent. " 'We must be consistent—recognize the colored man [and woman] in every aspect as a man and a brother.' " In doing this, Wright told them, there would be a cost. " '[We] will have to encounter scorn; we shall have to breast the storm' " (Aptheker, 1967, p. 172). "We" referred to both blacks and whites in the antislavery movement. The "storm" referred not to the normal criticism that some segments of white society reserved for whites and blacks within the antislavery movement but, rather, the passionate hatred and bitterness that came forth when the core racial beliefs of white America were challenged, such as the belief in white racial superiority. This racial belief was the foundation of what Wright described as " 'the giant sin of prejudice . . . this foul monster' " (p. 172).

Wright challenged white abolitionists to take a higher moral road than just the abolition of slavery. He challenged them to abolish the white racial prejudice that most of them shared, to a lesser or greater degree, with white slave owners. Such a challenge placed a great burden on the sometimes fragile interracial cooperation within the antislavery movement. To " 'breast the storm,' " Wright told white abolitionists that they would " 'do well to spend a whole day in thinking about it and praying over it. Every abolitionist would do well to spend a day in fasting and prayer over it and in looking at his own heart' " (Aptheker, 1967, p. 172).

Wright ended this talk with an example of the effects of white racism on the antislavery movement. Although acknowledging that the " 'successors of Penn, Franklin and Woolman have shown themselves the friends of the colored race' " and that they have " 'done more in this cause than any other church and they are still doing great things both in Europe and America . . . and lifted up their voices against slavery and the slave trade,' " Wright claimed that with but few exceptions, " 'they go but halfway.' " According to Wright, " 'When they come to the grand doctrine, to lay the ax right down at the root of the tree, and destroy the very spirit of slavery—there they are defective. Their doctrine is to set the slave free and let him take care of himself.' " As a result, Wright commented, " 'We hear nothing about their being brought into the Friends' Church, or their being viewed and treated according to their moral worth' " (Aptheker, 1967, p. 172). Wright then related a classic example of how well-meaning white abolitionists maintained certain aspects of white racial dominance:

"Our hearts have recently been gladdened by an address of the Annual Meeting of the Friends' Society in the city of New York, in which they insist upon the doctrine of immediate emancipation. But that very good man who signed the document as the organ of that society within the past year, received a man of color, a Presbyterian minister, into his house, gave him his meals alone in the kitchen, and did not introduce him to his family. That shows how men can testify against it at the South, and not assail it at the North, where it is tangible. Here is something for Abolitionists to do. What can the friends of emancipation effect while the spirit of slavery is so fearfully prevalent? Let every man take his stand, burn out this prejudice, live it down, talk it down, everywhere consider the colored man as a man, in the church, the stage, the steamboat, the public house, in all places, and the death-blow to slavery will be struck." (pp. 172-173)

Wright's candid views on white abolitionists' racial attitudes and conduct represented some of the burning concerns, tensions, conflicts, and frustrations facing blacks within an interracial movement in which some whites were still clinging to some aspects of the racial status quo. Blacks demanded much more from their interracial interactions than many white abolitionists were willing to give. Black abolitionists saw the antislavery movement as a demonstration of full equality between blacks and whites in an interracial fellowship. Many white abolitionists saw the movement as an interracial effort to free blacks from slavery but not to free themselves from their prized heritage of white-skin privilege.

A major point of tension and conflict between black and white abolitionists centered on the issue of how the movement would benefit free blacks. Few could question the great work that many white abolitionists had done in the areas of civil rights and educational opportunities for the free black community. Yet "little had been done in the way of economic assistance, except to call upon Negroes to improve themselves" (Litwack, 1965, p. 141). Blacks were struggling to improve themselves against all odds, but they needed white abolitionists to live up to their professed belief in interracial cooperation by providing employment opportunities in businesses they owned. The *Colored American* in 1837 surveyed the economic plight of blacks in its community and could not find " 'one local abolitionist [who] had placed a Negro in any conspicuous position in his business establishment; in fact, it could not even find a Negro in the offices of the New York Anti-Slavery Society' " (pp. 141-142).

By 1852, very little progress had been made in this vital area. This prompted black delegates to an antislavery convention to accuse the antislavery movement of falling short of its responsibility (Litwack, 1965). Leading white abolitionists had been approached to hire blacks in their businesses but to no avail. One leading white abolitionist, Arthur Tappan, did hire some blacks in his department store but only in menial jobs. In describing this situation, a black delegate to the antislavery meeting mentioned earlier lamented, " 'wherever the colored man is connected with the houses of these gentlemen, it is as the lowest drudges' " (Litwack, 1965, p. 142).

Pleading for desperately needed employment must have been painful for black abolitionists who, on one hand appreciated their white allies in the struggle against slavery, yet on the other hand probably wondered why these white coworkers did not understand the extent of despair and need among them. As Litwack (1965) argues,

> [In] demanding economic assistance, the Negro denied any desire for preferential treatment; he simply wanted an equal opportunity to compete for respectable employment. And since many white abolitionists were in a position to make this possible, they were asked to give practical implementation to their antislavery professions. (p. 142)

From the perspective of black leaders, white abolitionists who failed to understand this vital role that their black coworkers were asking them to play did not understand that the fight for equal rights could not be won on "the bare ground of abstract principles" (Litwack, 1965, p. 129). Black abolitionists expected more and demanded more from white abolitionists. White abolitionists had to understand that they were engaged in two struggles: one to eliminate slavery and one to eliminate the slavery of free blacks, "which doomed the free Negro to economic dependence and pauperism" (p. 142). One black leader was very concerned about the fact that many white abolitionists had time for a variety of other reforms, such as capital punishment, temperance, and women's rights, but denied employment to free blacks who desperately needed it.

At a 1855 black convention, a delegate argued that some white abolitionists who claimed to be the most ardent antislavery advocates had not given blacks any economic assistance and avoided putting their principles into practice:

> [Some white abolitionists] might employ a black youngster as a porter or packer, but the majority would as soon put a hod-carrier to the clerk's desk as a colored boy, ever so educated though he be. (Litwack, 1965, p. 173).

Frederick Douglass challenged white abolitionists to address the issue: " 'What boss anti-slavery mechanic will take a black boy into his wheelwright shop, his blacksmith shop, his joiner shop, his cabinet shop? Here is something practical; where are the whites and where are the blacks that will respond to it?' " (p. 143).

Were many of these white abolitionists hypocritical, saying one thing while practicing something else? Or did black abolitionists expect too much of their white coworkers in the antislavery struggle, who, as Sarah Forten observed, were " 'being forced to make great sacrifices to public sentiment' " (Litwack, 1965, p. 140). Certainly, many white abolitionists felt they were doing enough in struggling to free the slaves when the institution of slavery was strong and unyielding. Yet black abolitionists expected much more from white abolitionists and felt abandoned and betrayed when white abolitionists who owned businesses did not employ free blacks who desperately needed jobs. Blacks also felt betrayed and frustrated when those white abolitionists who did employ blacks employed them only in menial jobs.

At this juncture of our analysis, one should remember the earlier discussion on white-skin privilege. The antislavery movement was the first large-scale interracial movement for any kind of racial justice in the United States. It was America's first sustained—however flawed, inconsistent, and at times ideologically fragmented—interracial social reform movement. It evolved within the larger white racial culture grounded in a belief in white racial superiority and black inferiority. One could be "antislavery" and hold on to one's white-skin privilege at the same time. White involvement in the antislavery movement did not require the abandonment of all of one's racist baggage or a commitment to antiracism in one's personal life. A full commitment to antiracism would have required whites to scrutinize their lives for any and all aspects of racial prejudice. Apparently this was too much of a burden for many white abolitionists. Whereas black abolitionists expected white abolitionists to work on their prejudices and assist free blacks in obtaining much needed jobs, many white abolitionists viewed their role differently.

These different views and expectations of the role of whites within the struggle for racial equality, including both the abolition of slavery and the uplifting of free blacks, are indicative of the developmental stage of interracial cooperation within the antislavery movement. White and black abolitionists were still struggling to come to grips with certain aspects of the racial status quo.

Perhaps no other aspect of the racial status quo was so glaring a violation of the dignity and pride of black abolitionists than the paternalism of white abolitionists toward their black coworkers. Paternalism has always been a by-product of majority-minority power relations in the United States, especially within black-white relations. Paternalism is one of the highest forms of benign white racism and often the most insidious form of white-skin privilege. It is a silk glove covering the harsh hand of white racial power.

White paternalism manifested itself in various forms within the antislavery movement. One such form was the double standard that white abolitionists applied to the achievements of blacks. For example, some black abolitionists accused white abolitionists of expecting less of black students in the classroom, speaking "exultantly of the academic work of Negroes which would have been barely passable if performed by whites, and willingly tolerat[ing] Negro ministers and teachers who fell far short of the qualifications of whites for the same positions" (Litwack, 1965, pp. 140-141).

Another form of paternalism related to the special role that some white abolitionists wanted ex-slaves to play on the antislavery lecture tour. A fugitive slave with a good tale could swell the audiences at antislavery gatherings. Many Northern whites were eager to hear such tales from the mouths of those who had escaped from slavery. But this role had to be consistent with the "image" of the slave held in the mind of Northern white audiences, that of a poor creature bent and worn by oppression, barely able to speak intelligently. This image was contradicted by many great ex-slaves such as Sojourner Truth and Frederick Douglass, often to the chagrin of some white abolitionists. Not long after he joined the antislavery lecture circuit, Douglass contradicted this image by such excellent speaking that some white abolitionists advised him to stick to tales of his life as a slave, because that was what audiences wanted to hear. More revealing of both the paternalism and the view of the intellectual division of labor within the interracial structure of the antislavery movement was the advice white abolitionists offered to give them the facts and they would take care of the philosophy. " 'People won't believe you were ever a slave, Frederick, if you keep on this way,' " he was told. " 'Be yourself and tell your story. Better have a little of the plantation speech than not; it is not best that you seem too learned' " (Litwack, 1965, p. 147).

The white abolitionists who advised Douglass to confine himself to the facts while they took take care of the philosophy had clearly determined the role that ex-slaves and, by extension, most black abolitionists should play in the antislavery movement. Their attitudes were influenced by their perception of their role in this movement. Most white abolitionists, even the much beloved Garrison, were not immune to notions of their privileged role in the antislavery movement.

The breach in 1851 between Garrison and Douglass, the two most famous and best-known symbols of interracial cooperation in the antislavery movement, was caused by more than just ideological differences between the two (Quarles, 1968). Douglass could not restrict himself to the confines of the Garrisonian camp. In many ways, Douglass was a threat to the mode of interracial cooperation that appealed to most white abolitionists. He was too bold, intelligent, and independent, at a time when blacks were expected to be satisfied with whites playing the dominant role in their salvation. When Douglass decided to start his own antislavery newspaper against the advice of Garrison, once his hero and mentor, he was challenging the racial status quo within the antislavery movement.

In January 1848, Douglass published an article in defense of the establishment of black newspapers that revealed how he felt about the interracial division of labor within the antislavery movement. It also revealed the points of tensions and conflicts between whites and black abolitionists: " 'COLORED NEWSPAPERS. They are sometimes objected to, on the grounds that they serve to keep up an odious and wicked distinction between white and colored persons and are a barrier to that very equality which we are want to advocate' " (Foner, 1950, p. 291). Douglass strongly disagreed with such views of interracialism.

> "So far from the truth is the notion that colored newspapers are serving to keep up that cruel distinction, the want of them is the main cause of its continuance. . . . In order to remove this odious distinction, we must do what white men do." (Foner, 1950, p. 291)

Douglass attacked the racist root of the racial division of labor that many abolitionists no doubt accepted:

> "It must be no longer white lawyer, and black woodsawyer,—white editor, and black street cleaner: it must be no longer white, intelligent, and black, ignorant; but we must take our stand side by side with our white fellow countrymen in all the trades, arts, professions and the callings of the day." (Foner, 1950, p. 291)

Douglass's view of interracial cooperation was based not on an unequal relationship in which whites dominated all the positions of wealth and talent and blacks remained perpetual wards of their benevolence but, rather, on a relationship in which both races stood side by side in all areas of life. This view placed heavy demands on the racial status quo within the antislavery movement.

By the late 1830s, some black abolitionists were already challenging the prevailing mode of interracial cooperation. Black leaders began rethinking the roles forced on them by ideological battles among white abolitionists and demands within the black abolitionist camp for "ideological and political independence" (Litwack, 1965, p. 143). Black abolitionists became increasingly articulate and eager to speak for themselves. As Litwack (1965) puts it, "They tended increasingly to voice their own aspirations and to question the white abolitionist's prerogative to speak for them" (pp. 143-144). In 1839, the *Colored American* warned its readers about being too dependent on white abolitionists. " '[As] long as we bow to their opinions, and acknowledge that their word is counsel, and their will is law; so long they will outwardly treat us as men, while in their hearts they still hold us as slaves' " (p. 144).

The emergence of the *Colored American* represented a crucial stage in both the intellectual development of the black community and the shifting power relations in the antislavery movement. As a black newspaper, the *Colored American* "was the most prominent voice of this quest for independence expression" (Litwack, 1965, p. 144). It was part of a larger independent movement of blacks to speak for themselves through instruments of their own choosing, such as annual conventions, which started in 1831 in Philadelphia (Aptheker, 1967). Annual black conventions and black newspapers forced significant changes in the structure of interracial cooperation within the antislavery movement. Although some white abolitionists opposed what they considered to be separatist tendencies among black abolitionists, other whites understood and supported independent black development. These whites were in essence accepting a needed shift in the power relations within the antislavery movement. Many also supported the *North Star,* a new antislavery paper started by Douglass (Quarles, 1969).

The movement toward black independent development within the larger antislavery movement proved crucial during the ideological battles among white abolitionists, who were prone to debates over abstractions just as the plight of blacks, slave and free, was becoming increasingly desperate. These ideological battles split the antislavery movement into warring factions. Many black leaders found that these battles directed attention away from the larger struggle against slavery and racism. This was all the more reason for blacks to take their struggle into their own hands and determine what strategies and methods best suited their needs (Quarles, 1969).

The urgent need to take control of their own struggle meant deviating from some of the ideological "sacred cows" of some prominent white abolitionists such as Garrison, who opposed both political action and separate black conventions (Litwack, 1965). The *Colored American* took the lead in disregarding these ideological sacred cows. Not only did the newspaper criticize the ideological battles among abolitionists because of their destructive effect on the unity of the antislavery cause, it went even further and urged qualified blacks to vote. To add further injury to profound insult, in response to an attack from the Garrisonians for its ideological deviation, the *Colored American* scolded the Garrisonians for presuming to " 'dictate antislavery doctrine to the Negro.' " Furthermore, " 'Sooner than abate one jot or tittle of our right to think, speak and act like men, we will suffer our enterprise to perish, and the *Colored American* will be numbered with the things that were' " (Litwack, 1965, p. 145).

The *Colored American* continued to defend the right of blacks to chart their own course of struggle against the Garrisonians—some of whom were black—when the Garrisonians also criticized separate black conventions. Samuel Ward, a black supporter of independent development, took his white friends to task on this question, stating that they would understand the need for such independent action among blacks if they had " 'worn a colored skin from October 1817 to June 1840, as I have in this pseudo-republic.' " Although recognizing the contributions of white abolitionists to the antislavery cause, Ward was less than satisfied " 'with a certain type of white abolitionists who had failed to confront their own racism.' " He felt that " 'too many best love the colored man at a distance' " (Litwack, 1965, p. 145).

The independent movement among blacks continued through the following decades, creating tensions and conflict within the traditional structure of interracial cooperation. By the early 1840s, blacks had been conducting their own annual conventions for over a decade. Gone were the days when many blacks thought that Garrison walked on water. Although many blacks still respected those white abolitionists who had sacrificed so much for both the slave and the freed, many also recognized the need to move to the front of the antislavery struggle—to be more than a prize exhibit on lecture tours organized by whites.

The need for black independent development was also a sign of the growing ineffectiveness of the traditional mode of interracial cooperation, which was unable to address the growing concerns of the black community or accommodate its rapid ideological growth. Radical black leaders such as Henry Highland Garnet were too bold for those white abolitionists who were used to more passive and grateful blacks who accepted their assigned roles.

In August 1843, Henry Highland Garnet presented one of the most militant speeches ever delivered by a black abolitionist up to that time. It was delivered before the delegates to the National Negro Convention, which was held in Buffalo, New York, against some opposition. The speech, titled "An Address to the Slaves of the United States," attracted national attention because it called out to the slaves to rebel against their masters:

> "Brethren, the time has come when you must act for yourselves. . . . If you must bleed, let it all come at once—rather die freemen than live to be slaves. Brethren, arise, arise! Strike for your lives and liberties. Now is the day and the hour. Let every slave throughout the land do this, and the days of slavery are numbered. You cannot be more oppressed than you have been. . . . rather die freemen than live to be slaves. Remember you are four millions." (Aptheker, 1967, p. 226)

Garnet told the gathering that it was in slaves' power to " 'so torment the God-cursed slaveholders that they will be glad to let you go free.' " He then criticized slaves' patience:

> "But you are a patient people. You act as though you were made for the special use of these devils. You act as though your daughters were born to pamper the lusts of your masters and overseers. And worse than all, you tamely submit while your lords tear your wives from your embrace and defile them before your eyes. In the name of God, we ask, are you men? Where is the blood of your fathers? Has it all run out of your veins? . . . Awake, awake; millions of voices are calling you! Your dead fathers speak to you from the dead. Heaven, as with a voice of thunder, calls on you to arise from the dust. Let your motto be resistance! Resistance! RESISTANCE! No oppressed people have ever secured their liberty without resistance." (Aptheker, 1967, pp. 231-233)

Garnet's call to slaves to rise up against their masters fell short by one vote of being adopted by the convention as its official view on the subject of slavery. It was yet another sign of the times: Black abolitionists were becoming more desperate and frustrated with the state of racial oppression in the country. Even more significant than the speech was the response of Maria Weston Chapman, a well-known abolitionist writer and poet, who condemned not only the convention of blacks but also Garnet's speech. Garnet's response to Chapman was yet another example of the stresses and strains within the traditional structure of interracial cooperation.

After Chapman wrote an article that appeared in the *Liberator* condemning the convention and Garnet, Garnet wrote a rebuttal in which he scolded Chapman for treating him like a slave:

> "I was born in slavery, and have escaped, to tell you, and others, what the monster has done, and is still doing. It, therefore, astonished me to think that you should desire to sink me again to the condition of a slave, by forcing me to think just as you do. . . . My crime is that I have dared to think, and act, contrary to your opinion. . . . [If] it has come to this, that I must think and act as you do, because you are an Abolitionist, or be exterminated by your thunder, then I do not hesitate to say that your abolitionism is abject slavery." (Aptheker, 1967, pp. 234-235)

Garnet's rebuttal focused on the racial paternalism of white abolitionists that had already begun to alienate the more radical and outspoken black abolitionists, who were seeking more independent actions outside of the traditional mode of interracial cooperation. He was particularly concerned about Chapman's reference to his speech in which she said he had " 'bad counsel.' " In response, Garnet commented,

> "You are not the only person who has told your humble servant that his humble productions have been produced by the 'counsel' of some Anglo-Saxon. I have expected no more from ignorant slaveholders and their apologists, but I really looked for better things from Mrs. Maria W. Chapman, an antislavery poetess and editor pro tem of the *Boston Liberator.*" (Aptheker, 1967, p. 235)

One can sense Garnet's anger when he comments, " 'I can think on the subject of human rights without 'counsel,' either from the men of the West, or the women of the East.' " Garnet ended his rebuttal by informing Chapman that he hoped to publish his address so that she could " 'judge how much treason there is in it.' " She, meanwhile, should " 'be assured that there is one black American who dares to speak boldly on the subject of universal liberty' " (Aptheker, 1967, p. 236).

Evidently, Chapman did not learn much about her brand of racial paternalism from Garnet's response; 3 years later, she confided to an English friend about her doubts concerning Douglass's ability to withstand pressure from the anti-Garrison camp. Here again is an example of an established white abolitionist lacking faith in the abilities of a black coworker. Douglass responded to Chapman's racial paternalism much as Garnet had:

> "I have felt somewhat grieved to see by a letter from you to Mr. R. G. Webb of Dublin that you betray a want of confidence in me as a man, and an abolitionist, utterly inconsistent with all the facts in the history of my connection with the anti-slavery enterprise." (Foner, 1981, p. 143)

He detailed his concerns, which cut to the core of the racial paternalism that certain blacks had to face as they continually struggled to overcome the unequal interracial power relations within the antislavery movement:

> "In that letter you were pointing out to Mr. Webb the necessity of his keeping a watch on myself and friend Mr. Buffum, but as Mr. Buffum was rich and I poor while there was little danger but Mr. Buffum would stand firm, I might be bought up by the London committee. Now, dear Madam, you do me great injustice by such a comparison. They are direct insinuations, and when whispered in the ear of a stranger to whom I look up as a friend, they are very embarrassing. . . . I can assure you, Dear Madam, that you have mistaken me altogether if you suppose that the love of money or the hate of poverty will drive me from the ranks of the old Antislavery Society. But had I no more confidence in them than you seem to have in me, I would not take a second breath before leaving them.

> "You have trusted me or seemed to do so at home. Why distrust me or seem to do so abroad? Of one thing I am certain, and that is I never gave you any just cause to distrust me, and if I am to be watched over for evil rather than for good by my professed friends, I can say with propriety, save me from my friends, and I will take care of my enemies. Had you, kind friend, previous to my leaving America, given me face to face that advice and friendly counsel which your long experience and superior wisdom has richly enabled you to do . . . my feelings towards you . . . would be those of ardent gratitude. If you wish to drive me from the Antislavery Society, put me under overseership and the work is done. Set someone to watch

over for me for evil and let them be so simple-minded as to inform me of their office, and the last blow is struck." (Foner, 1981, pp. 143-144)

Although race was not explicitly stated, it is clear that Chapman's conduct was based on her perceptions of Douglass's abilities. Douglass's response reflected the anger and frustration of black abolitionists who refused to accept the veiled slights and insults of white abolitionists. It was no doubt difficult for famous and well-established white abolitionists such as Chapman not to feel paternalistic toward former slaves like Garnet and Douglass, notwithstanding the fact that they had clearly beaten the odds and developed impressive intellectual capacities equal or superior to those of many white abolitionists. Perhaps that was the problem. In a rather short period of time, black abolitionists were forced to engage in rapid intellectual and organizational development because their survival depended on it. They could not allow white abolitionists to determine when and where and through what means they should engage in independent action. This was traumatic for some white abolitionists, who were more comfortable with blacks as followers instead of leaders.

As the 1840s drew to a close, blacks became increasingly militant, placing even more strain on the traditional mode of interracial cooperation. Although a black national convention in Troy, New York, in October 1847 rejected violence as a means of struggle, 2 years later a black convention in Ohio voted to obtain 500 copies of Garnet's 1843 speech. In 1849, speaking in Boston, Douglass abandoned the pacific position he had taken in 1843 and ended a speech with the statement that he would welcome the news that the slaves had arisen. The 1850s brought even more militancy among blacks, sparked by the Fugitive Slave Law. A state convention of blacks in Ohio in 1850 encouraged blacks to organize military companies "where it was practical and where they could not be enrolled with whites" (Quarles, 1969, pp. 228-229). By the time of the *Dred Scott* decision, "the militant spirit among the Negroes was fanned full sail" (p. 230). When John Brown was executed on December 2, 1859, blacks lost their greatest white coworker, and the tradition of interracial cooperation was given its greatest martyr.

John Brown's death had a galvanizing effect on the interracial movement of abolitionists. Not all white abolitionists approved of Brown's attempt at insurrection on behalf of the slaves, but the vast majority of blacks did. This disparity could have further weakened interracial cooperation between many black and white abolitionists, but Brown's martyrdom brought thousands of blacks and whites together. In several cities, racially mixed gatherings held memorial services to honor Brown for his dedication to the struggle for racial justice. Whatever shortcomings had prevented interracial cooperation in the antislavery movement from reaching its full potential were forgiven in these gatherings of black and white.

Relations between white officers and black troops in the Union Army represented another stage in the history of interracial cooperation. I noted earlier that many white officers who commanded black troops shared the same racist beliefs as white Southerners. Actual service alongside black troops helped these white officers shed much of their prejudice, however. Yet many white officers, as well as many Northern whites, had to struggle with deeply entrenched notions of white-skin privilege and white racial superiority as they attempted to come to grips with the psychological implications of black-white cooperation within the Union Army.

As soon as it became clear that black troops were a military necessity for waging the war against the South, the full implications of interracial cooperation hit the psyche of many Northern whites like the proverbial ton of bricks. Most whites, Northern and Southern, not only shared the same racial stereotypes about blacks but could not conceive of arming blacks. "Racial prejudice was so powerful," Glatthaar (1990) argues, "that most whites regarded the notion of arming blacks and encouraging them to fight for their freedom as lunacy" (p. 1). Sixteen months into the war, however, the federal government was forced to establish the policy of recruiting black soldiers. But there was more at stake than simply winning the war: The racial status quo was also at stake. To allow blacks to fight in a "white man's war" was in some ways to admit that Northern whites needed blacks to win. This would cause a gradual erosion of white superiority. To slow down this erosion and to protect their sense of white-skin privilege, Northern white policymakers and politicians started out by encouraging a structure of interracial cooperation within the Union Army that would not upset the racist sensibilities of white Northerners.

Perhaps in no area of interracial cooperation were white sensibilities more vulnerable than in the area of black officers. It was difficult enough for the Lincoln administration to "convince the military and public to accept black units. Having black officers was a step beyond that" (Glatthaar, 1990, p. 177). What was behind this racial fear and anxiety of whites? Glatthaar (1990) explains, "Whites had great difficulty dealing with blacks on an equal basis, let alone one of inferiority, a condition that would be created by the appointment of blacks to officers' rank" (p. 177). Notwithstanding the fact that blacks were fighting on their side, white Union troops felt racism so deeply that many could not stand the sight of a black officer. On one occasion, when white soldiers of the 70th Indiana Infantry marched past the 15th U.S. Colored Infantry, the white troops said nothing until they spotted a black lieutenant's shoulder straps. Then cries of " 'jerk them off, take him out, kill him resounded all along the line.' " According to one observer, it was only because they were in the line of march that prevented the white troops from " 'dealing severely with him' " (p. 177). Why this reaction? Because their perception of themselves as whites would not allow them to accept a black man on a level above them.

Not even the fact that both white and black soldiers were wearing the Union blue mattered. White troops could see only the erosion of their racial status in any structure of interracial cooperation that challenged their image of themselves as white men above all black men.

This racist need to feel superior to blacks, no matter what their rank, also existed among whites who volunteered to serve in black units. Six white doctors were so upset when they discovered that their commander was a prominent black surgeon that they threatened to resign. They wrote a letter of protest to President Lincoln in which they expressed their concern. This letter is revealing because it shows how important it was to these white doctors to serve in a black unit only if their status as whites was not threatened:

> "When we made application for position in the Colored Service, the understanding was universal that all commissioned officers were to be white men. Judge our surprise and disappointment when upon joining our respective regiments, we found that the Senior Surgeon of the command was a Negro. We claim to be behind no one, in a desire for the elevation and improvement of the Colored race. . . . But we cannot in any cause willingly compromise what we consider a proper self respect." (Glatthaar, 1990, p. 177)

The doctors "requested that this 'degradation . . . in some way be terminated' " (p. 177).

This protest reveals the contradictions in the racial thinking of those whites who, on one hand, claimed " 'to be behind no one in a desire for the elevation of the Colored Race,' " but on the other hand, could not

" 'in any cause willingly compromise what [they] consider[ed] a proper self-respect.' " To serve under a prominent black senior surgeon was a "degradation" that these whites hoped could be terminated. It did not matter that the black commanding officer was competent. All that mattered was their self-respect as white men. They would work for the elevation of blacks only if they could maintain their white-skin privilege. Ironically, these men and many who shared their racist views did not see, or perhaps were unwilling to see, that any real elevation of blacks could occur only at the expense of the racial status quo, because white racial privilege by its very nature was based on the social, economic, and political oppression of blacks.

The underlying reason for the racist attitudes of the white physicians was rooted in the belief common among most whites that blacks had very little leadership ability. Not even some white friends and supporters of black soldiers who played key roles in the structure of interracial cooperation during the war believed that blacks could be leaders. Chaplain John Eaton, who served as a colonel in the U.S. Colored Troops and made great contributions to the welfare of freed slaves during the war, believed that only whites were qualified to command black soldiers. Brigadier General Rufus Saxon, who ranked as another "friend of the Negro," believed that black soldiers preferred white officers because "they have been brought up to have a special respect for the guidance of white men" (Glatthaar, 1990, p. 177). These two men honestly cared for black soldiers, but their caring was rooted in the worst type of racial paternalism, which allowed them to be caring and racist at the same time. For all of their caring, "neither of them," Glatthaar (1990) remarks, "could envision black soldiers with enough character and good judgment to train and lead a company or a regiment in battle" (pp. 177-178).

Although black soldiers appreciated the sacrifices many white officers were making by serving in black units, they nonetheless rejected these officers' racial paternalism. Throughout the war, black soldiers voiced their complaints about being excluded from becoming officers. Black soldiers rejected the notion that they preferred white officers. One black soldier explained it best when he pointed out the distinction between Northern white men fighting for the Union and black men fighting for liberty: " 'And if we have to fight for our rights, let us fight under Colored officers, for we are the men that will kill the Enemies of the Government' " (Glatthaar, 1990, p. 179). Another black soldier wrote,

"My friend, we want black commissioned officers; . . . because we want men we can understand, and who can understand us. We want men whose hearts are truly loyal to the rights of man. . . . We want to demonstrate our ability to rule, as we have demonstrated our willingness to obey. In short, we want simple justice." (Aptheker, 1967, pp. 486-487)

Some blacks did make it into the ranks of officers, and a few even earned respect from both black enlisted men and white officers, but the price was high (Glatthaar, 1990).

Of perhaps more significance to the maintenance of some aspects of the racial status quo during the Civil War was the policy of differential payment for black and white soldiers. Here again, the root of this policy was the need to pacify white Northerners who rejected the use of blacks in what they considered to be a white man's war and whose sense of white superiority was threatened by black men in uniform. Initially, when the War Department authorized black enlistment into the Union Army, it did so on the basis of equal pay for white and black troops. It later reversed its policy, however, and decided to pay black troops $10 a month and white troops $13 a month. Black troops protested but could not do much because they were in war. Still, the troops of the 54th and 55th Massachusetts (Colored) Infantry refused to accept "inferior pay for equal work" (Glatthaar, 1990, pp. 169-170).

Upset over this injustice to black troops, and especially the black troops from his state, Massachusetts Governor John A. Andrew made an offer to compensate his men by paying them the difference, but the men refused. The commander of the 54th Massachusetts (Colored) Infantry explained to the governor:

"They feel that by accepting a portion of their just due from Massachusetts and a portion from the United States, they would be acknowledging a right on the part of the United States to draw a distinction between them and other soldiers from Massachusetts, and in so doing they would compromise their self respect." (pp. 170-171)

Writing to President Lincoln concerning the discriminatory pay policy, one black soldier asked Lincoln,

"Are we Soldiers, or are we laborers? We are fully armed and equipped, have done all the various duties pertaining to a Soldier's life, have conducted ourselves to the complete satisfaction of General Officers, who were, if anything, prejudiced against us, but who now accord us all the encouragement and honors due us; . . . Now, your Excellency, we have done a Soldier's duty. Why can't we have a Soldier's pay?" (Aptheker, 1967, pp. 482-483)

As a result of the refusal of black troops to accept their discriminatory pay, black families had to carry the burden of that hardship. The Lincoln administration and some liberal congressmen had hoped that the policy of discriminatory wages would help make black soldiers more accept-able to those Northern whites who needed to be reassured that blacks in uniform were less of a threat to white-skin privilege if they were paid less than whites. But the policy backfired because it angered racist whites who could see that it was an attempt to pacify them and it angered blacks and whites who supported the use of black troops. Governor Andrew understood the racial politics of the Lincoln administration when he made the following comment:

"For fear the uniform may dignify the enfranchised slave, or make the black man seem like a free citizen, the government means to disgrace and degrade him, so that he may always be, in his own eyes, and in the eyes of all men, 'only a nigger.' " (Aptheker, 1967, p. 172)

Mounting pressure from several quarters finally forced the govern-ment to relent. In June 1864, Congress allowed equal pay for all soldiers "from January 1, 1864, and back pay [for black soldiers] to the level of white soldiers holding the same rank, providing the black soldiers had been free on April 19, 1861." There was a catch: "Thus, only prewar free blacks received equal pay for 1862 and 1863, it was another insult to the black race" (Aptheker, 1967, p. 174).

The preceding examples of white reactions toward black officers and the government policy of discriminatory wages would not have been an issue had there not been the need for black troops to aid in winning the war. The racial status quo and the structure of white-skin privilege would not have been so threatened had the North not attempted an experiment in interracial cooperation between black soldiers and white officers. As in earlier experiences of interracial cooperation, whites and blacks held vastly different expectations of their interracial relation-ships. Many whites wanted to maintain some aspects of the racial status quo even while they cooperated with blacks in fighting the war. Witness again the white doctors who would work for the advancement of blacks as long as they occupied a place above them. Black soldiers, on the other hand, saw interracial cooperation as a challenge to the racial status quo. Thus, whereas interracial cooperation between black soldiers and white officers within the Union forces changed many aspects of the racial status quo, other aspects were maintained and transmitted to the next stage of American race relations.

NEW FORMS OF
INTERRACIAL COOPERATION

The next stage of American race relations was characterized by the most revolutionary changes in the racial status quo in over two and a half centuries. These changes were triggered by the Civil War and the emancipation of 4 million black slaves. The trauma of this change, at least in some Northern circles, was softened by the long history of interracial cooperation between blacks and whites in the antislavery movement. Notwithstanding the many shortcomings of the antislavery movement in terms of white racism and black bitterness, the movement as a whole provided the American public with some of the best and worst examples of how blacks and whites could interact outside of the roles of black slave and white master. In some ways, the interracial activities of the antislavery movement were dress rehearsals for the next stage of interracial cooperation in the United States.

Not unlike the earlier stages of interracial cooperation, which witnessed some whites holding on to certain aspects of the racial status quo, there was a similar pattern of white attempts at maintaining the racial status quo within the context of interracial cooperation between the end of the Civil War and the end of World War I. The major difference between these two periods of interracial cooperation was that the former held great potential for radical changes in the racial status quo. The post-Civil War period started out with the demise of a regional, social, economic, and political system, which cleared the way for the first large-scale experiment in biracial democracy in the history of the modern Western world. Lerone Bennett (1969) describes this momentous stage of American race relations best:

> At the end of the Civil War, America embarked on a racial experiment unprecedented in the inner precincts of the Western World. In a remarkable turnabout, the former slaves were enfranchised and lifted to a position of

real political power vis-à-vis their former masters. And the new national purpose was expressed in the ratification of the Fourteenth and Fifteenth Amendments and passage of the most stringent civil rights legislation ever enacted in America. It was in this climate that black and white men made the first and, in many ways, the last real attempt to establish an interracial democracy in America. (p. 11)

For a brief period in the long and tragic history of American race relations, blacks and whites struggled to lay the foundation for the first interracial democracy. During the period of radical Reconstruction, 1865 to 1877, a motley crew of ex-slaves, pre-Civil War free blacks, ex-Confederates, and Northern whites worked together to set up new state constitutions and put in motion reforms such as universal education. "Never before—never since—had there been assemblies like these," Bennett (1969) writes. "Confederates, Unionists, poor men, rich men, black men, white men . . . elected by a poor white and black constituency and composed of Northern-born and Southern-born blacks, the Reconstruction conventions represented the first democratic assemblies in America" (pp. 96-97).

For all the pain and anguish that they had suffered at the hands of Southern whites, the black participants in this first experiment in interracial democracy were surprisingly magnanimous and forgiving. According to Kenneth M. Stampp (1967),

> The Negroes were seldom vindictive toward native whites. To be sure there were plenty of cases of friction between Negroes and whites. . . . But in no Southern states did any responsible Negro leader, or any substantial Negro group, attempt to get complete political control into the hands of freemen. All they asked for was equal political rights and equality before the law. (p. 168)

But equal political rights and equality before the law were often too much to ask of many whites who were forced by circumstances to engage in interracial political cooperation. The Unionist-scalawag element within this interracial political coalition, Stampp explains,

> had little enthusiasm for one aspect of the Radical program: the granting of equal civil and political rights to the Negroes. They favored the disenfranchisement of the Confederates to enable them to dominate the new state governments but they were reluctant to accept Negro suffrage. (p. 162)

The Republican party and the Northern industrialists who controlled it supported interracial political cooperation as part of a political agenda to use blacks to consolidate political hegemony within the South. "Practical Republicans," Franklin and Moss (1988) point out, "fearful of the political consequences of a South dominated by Democrats, became convinced that Negro suffrage in the South would aid in the continued growth of the Republican Party" (p. 206).

These Republicans,

> whatever their altruistic motives, were moved to adopt the cause of the Negro almost solely by consideration of political expediency and strategy. It would have been unnatural for them not to have strengthened their party by enfranchising the Negroes and enlisting them as loyal voters. (Franklin & Moss, 1988, p. 225)

Northern industrialists needed to stabilize the South through the Republican Party "in order to hasten the exploitation of Southern resources and to capture Southern markets" (p. 222). Unfortunately, the first experiment in interracial democracy was abandoned when it no longer served the purposes of the Northern industrial class.

Although blacks did engage in interracial political cooperation to advance themselves politically and economically, they tended to be much more willing than whites in these interracial political coalitions to seek benefits for the other race. During the South Carolina state constitutional convention, black delegates pushed for "a petition to congress to remove all political disabilities from white citizens" (Du Bois, 1935/1964, p. 396). Blacks also demonstrated a greater willingness to cooperate with whites in reform movements such as the Populist Party. Despite the willingness of blacks to engage in interracial cooperation for the mutual benefit of themselves and whites, white Republicans, Democrats, and Populists tended to view interracial cooperation as a means of carrying out white political and economic agendas (Crowe, 1970; Saunders, 1969).

Nowhere was this tendency to use interracial cooperation to maintain the racial status quo more blatant than within the Populist movement. In Georgia, white Populists demanded racial segregation at political meetings. Crowe (1970) writes,

> Most of the Populists were simply more committed to white supremacy than to reform and many blacks voters seemed well aware of this fact. . . .

> It is clear that Populist leaders wished to harvest black votes without compromising any major doctrines or practices of white supremacy. (pp. 110-111)

If there was any lesson to learn concerning interracial cooperation during the radical and post-Reconstruction periods, it was this: Most whites rarely engaged in interracial cooperation with the idea of radically changing the racial status quo. The Republicans, who had been the pioneers of the grand experiment in interracial democracy, soon lost interest and sacrificed this infant experiment to their political and economic ambitions. The industrialists of the North who controlled the Republican Party wanted Southern markets and resources, and to that extent, most supported black political development that would ensure their political and economic hegemony over the South. "But when the program [radical Reconstruction] failed to bring peace and order, thereby postponing prosperity, they helped to restore home rule in the South" (Franklin & Moss, 1988, p. 222). Thus ended the first interracial attempt to lay the foundation for an interracial democracy.

The betrayal of radical Reconstruction, brought on in large part by the Republican-Northern industrialist acceptance of home rule, paved the way for the virulent ideology of Southern white supremacy. This ideology was best manifested in the movement to disenfranchise Southern blacks. This triumph of white supremacy in the South, and the North's acceptance of it, created a climate that would tolerate only a type of interracial cooperation that maintained the ideology of white supremacy—or, at the very least, basic components of this postradical Reconstruction racial status quo. Such basic components included the belief that blacks were politically, morally, and socially inferior or rapists of white women and not ready to participate in white civilization on their own terms (Williamson, 1986).

It took the genius of Booker T. Washington to develop a mode of interracial cooperation that could function on behalf of blacks in the midst of this climate of virulent white racism. He had to appear, in the eyes of whites, to be maintaining certain "sacred cows" of white supremacy. The recent history of Southern racial oppression of blacks was not lost on Washington. He knew only too well that for blacks to survive, they needed access to an effective mode of interracial cooperation; the only available mode, given the racial climate of both the South and the North, was one that walked delicately around whites' racial phobias and anxieties. In July 1884, in a speech before the National Educational

Association in Madison, Wisconsin, Washington presented a mode of interracial cooperation that left inviolate the racial status quo.

In this speech, Washington explained that any "movement for the elevation of the Southern Negro, in order to be successful, must have, to a certain extent, the cooperation of Southern whites. They control government and own the property—whatever benefits the black man benefits the white man" (Harlan, 1972b, p. 256). Washington was being very realistic. He acknowledged the fact that whites had the power in government and property ownership and implied that such power determined both black educational success and the mode of interracial cooperation on which that success would be based. He then set forth the respective benefits that would accrue to blacks and whites within such a mode of interracial cooperation as if they had equal value.

Continuing his speech, Washington said, "Brains, property, and character for the Negro will settle the question of civil rights. . . . The best course to pursue in regard to the civil rights bill in the South is to let it alone; let it alone and it will settle itself" (Harlan, 1972b, p. 260). Here again, Washington remained on safe ground, because any discussion of civil rights for Southern blacks would destroy any hope of interracial cooperation in support of black education. Washington made it clear, however, that he was not counseling submission of blacks to whites:

> There should be no unmanly cowering or stooping to satisfy unreasonable whims of Southern white men, but it is charity and wisdom to keep in mind the two hundred years' schooling in prejudice against the Negro which the slaveholders are called upon to conquer. (p. 260)

Industrial education would be the key. "Educate the black man, mentally and industrially, and there will be no doubt of his prosperity" (p. 260).

This speech and the more famous one Washington made in Atlanta in 1895 became the ideological pillars of the accommodationist mode of interracial cooperation that maintained core components of the system of white supremacy in the South. This mode of interracial cooperation went hand in glove with the Northern industrialist-philanthropists' financial support of black education in the South. Southern white supremacists accepted Northern industrialist-philanthropists' financial support of black schools, because, as Franklin and Moss (1988) explain, "there was general approval of Northern philanthropy when the white citizens of the South discovered that their benefactors showed little or no interest in establishing racial equality or upsetting white supremacy" (p. 242).

Northern capitalists knew the benefit of working within the system of Southern white supremacy, a system that was made somewhat less distasteful by its acceptance of the accommodationist mode of interracial cooperation. "Northern capitalists and philanthropists had no exalted idea of Negro equality," according to Meier (1963), "but felt a sense of noblesse oblige and wanted a supply of trained labor available for the industrialization of the South and saw in industrial education an eminently 'practical' method of educating Negroes" (p. 93). Washington assisted in crafting and facilitating a mode of interracial cooperation that Northern capitalists could live with and Southern white supremacists could tolerate.

World War I set the stage for new forms of interracial cooperation geared, in large part, to control the movement of Southern black workers. Northern demands for cheap Southern black labor, brought on by the decline of European immigrant labor, forced Southern planters, Northern capitalists, and the federal government to employ various modes of interracial cooperation to further their respective aims. As thousands of black peasants left the land, Southern white businessmen and some black leaders held conferences on interracial cooperation and, among other efforts, worked on cleaning up black areas to dissuade black workers from migrating North. For example, black and white citizens in places like Thomasville and Waycross, Georgia, held large interracial meetings and several days of conferences to map out ways in which blacks and whites could cooperate in stopping the migration of Southern black labor to the North. In 1916, Tuskegee Institute held conferences with bankers and planters to seek ways to improve the conditions of blacks as a means to check the migration. All of these efforts were triggered by fear among the Southern white business community that it was losing control of its cheap black labor (Scott, 1920/1969).

Northern industrial capitalists and the federal government also used certain modes of interracial cooperation as a means to their respective ends—the systematic acquisition and stabilization of Southern black workers. Many Northern industrial capitalists feared the potentially disruptive conditions that could occur in the wake of large-scale black migration from the South. The bloody interracial conflicts that erupted in East St. Louis in 1917 and in Chicago in 1919 were brutal reminders of the need for interracial cooperation among the black and white leadership to come up with solutions; these solutions had to include regulating the flow of Southern black migrants to Northern industrial centers and setting up social programs designed to transform these migrants into effective and productive industrial workers (Rudwick, 1972).

Industrial capitalists and the federal government could not solve the complex problems of the demand for Southern black labor, mass migration, disruptive interracial conflicts in industrial centers, and a need for the stabilization of black workers without help from black leaders. As early as 1918, the Ford Motor Company in Detroit started using local black leaders to help manage racial conflicts in the plants (Lewis, 1954). Realizing the need for some type of interracial cooperation to cope with the myriad of problems associated with wartime deployment of black labor, in February 1918, a group that included some of the major black leaders in the country came up with a partial solution to the preceding problems. But their solutions required interracial cooperation at the highest governmental level. In a letter to Secretary of Labor William D. Wilson, Eugene Kinckle Jones, president and secretary of the National Urban League; John R. Schillady, secretary of the NAACP; Robert R. Morton and Emmett J. Scott, principal and secretary, respectively, of Tuskegee Institute; among others, requested the appointment of a "Negro expert on labor problems." This expert, they explained, would help the nation solve the critical labor problems by effectively deploying black labor. "If the forces at the front are to be munitioned and kept supplied by a continuing stream of labor and food producers, and if the needs of the home population are adequately to be met," these leaders argued, "every resource of labor and skill must be utilized in the most effective manner."[1]

The group saw itself as playing a key role in the war via the deployment of black labor. As representatives of organizations "most intimately acquainted with the colored people," it urged the government to see as an advantage to the public welfare a proposed labor program that included "the best possible use and distribution of the tremendous potential labor supply to be found among the 12,000,000 Negroes of this country."[2] The extensive migration of black workers to Northern cities would cause disturbing maladjustments that would, in turn, "react unfavorably upon maximum productive efficiency," unless they were wisely directed. According to these leaders, this could only be done by appointing a "Negro expert on labor problems." The group pointed out the precedent set by the secretary of war in appointing a black, Emmett J. Scott, as a special assistant for counseling on matters affecting black people and their relation to the war.

In May 1918, Secretary Wilson appointed Dr. George E. Haynes, professor of sociology and economics at Fisk University, Nashville, Tennessee, as director of Negro economics. His two main duties were

> to advise the Secretary and the Directors and Chiefs of the several bureaus and divisions of the Department of Labor on matters relating to Negro wage earnings, and to outline and promote plans for greater cooperation between Negro wage earners, white employers and white workers in agriculture and industry. ("Appointment and Function of the Director of Negro Economics," 1918, p. 37)

Haynes began his new job by visiting strategic centers in states where the problems of black workers had reached a critical stage. In response to these problems, Haynes assisted in establishing conferences and special interracial committees called Negro Workers' Advisory Committees. The committees were formed to

> study, plan and advise in a cooperative spirit and manner with employers of Negro labor, with Negro workers, and with the United States Department of Labor in securing from Negro laborers greater production in industry and agriculture for the purpose of winning the war through increased regularity, application and efficiency, through increasing the morale of Negro workers, and through improving their general conditions. (Haynes, 1921, p. 12)

Clearly, the necessity of stabilizing black labor as a means for contributing to the war effort was the main rationale for interracial cooperation. In one sense, the war had created an opportunity for the development of yet another mode of interracial cooperation. As with other such modes, however, this one accommodated itself to the racial status quo. Nothing changed essentially in the pattern of white racial dominance. Despite the fact that Secretary of Labor Wilson decided that the advice of the director of Negro economics should be sought before any work affecting black workers was undertaken and that he be kept aware of the progress of such work "so that the Department might have at all times the benefit of his [Haynes's] judgment in all matters affecting Negroes," Wilson still determined the context in which Haynes operated (Haynes, 1921, p. 139). Haynes's position as director was only advisory. Interracial cooperation between Haynes and Wilson was based on unequal power relations.

The end of the war saw an end to the Division of Negro Economics as a short-term mode of interracial cooperation. However short term, there were valuable lessons to be learned from the experience. Namely, in a national crisis, interracial cooperation is essential to the welfare of the entire nation. After having served that function, however, it can easily be jettisoned by the dominant white elite as it resumes its partial function of maintaining the racial status quo.

TENSIONS AND CONFLICTS
IN NEW INTERRACIAL MOVEMENTS

Postwar American race relations were anything but smooth, with a rise in lynching and bloody race riots throughout the country in 1919 (Franklin & Moss, 1988). Although new modes of interracial cooperation were steadily increasing, many did not challenge major aspects of the racial status quo and in some ways even reinforced it. The war, however, had stimulated a rise in black expectations that placed new, more radical demands on American democracy and interracial cooperation. Blacks were no longer willing to allow whites to dictate the norms of interracial cooperation or maintain the status quo under the cloak of benign interracial cooperation. Interracial cooperation would come to mean more than just relations between blacks and whites with little or no suggestion of integration, equal rights, or balance of power, as was the understanding during the early 1920s (Knotts, 1988).

Blacks required more from their participation in interracial cooperation than many whites were willing to give. For example, during the 1920s, white Methodist missionary women "donated used clothing and baskets of food, taught Sunday school for black children, trained black Sunday school teachers, and helped organize clubs for black women" (Knotts, 1988, p. 207). But one of their leaders, Bertha Newell feared and rejected social equality with blacks. In fact, as late as 1938, she decried " 'such forms of intercourse as promote miscegenation of the races. . . . Such a process—by and large—always leads to deterioration of both racial strains' " (p. 207).

Both the Commission on Interracial Cooperation (CIC) and the Women's Missionary Council (WMC) tended to accept the racial status quo even as they continued to support the interracial movement in the South. According to Knotts (1988), this failure to challenge racial segregation within the interracial movement did not prevent the WMC from "changing race relations in the South." Despite the fact that the leaders of the

WMC failed to call for an end to segregation or for changes in segregation laws, they were changing race relations in the South:

> These women, who expressly opposed "social equality of the races" and
> interracial marriage, and who staunchly supported segregation, were lead-
> ers in the interracial movement. The interracial movement gained immedi-
> ate success and grew rapidly, especially because it was led by Southern
> women who were widely recognized by other white women as people much
> like themselves. (Knotts, 1988, p. 207)

Knotts argues, "Neither the leaders nor their grassroots supporters
planned to do more or less than fulfill their Christian and neighborly
responsibilities. If the leaders had advocated legal and social equality
of the races, they would not have gained a hearing" (p. 207). As a
consequence of these white women's maintenance of the racial status
quo, however, they lost the support of radical black women.

Tension and conflict were inevitable within any mode of interracial
cooperation that maintained even the slightest aspects of the racial
status quo. By the 1930s, new forms of interracial cooperation were
dotting the landscape of American race relations; along with these new
modes came some sharp criticism about common flaws in interracial
cooperation. In September 1933, an instructor of sociology at the
University of Cincinnati published an article in the National Urban
League's publication, *Opportunity,* in which he outlined the basic weaknesses of the interracial cooperation movement:

> The unequal placement of the Negro and the white man in our social system
> is an obvious fact. And this condition limits interracialism. It inhibits
> interracial cooperation in various ways. . . . There is a tendency for inter-
> racial organizations to come to terms with this condition. They adjust to
> the fact of inequality of status, the very condition out of which the race
> problem in its manifest forms emerges. Interracial cooperation thus tends
> to be conservative rather than bold or radical. (Brown, 1933, p. 272)

Interracialists might protest against

> lynching, economic persecutions of the Negro, political disabilities, in-
> equality of educational provisions, and the harsh practices in which the
> Negro is a victim due to his low status. But seldom do they proclaim the
> obvious fact that all of these conditions express the inferior status of the

Negro, symbolized in the color line. To attack the color line is dangerous. Yet the color line is the crux of the whole matter. (p. 272)

Moving into the heart of the problem as he perceived it, Brown (1933) argues that on the issue of attacking the color line, that is, the racial status quo, the

> interracial cooperators feel that they must soft-pedal here. They protest their disbelief in "social equality," implying in effect that they are not going to appreciably disturb the status quo in race relations. Apparently, tolerance and support for interracialism requires the payment of this price. (p. 272)

Many whites would probably not engage in interracial cooperation, Brown claims, "if they felt that this implied a basic disturbance of the relative positions of the races in the social order" (p. 272). This could be the litmus test for liberals and "confirmed interracialists, at least among the whites" (p. 272). He concludes, "Interracial cooperation thus turns out to be an effort to control the incidental evils of white domination, rather than a movement for equality of status" (p. 272).

According to Brown (1933), another problem with the interracial cooperation movement at the time was its inability or unwillingness to cope with black radicals:

> The unequal placement of the races is reflected also in the tendency for interracial groups to eliminate the "radical" element from the work of cooperation. The radical Negro, the man who is uncompromising in his demand for equality in all of its forms, is often an irritant among interracialists. (p. 272)

These radicals are blamed for not having tact. As a result, "they create fears and suspicions, causing the public to wonder as to the 'soundness' of interracial activities. A radical Negro at large in interracial work may do much to inhibit the sentiments of white people for such work" (p. 272).

Brown (1933) points out how the black radical can create problems for the black interracial cooperator. "Negro cooperators may secretly agree with the radical, but they fear the consequences of his utterances. They know well the sensitivity of the dominant white world relative to anything smacking of real and fundamental demands" (p. 272). The black cooperator finds him- or herself in the awkward position of agreeing with the black radical in the abstract but disagreeing with the black radical's tactics, seeing them as impractical. Therefore, radical blacks tend to be "out of place in interracial work. The 'practical,' smooth, compromising type will probably get along much better" (p. 272).

White racial dominance in the interracial cooperation movement was yet another problem. "Given this inequality of status previously referred to, it is perhaps inevitable that whites should tend to dominate interracial activity. This in spite of the fact that Negroes tend to furnish the followers and devotees of interracialism" (Brown, 1933, p. 272). According to Brown, one explanation for this white dominance is that

> a white leadership is essential to the conversion of the white masses to the gospel of interracial cooperation. It is often assumed that since whites have more prestige and power, a white leader can win more for the cause than could a Negro leader. (p. 272)

This in itself, he points out, "reflect[s] well the subordination of the Negro in the social order" (p. 273). Compounding the problem of the dominance of white leadership in the interracial cooperation movement is the problem of racial paternalism in which whites "have been known to adopt a condescending, superior attitude toward their Negro co-workers" (p. 273). These whites

> expect the Negro to be grateful for support of white people in the solution of the Negro's problems. Gracious appreciation, they feel, is small reward for their labor in the interest of the "poor" Negro. Often, in interracial work, the Negro must stay in his place. (p. 273)

Racial isolation of blacks and whites was a real problem for the interracial cooperation movement. "The races are mutually ghettoized. They seldom meet at the level of natural and spontaneous social contacts. Intimacy at the equality level is relatively rare. The fact of bi-racialism is more potent than the idea of interracialism" (Brown, 1933, p. 273). The masses of blacks and whites are "heir[s] to distorted beliefs and absurd mythologies about each other. Naturally, to build the bridge of interracialism across this gulf of separation is a difficult task" (p. 273). Racial isolation, Brown argues, makes it difficult to

> translate ideals of interracial amity into practice. We interracialists come from our respective racial ghettoes to our interracial meetings. We "cooperate" and then return to our respective racial worlds. The whole procedure

has an element of the farcical in it. Our interracial cooperation appears artificial and futile under such circumstances. (p. 273)

The question as to whether interracial work has any effect on racism is "problematic."

> We cross the color line to cooperate, but do we actually break or even bend this line through this cooperation? Perhaps this is not the aim, but if it is not, what merit ultimately has interracial work? The unbelieving outsider is apt to view with sardonic disdain our achievements, amused at the antics of the embattled warriors of interracial goodwill. (p. 273)

This isolation, Brown (1933) contends,

> often makes even the contacts between interracialists formal and distant. In the interracial world barriers to basic intimacies obtain. Not being used to natural and free association at the equality level, even the partisans of interracialism in committees assembled at times suffer from some strain. (p. 273)

Interracialists tend to be

> elaborately polite. And on occasions they lie to each other, telling what each would like to believe is true rather than the truth. Or again, whites will listen to their Negro colleague berate the white man, the white cooperators thereby acquiring a sense of their tolerance and broadmindedness. (p. 272)

Another of Brown's (1933) indictments of the contemporary interracial cooperation movement is "the tendency to substitute belief and hope for actual achievement." Interracialists, he claims,

> are apt to be incurable optimists. Every skirmish won appears to us as a major victory. We are always in danger of becoming silly romanticists, mistaking gestures for action, our programs for achievements, our dreams for realities. We want a world freed of prejudice, proscription and racial hate; and every bit of evidence indicating this to be a fact we seize with avidity, assuming it to imply revolution along the racial front. (p. 273)

Interracialists need to believe that "the kingdom of goodwill is at hand." They believe these things "because hope and faith compel, not because of the facts." The sad truth is that the interracial movement is a movement of the elite of both races, the select few, not a movement of the masses of either or both races. It is not a folk movement, spontaneously generated by mass feeling and sentiment. . . . Up to now the white masses no doubt sense a vested interest in securing the political, economic and social subordination of the Negro. And the Negro masses are more or less impotent and inert. Seen from this frame of reference, interracial work appears rather Lilliputian in its possibilities. (p. 273)

In addition to the preceding, Brown (1933) points to the

factionalism among Interracialists. . . . It should be remembered that there is not perfect amity and solidarity among interracialists. There is disagreement as to aims, ideologies and methods. And sadly today there is . . . organizational jealousy. (p. 285)

These interracialists are competing "for place and prestige" (p. 285).

Notwithstanding all these "handicaps and weaknesses," Brown (1933) believes "interracialism has justified itself" (p. 285). One of its contributions was "increased tolerance." He states,

To many it has brought a new point of view. Incident to its work, many whites and Negroes have discovered each other as persons, race falling into the background, or eliminating itself entirely. It has served as a tension breaker in crises. And it has furnished inspiration, hope and strength to men of goodwill in both races. (p. 285)

By the 1930s, rising black social and political consciousness was increasing the tensions and conflicts within traditional modes of interracial cooperation and exerting more influence on the balance of power within newly emerging modes of interracial cooperation. One of the best examples of how rising black social and political consciousness increased tensions and conflicts occurred during the organizing drive of the United Auto Workers-Congress of Industrial Organizations (UAW-CIO) among black auto workers in Detroit in the mid-1930s to the late 1930s. In 1918, Henry Ford had developed a mode of interracial cooperation that used black leaders to manage racial crises involving black and white workers in his plants. Before long, this system evolved into a sophisticated mode of interracial cooperation that used several powerful black ministers and their equally powerful churches to control the politics of larger segments of the black community. Blacks were punished if they voted for the Democratic Party or joined the union. It took the radicalization of a new working-class leadership to break the hold that the Ford corporate paternalism had had on the Detroit black community for decades. This black working-class leadership was able to achieve the break from this corporate paternalistic mode of interracial cooperation only by forging a more radical and equal partnership in the UAW-CIO (Thomas, 1992).

During the 1930s, the blacks and whites who cooperated in the Democratic Party and the new unions within the CIO represented significant departures from the more traditional modes of interracial cooperation, but many tensions and conflicts prevailed as black demands and expectations conflicted with certain aspects of the racial status quo. President Franklin Roosevelt's so-called black cabinet, composed of some of the most professionally qualified and talented black men and women in the country, such as Mary McLeod Bethune and Robert C. Weaver, was one of the best examples of interracial cooperation within the Democratic Party. As Franklin and Moss (1988) point out, however,

> The task of "top" Negroes in the federal government was a difficult and delicate one: to press for economic and political equality of the black man in America. This task was all the more peculiar because they were seeking to bring about an integration that was antithetical to their own roles. (p. 351)

Tensions and conflicts were inevitable because all of the members of Roosevelt's black cabinet "were unalterably opposed to racial segregation." Therefore, according to Franklin and Moss (1988), "When the suggestion was made that there should perhaps be a Negro bureau to deal with all matters affecting the Negro, several of the black cabineteers combined their energies to oppose it on the grounds that it would tend to make Negroes wards of the government" (p. 351).

Tensions and conflicts continued to strain the New Deal mode of interracial cooperation during the early 1940s. Some blacks began accusing the Roosevelt administration of racial discrimination in "some of the relief agencies and of excluding Negroes from preliminary defense preparation" (Franklin & Moss, 1988, pp. 346-347). Some of these blacks began to desert the Democratic party, calling the New Deal "the dirty deal." This led to a significant decline in black votes for Roosevelt in 1940. By the summer of 1941, the mode of interracial cooperation exemplified by the black cabinet and white New Dealers was being seriously challenged by the rising demands of the March-on-Washington Movement (MOWM), founded by A. Philip Randolph in early 1941 to protest the government's failure to abolish racial discrimination, particularly in defense industries (Foner, 1981).

This period was characterized by mounting frustration among blacks over the lack of government response to racial discrimination. Much of this frustration was rooted in the fact that certain modes of interracial cooperation were still dominated by whites. For example, after the split at the 1940 National Negro Congress (NNC) between Randolph, the NNC president, and the CIO-Communist Party delegation, Randolph not only resigned but accused the NNC of being dominated by whites and Communists. Later, when he founded the MOWM, he excluded whites (Foner, 1981). This exclusion of whites by a major black leader who, decades earlier, had started his radical career working with white socialists and had fought for years for the recognition of black workers within the predominantly white labor movement, was an indication of the tensions and conflicts that would continue to arise within modes of interracial cooperation that consciously or unconsciously maintained certain aspects of the racial status quo.

The CIO, the most dominant and impressive mode of interracial cooperation within the labor movement during the 1930s and early 1940s, also struggled with tensions and conflicts arising from the efforts of some of its white members to maintain certain aspects of the racial status quo. Several times during World War II, white workers went on strikes against the upgrading of black workers, because such upgrading challenged their traditional white-skin privileges to certain occupations. The CIO white leadership was able to keep such racism in check by demonstrating, at least for the time being, that it understood the relationship between attempts by white workers to maintain the occupational racial status quo and the tensions and conflicts within the CIO because of its position as the dominant mode of interracial cooperation within the larger movement (Foner, 1981).

Interracial cooperation and the maintenance of certain aspects of the racial status quo plagued the political coalition of white liberal democrats and black democrats and the black community-labor alliance for decades. Notwithstanding the great interracial advances accomplished by the dominant modes of interracial cooperation, their efforts were often hampered by their maintenance of the racial status quo.

CONCLUSION

Throughout the history of interracial cooperation, there has been a tendency for the dominant white group to maintain certain aspects of the racial status quo, even while they were engaged in joint efforts against slavery and racism. This tendency can be explained best by understanding white-skin privilege. White-skin privilege enabled whites to hold on to a sense of superiority as they worked with blacks against slavery and racism. This very act tended to strip away some of whites' feelings of superiority. Given the pervasiveness of racism in the United States, however, many whites in interracial movements felt that they should not be expected to give up all aspects of the racial status quo. Many felt that they were doing well just to work with blacks in the struggle against slavery and, later, racial segregation. But many blacks within these interracial movements wanted whites to give up all aspects of the racial status quo. To many whites, such requests or expectations were too radical.

Some white abolitionists could not get beyond viewing African American abolitionists as either former slaves who needed help or free persons of color who needed guidance. They did not mind struggling to free slaves, but they did not want freed slaves to be on an equal level with them. African American abolitionists had to force many of their white coworkers to abandon their racist attitudes. As a result, African Americans and a few of the more radical white abolitionists expanded the antislavery movement to include the budding antiracism movement.

White Union officers and enlisted men had a difficult time being on the same side as blacks. These whites shared the same racist beliefs about blacks as their Southern counterparts. The Union Army needed black troops, but many whites could not give up the belief in white-skin privilege; this was just too much to give up, even to win the war. Many white officers and enlisted men could not stand the sight of a black officer. By the end of the war, however, white Union officers commanding African American troops relinquished many of their racist views. But interracial cooperation did not completely eradicate many aspects of white racism.

The first experiment in interracial democracy during the radical and post-Reconstruction periods marked a watershed in interracial political cooperation between blacks and whites. For a while, there was hope that this great interracial experiment would work. But it could not overcome the social, political, and economic forces attributed to the maintenance of white-skin privilege.

Certain modes of interracial cooperation had to accommodate themselves to the power realities of the time. For example, Booker T. Washington was forced to work within an accommodationist mode of interracial cooperation, as was the National Urban League. This mode of interracial cooperation maintained a key aspect of the racial status quo: white paternalism.

African American migration to the North during World War I created the need for interracial cooperation between black leaders and the government to stabilize the flow of black labor. Industrialists such as Henry Ford entered into interracial cooperation with local black leaders to assist black laborers in his plants. Interracial cooperation in both cases served the racial status quo.

From 1920 to 1945, several modes of interracial cooperation failed to challenge the racial status quo. The CIC and the WMC tended to accept the racial status quo, even as they continued to support the interracial movement in the South. Interracial cooperation reached a new stage during the 1930s within both the New Deal government and the labor movement, but blacks in the federal government had a hard time pressing for economic and political equality for African Americans. Their roles were, at best, token. Interracial cooperation in the CIO was by far the most impressive of the period. Yet as we shall see in Chapter 4, it too had its problems.

A key reason why so many modes of interracial cooperation were not able to eradicate racism fully is that so many were dominated by whites who were not willing or able to see the necessary connection between interracial cooperation and antiracism. Operating in such a racist society, many well-meaning whites felt that they were doing enough just to be associating with blacks. To do much more was, to their way of thinking, asking too much. Of course there were whites who embraced interracial cooperation, social justice, and antiracism. These were the white saints of the "other tradition."

Invariably, tensions and conflicts arose within those modes of interracial cooperation that tended to maintain the racial status quo. Blacks were no longer willing to allow whites to dictate the norms of interracial cooperation or maintain the racial status quo under the cloak of benign interracial cooperation. Black expectations and demands began to increase the tensions and conflicts within several dominant modes of interracial cooperation. Viewed from a developmental perspective, such tensions and conflicts were perhaps inevitable.

NOTES

1. Letter, Robert R. Morton, James H. Dillard, L. Hollingsworth, John R. Shillady, Eugene Kinckle Jones, and Thomas Jessie Jones to William D. Wilson, February 12, 1918, chief clerk files, record group 174, National Archives, Washington, DC.

2. See note 1.

4

Black Expectations and Demands

BLACK AND WHITE DEMOCRATS IN POLITICAL COALITIONS

Despite economic, political, and social advancements made by many blacks between the New Deal and the civil rights era, major aspects of the racial status quo were maintained. Housing and job discrimination continued, and in many cases increased, as thousands of Southern blacks migrated to Northern cities. "Progress had been made in upgrading blacks to semiskilled and skilled jobs during the war," Foner (1981) explains, "but the vast majority of black workers had not risen above the unskilled categories" (p. 269). Interracial cooperation was still a force operating against racism and opening opportunities for blacks, but it was plagued by tensions and conflicts as many whites dragged their feet on racial equality and many blacks fought to speed the pace of racial change.

Between the New Deal and the civil rights movement, black-white political coalitions within the Democratic party and the black community-labor alliance represented two of the dominant modes of interracial cooperation. Both modes evolved out of the political, social, and economic turmoil of the 1930s and converged into workable but tense alliances for several decades. The black-white liberal coalition within the Democratic party was shaken by the March-on-Washington Movement (MOWM) and the fact that, in 1940, some blacks had already begun to desert the Democratic party because they felt that the New

Deal had gone sour on racial issues. By this time, many blacks had recovered from a heady admiration for Roosevelt and had begun to look more critically at his administration's policies on racial issues. The novelty of Roosevelt's black cabinet as a symbol of political interracial cooperation was wearing thin under the wear and tear of racial discrimination. As a result, rising black expectations and demands for the elimination of racial discrimination forced the white liberal wing of the Democratic party, a key player in the political mode of interracial cooperation, to challenge significant aspects of the racial status quo.

The black community-labor alliance, the other dominant mode of interracial cooperation during this period, also experienced rising expectations and demands, which in turn triggered white resistance. This alliance and the white liberal wing of the Democratic party shared similar histories, constituencies, tensions, and conflicts as they attempted to keep their respective boats afloat amid storms of racial turmoil and change.

According to Donald McCoy (1984), the Truman period witnessed the growth and development of civil rights groups,

> especially black and Jewish ones [who were becoming] better organized, more vocal, and better coordinated than ever before. And they had a great deal of support from labor, liberal, and religious organizations. This influenced Truman to make civil rights part of his program and often to let the nation know how important it was. (p. 170)

The influence of these civil rights groups was tied to their ability to tap into long-established networks of interracial cooperation, which provided them with tremendous political leverage. This political leverage was particularly useful for black leaders such as A. Philip Randolph, who pressured the Truman administration to address racial discrimination. In March 1948, Randolph stood as a symbol of the rising demands of blacks during the postwar period when, in testimony before Congress, he stated that he would urge young men to refuse to serve in the armed services of the United States unless racial segregation was abolished. Randolph's idea struck a cord in many black Americans who, at the time, saw the issue as a "rallying point for exerting pressure, especially as the administration was exhorting Congress to reinstate the draft" (McCoy, 1984, p. 108).

The coalition of civil rights, labor, liberal, and religious organizations constituted the core of interracial political cooperation within the Democratic party during Truman's presidency and kept the pressure on him to stay on the course for civil rights against reactionary Southern Democrats and their Republican bedfellows. In 1946, President Truman appointed an interracial committee to look into the state of civil rights and to come up with recommendations for improvement. The committee produced a report that "strongly denounced the denial of civil rights to some Americans" and "called for a positive program to strengthen civil rights, including 'the elimination of segregation based upon race, color, creed or national origins from American life' " (McCoy, 1984, p. 412). That same year, Truman appointed another interracial committee to examine racial problems in higher education. This committee recommended "not only the elimination of inequalities in educational opportunities but the abandonment of all forms of discrimination in higher education" (p. 412).

In 1948, President Truman appointed another committee to look into racial discrimination in the armed services. The report of this committee, *Freedom to Serve,* "was a blueprint of steps by which integration was to be achieved" (McCoy, 1984, p. 58). In 1949, as a result of this report, the Army began instituting a new policy that opened all jobs to "qualified personnel, without regard to race or color and abolishing the racial quota" (p. 58). The Navy and Air Force soon followed. Truman continued on this path, using public statements and the prestige of his office to improve the status of black Americans. In 1948, Truman also issued the executive order that required fair employment in the Federal government (McCoy, 1984, p. 412).

Truman's actions won him and his party the respect of black leaders such as Walter White of the NAACP, who characterized the 1946 report, *To Secure These Rights,* as " 'the most uncompromising and specific pronouncement by a government agency on the explosive issue of racial and religious bigotry' " (Ashmore, 1982, p. 110). In addition, the uncompromising tone of the report was a testimony to the interracial committee that produced it because members did not cave in to the more conservative whites who wanted the language to be tempered "to minimize exacerbation of white sensibilities" (p. 110). As Ashmore explains, the report "had wide public support in the North, and in the South it served to finally cut the ground from under the gradualists" (p. 110).

These actions by Truman were not what finally caused the Southern firebrands to bolt from the party under the banner of the Dixiecrats, however. Rather, Ashmore (1982) writes, "the Dixiecrat bolt was touched off by an obscure young delegate, Mayor Hubert Humphrey of Minneapolis, who challenged the bland rewrite of the 1944 civil rights plank, . . . offering as a substitute a resolution unequivocally rejecting all forms of racial discrimination" (p. 124). In his speech before the 1948 Democratic Convention, Humphrey proclaimed, " 'The time has arrived for the Democratic party to get out of the shadow of states' rights and walk in the bright sunshine of human rights' " (p. 124).

Humphrey's 1948 rallying cry was aimed at the ultraliberals at the convention, who were successful in strengthening the civil rights plank and, in the process, made "Truman appear to be a reluctant lion in the cause of civil rights" (McCoy, 1984, p. 170). Truman had to walk a political tightrope in his attempt to address sensitive racial issues. He was understandably reluctant "to fragment the fragile Democratic coalition [and] tried long and hard to accommodate both civil rights liberals and Southern supremacists" (p. 170). According to William H. Chafe (1989), Truman was ambivalent in response to the "brutal repression of black efforts to register to vote after the war" (p. 144). As a result, during the spring and summer of 1946, an interracial coalition of black protest groups and their allies "demanded a response from Truman." More than 15,000 people marched to the Lincoln Memorial, and a national emergency committee "pleaded with the President to intervene." Truman responded with the appointment of the interracial committee that produced the report *To Secure These Rights* (Chafe, 1989, p. 167).

Unfortunately, Truman had a tendency to backtrack on civil rights under certain circumstances. For example, he tended to retreat from his strong support for civil rights to hold onto Southern Democrats, whose support he needed for his foreign policies, "and failed to introduce any legislation to implement the recommendations of his civil rights committee. Nor did he issue executive orders to end segregation in the military or in Federal employment until he had to do so in the midst of the 1948 presidential campaign in order to appeal to black voters in the North" (Chafe, 1989, p. 167). This form of racial political expediency represented a pattern that had eroded interracial cooperation for decades.

Another case in which racial political expediency took precedence occurred when Truman, after urging the enactment of a permanent Fair Employment Practices Committee (FEPC), failed to do anything to empower the committee. He even refused "to permit the FEPC to order Washington's transit system to hire black operators" (Chafe, 1989, p. 167). This so enraged the famous black civil rights lawyer Charles Houston that he resigned from the FEPC, denouncing the government's failure to enforce democratic practices and protect minorities in its own capital. Although the Truman administration "may have encouraged civil rights protests on a national level by giving renewed attention to the issues raised by civil rights groups, . . . in substance the situation facing those who challenged white supremacy in the South had not changed" (p. 167). This form of racial political expediency was explained by one of Truman's aides: " 'The strategy was to start with a bold measure and then temporize to pick up the right-wing forces. Simply stated, backtrack after the bang' " (p. 167).

Notwithstanding the Truman strategy of racial political expediency, the realities of racial politics both within and without the Democratic party did not always allow for a purist type of racial reform. In 1951, the black newspaper the *Pittsburgh Courier* understood this harsh reality of race and politics when it described Truman's Committee on Government Contracts Compliance as a "half-a-loaf FEPC" recognizing that it was the best Truman " 'could do under the circumstances' " (McCoy, 1984, p. 255). Truman, however, did help pave the way for future interracial cooperation.

Blacks and their white allies within the interracial coalition of the Democratic party would continue to demand more than half a loaf of equality, and reactionary whites within the party would continue to resist any changes in the racial status quo.

The Kennedy administration represented the best example of how the rising tide of black expectations and demands influenced the political coalition of white liberals and blacks within the Democratic party. The civil rights movement, which evolved into the primary vehicle of rising black expectations and demands, forced the Kennedy administration to challenge some key aspects of the racial status quo. Had the civil rights movement not existed, the Democratic party as the dominant mode of interracial cooperation in the political arena would have regressed to a mode of white-dominated interracial political opportunism (Giglio, 1991).

Both as a congressman and as a senator, Kennedy "favored civil rights legislation more as a matter of course than of deep concern" (Giglio, 1991, p. 160). This attitude disappointed civil rights leaders and advocates because they were aware that Kennedy's "political ambitions had sensitized him to Southern feelings" (p. 160). By the mid-1950s, "the NAACP and other civil rights organizations viewed [Kennedy] with greater suspicion" (p. 160). As soon as he began running for president, Kennedy, like other Democrats before him, realized he would need black votes. But his strategy was to try and woo black leaders "without alienating the South—a prerequisite for serious Democratic presidential contenders" (p. 160). He did not begin to focus on racial issues until the rising tide of black expectations and demands took the civil rights movement to a new level of intensity. He could not fool the many blacks in the movement, who booed him at a civil rights gathering. After he became the Democratic nominee for president,

> [Kennedy] vowed to pursue bold executive action and legislation to imple-
> ment the party's liberal civil rights commitments. Discrimination in hous-
> ing, he insisted, could end by a stroke of the presidential pen. He assured
> black Americans that a Democratic administration would move quickly on
> all fronts. (p. 160)

It did not take long for Kennedy to strain the mode of interracial cooperation within the Democratic party. The party's liberal civil rights commitment was the glue that held that cooperative mode together. Yet Kennedy's legislative strategy of wooing "recalcitrant Southern demo-crats on behalf of his liberal legislative program" dictated that he not propose any civil rights legislation in 1961 (Giglio, 1991, p. 161). This strategy greatly upset black leaders, particularly Roy Wilkins of the NAACP, who characterized Kennedy's strategy as tactically flawed because it sent the wrong signal to the opposition, telling them in effect that he was not " 'going to use the forward pass' " (p. 161). Wilkins had little faith in Kennedy's assumption that the South could be won over by "postponing" civil rights legislation. As a result, for the remainder of the Kennedy presidency, "Wilkins and fellow NAACP officials thought him inept as a legislative leader, no matter how they felt about him otherwise" (p. 161).

Kennedy did not contribute to the strengthening of the interracial cooperation within the Democratic party when he failed to mention civil rights in his inaugural address; he compounded the failure by not appointing a task force for civil rights, "an indication that matters of race warranted no such attention and that he wished no liberal input" (Giglio, 1991, pp. 161-162). By installing a civil rights adviser on the White House staff, Kennedy at least gave the impression that he was still connected to the liberal tradition of the Democratic party, in which interracial cooperation was a key factor. But even that move could not remove the perception that the adviser "served merely as a buffer between Kennedy and the civil rights leadership" (p. 162). Kennedy would have gladly maintained key aspects of the racial status quo, such as gradualism on civil rights and token and symbolic concessions to the more radical elements of the interracial political coalitions of his party. Irving Bernstein (1991) says,

> In civil rights Kennedy had begun his presidency with a policy of executive action now and legislation later. This was a political judgment that a civil rights bill in 1961 or 1962 would divide the country, shatter the Democratic party, and be rejected by Congress. (p. 115)

By 1963, however, the intense pressure from black activists forced Kennedy to "morally commit the presidency to the movement . . . resulting in the unavoidable Democratic party demise in the South in the years afterward (p. 286).

In March 1963, Martin Luther King, Jr. wrote a scathing critique of Kennedy's weak approach to civil rights, demonstrating the extent to which the credibility of the liberal mode of interracial cooperation within the Democratic party had eroded among black civil rights leaders. He wrote,

> The administration's circumscribed action in the civil rights field was generally accepted by the public; even liberal forces proved watchful rather than anxious, hopeful rather than insistent. The demand for progress was somehow drained of its moral imperative, and the issue no longer commanded the conscience of the nation as it had in previous years. The decline of civil rights as the number one domestic issue was a direct consequence . . . of the rise and public acceptance of "tokenism." (Washington, 1986, p. 113)

King acknowledged

> [the] impressive list of government actions which took place in 1963, including job opportunities, voting rights, desegregation of public facilities, the appointment of Negroes to official posts. . . . In fairness, it must be said that this administration has outstripped all previous ones in the breadth of its civil rights activities. (p. 113)

Notwithstanding these accomplishments, King accused the Kennedy administration of tokenism: "If tokenism were our goal, this administration has adroitly moved us towards its accomplishment. But tokenism can now be seen not only as a useless goal, but as a genuine menace" (p. 113). According to King, the tokenism of the Kennedy administration was a palliative which relieves emotional distress, but leaves the disease and its ravages unaffected. It tends to demobilize and relax the militant spirit which alone drives us forward to real change. Tokenism was the inevitable outgrowth of the administration's design for dealing with discrimination. (p. 113)

It was all part of a strategy to maintain key aspects of the racial status quo being challenged by rising black expectations and demands for racial justice.

The administration sought to demonstrate to Negroes that it has concern for them, while at the same time it has striven to avoid inflaming the opposition. The most cynical view holds that it wants the vote of both and is paralyzed by conflicting needs of each. (p. 113)

Kennedy was compelled by the rising expectations and demands of black activists to embrace the civil rights struggle. The civil rights movement forced him to abandon key aspects of the racial status quo, which implied abandoning the wooing of recalcitrant Southerners. According to Giglio (1991),

No domestic struggle occupied the Kennedy presidency more over a longer duration than civil rights. This was not, of course, by choice. Kennedy had intended to effect racial advances gradually, smoothly, and with a minimum of conflict. Civil rights activists, however, confronting considerable southern resistance, continually prodded the administration to move more forcefully against racial injustice, beginning with the Freedom Rides of 1961, desegregation efforts at the University of Mississippi in September 1962, and culminating in the demonstration in Birmingham in Spring 1963. . . . In the process, Kennedy became a more vigorous advocate of black America, his support leading to the Civil Rights Bill of 1963. Indeed his belated awareness of racial injustice—and civil rights contributions—paved the way for the greater successes of Lyndon Johnson. (p. 159)

The rising tide of black expectations and demands continued even after Kennedy's belated acceptance of parts of the civil rights agenda and his untimely death in 1963. During the 1964 Democratic convention, civil rights activists from Mississippi challenged the seating of the white-only Mississippi delegation with its own delegation representing the Mississippi Freedom Democratic Party (MFDP). Johnson, eager to win the white South, opposed the MFDP, "instructed the FBI to arrange surveillance of the MFDP delegates . . . [and] ordered his supporters and those of Hubert Humphrey to block the MFDP in the credentials committee" (Blum, 1991, p. 160). Although various compromises were offered to the MFDP, such as allowing delegates to participate in the discussion in the convention without voting, it refused them. Another compromise that included two token votes and a promise to ban segregated delegations from attending the 1968 convention also proved futile, even when supported by an interracial team of Democrats comprising Hubert Humphrey, Martin Luther King, Jr., and Bayard Ruskins. These three leaders were forced to sacrifice the MFDP not only to "keep the Democratic party peacefully united" (p. 160) but also to maintain it as a viable mode of interracial cooperation that could be drawn on to win other battles, such as the Voting Rights Act of 1965.

Black expectations and demands continued to rise during the Johnson administration, complicated by the emergence of black militancy within the civil rights movement. Johnson's signing of the Voting Rights Act in August 1965 increased the credibility of the white liberal Democrats and their black coworkers in the Democratic party and in the civil rights movement as those who were in the dominant mode of interracial cooperation in the political arena. The leaders of the major civil rights organizations present at the signing agreed with Johnson when he told a national television audience that "Today is a triumph for freedom." Some of them were so deeply moved by the Great Society programs that they described him as the "the greatest president American Blacks ever had" (Blum, 1991, p. 252).

The Voting Rights Act and the Great Society programs were insufficient to stop the urban disorders of the 1960s. Racial polarization began to permeate the entire political arena. More and more working class whites began abandoning the Democratic party. By 1976, however, "a Georgia governor had united white and black Democrats in a campaign that sent to Washington the first Southern planter to occupy the White House since Zachary Taylor" (Ashmore, 1982, p. 455).

President Jimmy Carter, not unlike other white Democrats, was forced by the harsh realities of racial politics to walk a tightrope to maintain the interracial coalition of the liberal wing of the Democratic party. During his campaign for governor in 1970, Carter unabashedly wooed those whites who had defected to George Wallace's third party, which was accused of "segging it up." In explaining his strategy to black leader Vernon Jordan, a fellow Georgian who would later become head of the National Urban League, Carter said, " 'You won't like my campaign, but you will like my administration' " (Ashmore, 1982, p. 455). True to his word, Carter delivered on that promise, "symbolically hanging a portrait of Martin Luther King in the statehouse and taking an uncompromising stand in support of the rights of blacks" (p. 455).

When Carter decided to run for president, he realized he would have to do what some political observers believed could not be done: "carry the black vote nationally while holding Southern whites in the Democratic ranks" (Ashmore, 1982, p. 446). In some ways, he disproved the Southern strategy when Southern voters who had defected to the Republicans in 1972 "came back in 1976—demonstrating that they had no reluctance in joining forces with the black politicians who were now holding office throughout the region" (p. 444). One must be careful with this assessment, though, because it was the black South that made the real difference for Carter. In fact, as Burton Kaufman (1993) points out, "Blacks . . . turned out in record numbers to support the Democratic candidate, casting five out of every six of their ballots for him. Without the unions and black vote, Carter would have lost the election" (p. 19).

Maintaining the fragile balance of interracial cooperation between black Democrats and white liberal Democrats while maintaining enough of the racial status quo to slow down the defection of Southern whites and Northern working class whites was becoming increasingly difficult for Democratic White House candidates. As a presidential candidate, Carter was trying to court the white ethnic vote when he "blundered into sensitive territory with an offhand remark about preserving 'ethnic purity' in urban neighborhoods" (Kaufman, 1993, p. 446). He later clarified the statement by explaining that he meant to say "that he was opposed to using the power of the federal government to 'artificially' change the ethnic character of a neighborhood, but that he would not condone discrimination against any family wishing to move into the neighborhood" (pp. 13-14). But the damage had been done; he was falling off the tightrope. Black leaders pounced on him. Jesse Jackson characterized Carter's statements as " 'a throwback to Hitlerian racism,' " and Mayor Richard Hatcher of Gary, Indiana, called him a " 'Frankenstein monster with a Southern Drawl' " (p. 14).

Carter refused to retract his statement because he felt that it had been taken out of context. Finally, after much coaxing, he acknowledged his error at a news conference, explaining that he, too, had been concerned about the use of the term *purity*. This satisfied most black leaders, including Detroit Mayor Coleman Young, who accepted Carter's apology and proclaimed that the entire matter had been a " 'phony issue' " (Kaufman, 1993).

Andrew Young also lent his support to Carter during this crisis over the ethnic purity remark. But Young played an even more critical role in holding together the fragile interracial coalition within the liberal wing of the Democratic party when he began campaigning for Carter, speaking on his behalf before black and liberal white audiences around the country. Along with Coretta King and Martin Luther King, Sr., Young "helped turn out the vote that gave the Georgian his narrow victory" (Ashmore, 1982, p. 446). When asked if he had "incurred any personal political obligations along the way" in winning the presidency, newly elected President Carter acknowledged that his only major debt was to Andrew Young who, at the time, represented the Atlanta district in Congress (p. 446).

The fact that the black vote was key in the election of President Carter was bound to lead to a rising tide of black expectations and demands that could destabilize the fragile political coalition between white liberal Democrats and black Democratic leaders. Notwithstanding president-elect Carter's appointments of blacks to high positions, such as Juanita Kreps as secretary of commerce, Patricia Harris as secretary of housing and urban development, and Andrew Young as ambassador to the United Nations, some black leaders felt that Carter was abandoning them. The Congressional Black Caucus went so far as to attack Carter's administration for not being responsive enough "to the fundamental needs of most blacks and even attacked . . . [Carter's] record on civil rights and federal appointments" (Kaufman, 1993, p. 26). In September 1978, the caucus sent a long document to President Carter in which it accused him of having provided "less federal funding for housing and economic development . . . than under Nixon and Ford." It also said that his urban policy "provided few direct benefits for poorer people." Furthermore, it claimed, the Carter administration had not gone far enough in creating new jobs; Carter had not "given a major speech on civil rights," and he had made only "limited black appointments to top positions," noting particularly "the absence of blacks in top economic positions" (p. 110).

In fact, Carter had not abandoned blacks, as some black leaders claimed, but had fulfilled many of his promises to blacks made during his campaign. For example, he had promised to increase the number of blacks and other minority federal judges, and he had done so. When he left office in 1981, Carter had appointed 28 black judges—more than any other president before him. As a result, the percentage of black federal judges increased from 4% in 1977 to 9% in 1981. In addition, he provided

more government contracts to minority firms, boosted substantially the
amount of federal deposits in minority-owned banks, strengthened the
Justice Department's enforcement of the Voting Rights statutes, and increased the effectiveness of the Equal Employment Opportunity Commission in settling job discrimination cases. (Kaufman, 1993, p. 110)

It was true, however, that poor blacks and other poor minorities failed
to benefit from these actions, largely because most of Carter's efforts
took place via "executive and agency action rather than through legislative initiatives, and their greatest impact was on mid- and upper-in-
come minorities, not the poor" (p. 110). This resulted in raising black
expectations and demands, which contributed to the increasing strain
on interracial cooperation within the liberal wing of the Democratic
party.

The Jesse Jackson campaign in 1984 had a profound effect on blacks
both within and without the Democratic party. His Rainbow Coalition
Movement raised the expectations not only of many blacks but of a host
of other marginalized groups within the Democratic party. As Sheila
Collins (1986), who worked in the campaign, explains, "The emergence
of the Jackson campaign in 1984 as a progressive, black-led, multiracial, anticorporate, and anti-imperialist movement that took an electoral
form must be appreciated as a daring and visionary innovation" (p. 86).
For many groups and sectional movements, Jackson's Rainbow Coalition provided "a unified political program." Of particular significance
was the undeniable fact that during this period, Jackson emerged as the
"symbol of the new black electoral insurgency" (Collins, 1986, p. 119).

Black political leaders were split over Jackson's candidacy. Julian
Bond, Andrew Young, Coleman Young, and Richard Arrington did not
support Jackson, fearing that he would cause a division within the ranks
of the Democratic party. However, other black political leaders, such as
Marion Barry, Walter Fauntroy, and Richard Hatcher, supported him.
Their support was based on the rationale that Jackson would provide
them with a "way of achieving black leverage with the white nominee"
(Collins, 1986, p. 345).

This split enabled the Democratic party to maintain key aspects of
the racial status quo. It was able to "retain the loyalty of blacks without
conceding anything of substance to them" (Collins, 1986, p. 285). In
the end, the party struck a bargain with Jackson: He would support the
ticket and "refrain from inflammatory remarks that would 'hurt the
party,' " and in return, he would be given a commission that included

money for a handful of staff to engage in voter education and mobilization for the Democratic ticket, a position for a close aide on Mondale's campaign staff, meetings between [him] and Southern Democratic party chairs, and the promise of support for Jackson campaign chairman Richard Hatcher's re-election to the vice-presidency of the Democratic National Committee. (pp. 285-286)

Given the climate of black political expectation generated by Jackson's campaign, Jackson could have refused to support a ticket that was "so obviously contemptuous of black needs" (Collins, 1986, p. 286). In fact,

Jackson might have led a walkout at the convention or a massive boycott of the November elections, or declared himself an independent candidate. In fact, there were many in the African-American community who were angered by the conciliatory posture he took and questioned his motives in deciding to support the Mondale/Ferraro ticket. (p. 286)

Given the grim political realities of the time and even the present, however, Jackson and the black community were simply "not in a position in 1984 to make a complete break with the only electoral vehicle which it had known" (p. 286). Thus, blacks with rising expectations and demands and a coalition of other marginalized groups that had found a home in Jackson's Rainbow Coalition Movement, were forced to give ground to the much stronger forces of the racial status quo operating within the Democratic party. Commenting on the state of affairs within the Democratic party at the time, Collins argues that "Democratic party leaders would rather forfeit the presidency than take the chance of having their own power usurped by an insurgency of new voters from below" (p. 255).

Like Democratic presidents going back to Roosevelt, President Bill Clinton has benefited from black loyalty to the Democratic party. And although he has made some impressive appointments of blacks to his cabinet, along with other lower-level appointments of blacks, the Democratic party is still struggling to come to terms with the rising tide of black expectations and demands within its always delicately balanced black Democrats-white liberal coalition. Clinton's withdrawal of Lani Guinier's nomination could have upset this delicate balance had he not had the support of blacks in his administration. Other blacks, such as Jesse Jackson, Spelman College President Johnnetta Cole, and Maxine Waters (D-Calif.) wasted little time in voicing their disapproval of Clinton's action (Berry, 1993).

In many ways, Clinton's decision to withdraw Guinier's nomination is a classic example of how white liberal politicians have traditionally maintained certain aspects of the racial status quo while engaging in interracial cooperation in less controversial areas. Clinton explained that his decision was based on the fact that Guinier's writings were inconsistent with the views he had expressed on civil rights during his campaign. As legal scholar and historian Mary Frances Berry (1993) points out, however, "In fact, candidate Clinton generally ignored the widening racial divide in our nation with the tacit approval of African Americans. . . . Their complacency in this regard gave him the freedom to dispatch Guinier" (p. 40). According to Berry,

> The ideas Guinier discussed concerning the use of the Voting Rights Act to increase the political power of African Americans and Latinos are being used successfully and with minimal controversy in many municipalities and legislative districts, particularly in the South. . . . Cumulative voting, which calls for allowing voters to cast multiple votes for a single candidate, lets minorities unite behind a single candidate to enhance the possibility of electing at least one minority official. Super majority plans, used in areas where blacks have been denied political opportunity, require white and black legislators to negotiate to increase the power of black elected officials. Both remedies have been used for decades. Alabama has a large number of such plans. Pennsylvania and Illinois have used cumulative voting plans in statewide elections. These plans have resulted from lawsuits, as in the case of Alabama, or from political compromise. (p. 38)

Clinton's remarks sparked concern from civil rights litigators, who worried about the effect on the Voting Rights Act. The White House responded with a general statement indicating that it would continue to use "the full range of remedies available under law." The statement failed to convince Berry (1993). "Given President Clinton's specific criticisms decrying some of these same voting rights remedies as discussed by Guinier, the statement shows, at best, confusion" (p. 40). Even more significant,

> Before the month of June was over, a five-person Supreme Court majority, including Clarence Thomas, using ideas similar to those expressed by Clinton in withdrawing Guinier, rejected a North Carolina reapportionment plan which had resulted in the election of the first black congress-person in that state since the 19th century. (p. 40)

Berry (1993) warns blacks that they will have to increase their expectations and demands on the Clinton administration:

> Essentially, Clinton, the politician, remains committed to avoiding controversy. This includes ignoring the white-hot reality of racism in American life. Other politicians across racial lines agree with him. . . . Only if African Americans mobilize to push their interest now, and make clear to Clinton that their votes are at stake, will his path be altered. (p. 42)

Berry's views are indicative of a historical pattern of rising black expectations and demands within the political coalition of white liberal Democrats and black Democrats that has characterized the political mode of interracial cooperation.

BLACK COMMUNITY-LABOR ALLIANCE

A similar historical pattern has characterized the other dominant mode of interracial cooperation, the black community-labor alliance. Although for the sake of analysis, I have separated these two dominant modes of interracial cooperation, they evolved together. The labor movement, the Democratic party, and the black community share a long history of coalition building and of similar problems. Labor leaders such as John L. Lewis, Philip Murray, and Walter Reuther were active supporters of civil rights for blacks. In 1940, Lewis spoke before the NAACP annual meeting. Murray and Reuther joined the NAACP's board of directors. Speaking at the 1952 CIO convention, a major NAACP official proclaimed that " 'the program of the CIO has become a Bill of Rights for Negro Labor in America' " (Marshall, 1964, p. 183). Two years later, after the 1954 Supreme Court decision overturning the separate-but-equal doctrine, the CIO stated that, " 'while the NAACP has taken the leadership in forging the law into an instrument of social precision to accomplish its objectives, the CIO has always been closely associated with the NAACP and other like-minded groups in this struggle' " (p. 183).

The black community-labor alliance proved invaluable for the Democratic party's victory in the 1948 national election. NAACP spokesman Walter White, speaking before the 1948 CIO annual convention after Truman's election, said that "the results would have been impossible for the Negro without labor, or for labor without the Negro vote. It was the job done by organized labor which narrowed the margin between the two major parties to the point where the Negro vote could be decisive" (Marshall, 1964, p. 183). Unfortunately, by the time of the 1955 merger of the American Federation of Labor (AFL) and the Congress of Industrial Organizations (CIO), the black community-labor alliance was beginning to unravel due to persistent patterns of white racism within major unions and the rising expectations and demands of black trade unionists and the larger black community (Marshall, 1964, pp. 184-185).

In June 1950, several black trade union leaders and their white allies had met in Chicago at the National Labor Conference for Negro Rights. They discussed racism in unions, factories, and apprenticeship programs. Paul Robeson, a veteran supporter of the black community-labor alliance, predicted that "black labor, supported by the whole Negro people together with progressive white working men and women could save the labor movement, CIO and AF of L, from the leaders who were betraying it" (Foner, 1981, p. 295).

This conference, led by black workers, reflected their lack of trust in the traditional black community-labor alliance and the nonlabor black organizations. They adopted a model FEPC, which they wanted to put into all union contracts, and set up a continuations committee comprised of three black trade unionists. These leaders opened up new fronts in the struggle against racism in unions and industry. Within a year, this committee set up 23 Negro labor councils in the major industrial centers of the country. One of the most active councils was led by William R. Hood, a radical black worker and member of the United Auto Workers (UAW) Ford Local 600. The Detroit Negro Labor Council waged a long battle against racism in industry. One of the council's major targets was the UAW leadership, led by Walter Reuther, which opposed the black workers' fight for a local FEPC; the council also attempted to elect a black member to the UAW all-white executive board. Reuther accused the black union members of being "communist inspired." But that did not dampen their spirits. Along with other local Negro Labor Councils from around the nation, they formed a National Negro Labor Council (NNLC) in Cincinnati, Ohio, on October 27, 1951. From 1951 to 1955, the NNLC was in the vanguard for change in the black community, until it fell victim to the attacks of the UAW leadership and the Committee on Un-American Activities (Foner, 1981, pp. 295-309).

The conflict between Walter Reuther and the NNLC was rooted in decades of ambivalence, tensions, and conflicts in the long tradition of black community-UAW interracial cooperation in Detroit. The black community-UAW alliance has been one of the best modes of interracial cooperation in the 20th century, although it has been plagued with the ambivalence, tensions, and conflicts that arise when such modes of interracial cooperation are structurally and ideologically unable to accommodate rising black expectations and demands.

From the very beginning of their relationship, the black community in Detroit and the UAW-CIO supported each other as they both struggled to forge an effective alliance to serve their mutual needs. The black community needed the support of the UAW in fighting for the rights of blacks against racism both in the workplace and in the larger community, and the UAW needed the black community, particularly black workers in the auto plants, to strengthen its ranks.[1] Yet even as the UAW-CIO struggled on behalf of black workers and the larger black community against racial discrimination (much of it from white workers in the unions), black UAW members had expectations and demands that exceeded the ability or willingness of some white UAW leaders.

By far one of the most difficult and seemingly intractable sources of tension and conflict revolved around the long struggle for black representation on the International Executive Board. This expectation and demand became a major bone of contention between black UAW members and the all-white International Executive Board between 1938 and 1962 (Meier & Rudwick, 1979). During the early factional struggles within the UAW in the late 1930s, black workers who had differences on other issues tended to agree on the issue of having a black on the board. In November 1938, a black representing one of these factions put forth the view that the UAW "should directly challenge the discriminatory employment policies of the auto manufacturers, elect a black to the International Executive Board, and give Negroes greater representation in running the locals" (Meier & Rudwick, 1979, p. 65). Another black worker representing another faction within the UAW put forth a similar view. He encouraged blacks to join the UAW because, if blacks were represented in large enough numbers, they could feasibly elect a black to the International Executive Board. Another black argued that a black seat on the executive board would attract blacks to the UAW. At the two conventions held by the rival factions in March 1939, one faction "took the unprecedented step of creating an at-large seat for blacks on their International Executive Board" (pp. 64-65) and electing a black to the position. In addition, a black was appointed as regional director-at-large. This forced blacks in the rival camp "to press their demand." But nothing resulted from their efforts. The call for a black member-at-large on the board stimulated debate at their convention but was ultimately defeated. Before the convention, a white UAW member had pointed out that it would take an intensive educational campaign among prejudiced whites in the union before a black could be added to the board (Meier & Rudwick, 1979).

More revealing of the different perspectives on the issue between black and white UAW members was the rationale offered by the new UAW president, R. J. Thomas. As the 1939 convention chairman, Thomas had intervened in person to block any discussion of the issue of adding a black to the International Executive Board. He explained that he desired all to know that although a black would be welcomed on the board, he " 'would no more support a specifically designated black seat than a Polish or an Italian seat.' " He flatly rejected the arguments of black UAW members that a black seat should be created because the defeated opposition had set up such a seat. Thomas took the position that he was opposed to segregation and, "to the applause of the delegates," said, " 'I don't believe that the majority of the Negro people themselves want a "Jim Crow car" attached to the International Union' " (Meier & Rudwick, 1979, p. 65).

Black UAW members refused to give up their expectations and demands for a black on the board. At the 1942 UAW convention, the issue "achieved considerable prominence" when black delegates "took the symbolic step" of nominating two black UAW members to new vice presidencies that had been slated for Walter Reuther and Richard Frankensteen, two major white leaders of the union (Meier & Rudwick, 1979, p. 211). By 1943, black expectations and demands had not subsided in the least. Much like their strategy during the factional fights in 1939, blacks sought to take advantage of the factional split in the union by using their balance of power to press their demands for a black seat on the board. After all the politicking, however, they were faced with the same results: no black seat. Insult was added to injury when two top UAW leaders, Thomas and Reuther, rejected their concerns. Thomas denounced the demand for a "special black seat as a 'hypocritical' demand for racism in reverse" (p. 211). This white perception and interpretation of black demands for equity within interracial coalitions would come to represent a major point of contention among members of these coalitions.

The issue surfaced again at the 1944 convention. Black delegates once again employed their balance-of-power strategy "in another fruitless effort to win their point" (Meier & Rudwick, 1979, p. 212). The issue was destined to surface with painful regularity at future UAW annual meetings. By 1959, 2 years after black unionists in Detroit formed the Trade Union Leadership Conference (TULC) to address the plight of black workers both in plants and in the union, TULC leader Horace Sheffield challenged the UAW leadership by nominating a black for a vice presidency. In many ways, this was an act of desperation by a veteran black trade unionist, reflecting the sentiments of other blacks in the UAW who had "become discouraged at the prospects of a black being elected through normal channels" (pp. 220-221). As before, this effort failed. But in 1962, as a result of pressure from the TULC combined with increased numbers of black workers in the plants, a black was elected to a new vice presidency. A second black was elected to the International Executive Board in 1968.

The long struggle of UAW members to get a black on the International Executive Board of the UAW, while fighting at the same time against racism in the plants, explains why blacks were forced to establish organizations such as the National Negro Labor Council (NNLC) and the TULC. From the very beginning, white labor leaders, such as Thomas and Reuther, failed to appreciate even the symbolic need for blacks to have a black on the board. When they interpreted such demands as "hypocritical" and "reverse discrimination," they revealed a common tendency that often emerges at developmental stages of major modes of interracial cooperation: the tendency of the dominant white power to rationalize the need to maintain certain aspects of the racial status quo. Because whites had most of the power in the coalition, blacks were forced to engage in divisive balance-of-power politics in countless abortive attempts to achieve their goal. The goal, to elect a black to the International Executive Board, was achieved only when blacks finally obtained the power, by sheer weight of numbers, to elect a black.

The NNLC emerged, in part, out of the unwillingness of white labor leaders such as Reuther to understand the expectations and demands of black trade unionists. For example, Reuther had a difficult time coming to terms with William R. Hood, the NNLC president who "had been a thorn in [his] side as recording secretary of Local 600, even before the National Negro Labor Council was formed" (Foner, 1981, p. 307). Local 600, River Rouge, was the power base for the black UAW. It had the "largest black membership in the union [and] had been in the forefront in urging the addition of a black vice-president on the International

Executive Board" (p. 195). Local 600 constantly criticized the Reuther leadership for "indifference to the upgrading of black auto workers" (p. 307). Black UAW members were particularly concerned that, notwithstanding the fact that hundreds of tool and die shops operated in the Detroit area and the technical schools graduated "a number of qualified blacks each year, not a single shop employed a Negro" (p. 307). This resulted in clashes between Local 600 and the UAW leadership before the formation of the Detroit NNLC, clashes that continued after the organization was formed. Clearly, the UAW white leadership and the Detroit NNLC represented unraveling threads of the fabric of the black community-labor alliance.

In March 1952, Reuther responded to the Detroit NNLC by appointing an administrator over Local 600, removing five of its most radical members from office, "and depriving them of the right ever to run for reelection" (Foner, 1981, p. 307).[2] Predictably, they were charged with being members of the Communist Party. Two of the five were black and had played a key role in the great unionizing drive in 1941—a drive that demonstrated a high point in the black community-UAW-CIO alliance and in turn contributed to the development of the larger black community-labor coalition. The five members appealed their dismissal at the 1953 UAW convention. The two black members issued a joint statement just before the convention:

> "If fighting against discriminatory policies of the Ford Motor Company and fighting for the rights of Negro men and women to be promoted to better jobs, if disagreeing with the International Union's lily-white executive board on issues affecting the good and welfare of Local 600 and the members of the UAW constitute 'membership in or subservience to the Communist Party,' then we say make the most out of it." (p. 308)

Reuther and his "automatic majority" defeated attempts by the delegates of Local 600 to reinstate the five dismissed leaders.

Reuther and other white labor leaders who were key players in the black community-labor coalition failed to understand that the rising expectations and demands of black trade unionists, often expressed in organizations such as the NNLC and the TULC, were only the tip of the emerging iceberg, the black revolution that would transform the relationship between blacks and labor.

This transformation was already underway before the 1955 merger of the AFL-CIO. According to labor scholar Ray Marshall (1964), "There was growing disenchantment with the CIO in the Negro community by the time of the AFL-CIO merger in 1955" (p. 187). This growing disenchantment was rooted in part in the rising expectations of the black community, stimulated by its constant struggle against entrenched racism and the slow pace of change within the labor movement. Despite this growing disenchantment, at the time of the merger the black community-labor alliance was still intact. As Marshall describes it, "By the time of the merger . . . the main Negro organizations . . . were still basically pro-union, Negro-labor political alliances showed little sign of splitting, and the Negroes had more strength within the unions than ever before" (p. 187). However, "a number of features of the AFL-CIO merger tended to widen the growing gulf between the labor movement and the Negro community" (p. 187).

The first feature of the merger that contributed to the growing gulf between the labor movement and the Negro community was the fact that the vast majority of the official positions of the new organization, including the position of the president, "went to the AFL, which was never able to overcome its unfavorable image in the Negro community, and which never had close relations with organizations like the NAACP and the NUL" (Marshall, 1964, pp. 187-188). The second feature, which was a slap in the face to the black community and had the greatest potential for destroying the very foundation of the black community-labor alliance, was the decision of the AFL-CIO Executive Council to admit two racist unions—the Brotherhood of Railway Trainmen and the Brotherhood of Locomotive Firemen—to the newly merged labor federation "even though they had race bars in their constitutions" (Marshall, 1964, p. 188). Worst of all, "none of the former CIO leaders cast a dissenting vote against these organizations" (p. 188). Only A. Philip Randolph, the black president of the predominantly black Brotherhood of Sleeping Car Porters, objected to allowing such avowed racist organizations to join the merger.

Black labor leaders were understandably alarmed at the violation of the principles on which the black community-labor alliance had been built. Marshall (1964) wonders how "such CIO civil rights stalwarts as James Carey and Walter Reuther [could vote] for the admission of organizations with constitutional prohibitions to nonwhite members" (p. 188). The other feature of the merger that incensed the black community and, by extension, created conflicts and tensions within the black community-labor alliance was the role that member unions of the AFL-CIO, such as locals of the International Brotherhood of Electrical

Workers, played in various cities, having engaged in years of intensive efforts to maintain their racial bars against blacks.

Five years after the merger, Herbert Hill, the labor secretary of the NAACP, gave a report on the status of race relations within the AFL-CIO at the 1961 NAACP annual meeting. Hill's report was later published as an article in the *Journal of Negro Education*. Hill (1961) puts forth a blistering attack on what he considers the major failures of the AFL-CIO in the area of race relations:

> The elimination of racism within trade unions was one of the major goals for organized labor announced at the merger convention of the American Federation of Labor and the Congress of Industrial Organizations in December, 1955. This was welcomed by many civil rights agencies and especially by the National Association for the Advancement of Colored People, which offered its full support to the labor movement. . . . Today, five years after the AFL-CIO merger, the national labor organization has failed to eliminate the broad pattern of racial discrimination and segregation in many important affiliated unions. (p. 109)

Hill attributes this failure to the lack of "a systematic and coordinated effort by the national labor federation to eliminate discrimination and segregation within local unions," which resulted in "piecemeal and inadequate efforts" that were usually "the result of protest by civil rights agencies acting on behalf of Negro workers." Hill indicates the national AFL-CIO as having "repeatedly refused to take action on its own initiatives" (p. 109). Although acknowledging that the "AFL-CIO adopted a much more liberal racial position than the CIO," Marshall (1964) writes that "the apparent ineffectiveness of the machinery set up by the merged organization led to the conviction that the AFL-CIO Civil Rights Committee, like its CIO predecessor, was mainly 'window dressing' " (p. 189).

Given the slow pace of change within the AFL-CIO and the rising tide of black expectations and demands within the black community-labor alliance, stimulated in large part by the civil rights and black power movements, conflicts and tensions were inevitable. Tensions continued to build as traditional allies within the black community-labor alliance began to fight over different perceptions of how best to address racial change within the labor movement. Jewish-led unions, such as the Amalgamated Clothing Workers and the International Ladies Garment Workers' Union, with a tradition of progressive policies with respect to civil rights and the black community, began to be affected by the conflict between the AFL-CIO and the black community. The Jewish Labor Committee (JLC), maintained by Jewish-led unions, tended, according to Marshall (1964), to side with the AFL-CIO in the union's conflicts with the NAACP. Such an alliance increased tensions within the black community-labor alliance. It also provoked a verbal attack on the JLC from the NAACP's labor secretary, himself of Jewish extraction, who stated that Jewish labor "would do well if they ceased to apologize for racists in the American labor movement, and instead of attempting to create a desirable public image for the AFL-CIO, join with Negro workers and the NAACP in directly attacking the broad pattern of racial discrimination" (p. 195).

Black demands and expectations within the labor movement increased with the increased militancy within the civil rights movement. Although black trade unionists during the 1950s founded black labor organizations, such as the National Negro Labor Council, the Trade Union Leadership Council, and the Negro American Labor Council (NALC), to focus on the exclusive needs of black workers (with the exception of the TULC, which encompassed the entire black community), they tended to reject the black nationalism that would come to characterize later black workers' movements. As A. Philip Randolph told the delegates at the founding convention of the NALC in New York in July 1959,

"While the Negro American Labor Council rejects black nationalism as a doctrine and practice of racial segregation, it recognizes the fact that history has placed upon the Negro and the Negro alone the basic responsibility to complete the uncompleted civil war revolution through keeping the fires of freedom burning in the civil rights movement." (Foner, 1981, p. 334)

The NALC, however, did reflect some aspects of black nationalism in its general mood and philosophy. Its constitution did not bar whites, but at the outset it confined itself to black membership and black financial support. Randolph defended this course of action as necessary to make it "possible for them to take a position completely independent of white unionists" (Foner, 1981, p. 334). Such a position did not mean the end of the black community-labor alliance. It did mean that the alliance was undergoing tremendous changes under the pressure of the conflicting demands being placed on it. The rising tide of black demands and expectations was clashing with the tendency of the labor movement to maintain aspects of the racial status quo. Power relations within the alliance were being contested; blacks no longer were willing to allow whites to determine or influence the nature of their demands and expectations within the alliance.

By the late 1960s, the black community-labor alliance was coming apart at the seams, as black workers within traditional unions became more radical and uncompromising. In the summer of 1968, 900 black members of Local 241, Amalgamated Transit Union, AFL-CIO, in Chicago staged a wildcat strike that shut down 60 bus lines and seriously affected 40 others, because the all-white union leadership (the local was 60% black) refused to revise the constitution, which used white pensioners' votes to maintain control. After a long struggle that included other demands, the black workers won a partial victory (Foner, 1981).

That same year, members of the Ad Hoc Committee, a black caucus within the United Steel Workers Union (organized in 1963 and representing over 200,000 black workers), placed picket lines around the entrance to the United Steel Workers (USW) Convention. They were protesting the lack of black representation in USW leadership and the "depressed status of Negro workers within the steel plants" (Hill, 1969, pp. 20-21). This was a period in which a score of black unions and caucuses within unions developed, including the Independent Alliance of Skilled Crafts in Ohio, the Maryland Freedom Labor Union, the United Community Construction Workers of Boston, the United Construction and Trades Union in Gary, and the National Ad Hoc Committee of Concerned Negro UAW members (Hill, 1969).

The most radical and well-known among the black unions posing the greatest challenge to the black community-labor alliance was the League of Revolutionary Black Workers, which originated in Detroit-area plants. Led by a group of young black revolutionaries who had grown to maturity in the age and spirit of the Student Nonviolent Coordinating Committee, Malcolm X, Che Guevara, Mao Tse-tung, and Fanon, the league went beyond the traditional political struggles of black UAW caucuses, such as the TULC, NNLC, and NALC. It was intent on destroying both capitalism and racism. It became clear to both union and management that the league meant business when it staged a walkout at the Dodge main plant on May 2, 1968. Later, the newly organized Dodge Revolutionary Union Movement (DRUM) led a march of black auto workers, students, and unemployed black youth to Chrysler headquarters in Highland Park, Dodge Local 3's offices, and Solidarity

House, the headquarters of the UAW. Two months later, DRUM established a picket line around the Dodge main plant. Close to 70% of the black workers walked out and stayed out for 2 days. This wildcat strike crippled production and forced Local 3 leadership to meet some of DRUM's demands. Other black revolutionary groups began emerging in other Detroit area plants, and strikes occurred in some of these plants (Foner, 1981; Georgakas & Surkin, 1975).

The league alarmed moderate black labor organizations, such as the TULC and the white leadership of the UAW, both of which were still part of the black community-labor alliance. The league's actions, however, benefited the more moderate TULC, because it forced the vacillating white UAW leadership to give ground to black moderates. As Foner (1981) points out, "Within a few months after the formation of the League of Black Revolutionary Workers, black workers were elected as presidents" (pp. 416-417) of previously white-dominated locals. For the first time in its history, Briggs Local 21 elected a black vice president. In other plants, black committeemen and shop stewards were also elected for the first time. The black union moderates used these black firsts as examples of how long and hard they had worked, whereas the white union leadership used these same examples to show that black workers could achieve their goals within the established union structure. Both ignored the league's radical influence on the sudden changes within the UAW. But this did not halt the activities of the league.

The league made several attempts to gain elected union offices in 1968, 1969, and 1970, but these efforts were largely unsuccessful. Coupled with these failures was internal dissension within the league as members became involved with nonplant political struggles, such as organizing a Detroit chapter of the Black Panther Party in the spring of 1969, establishing the International Black Appeal and a book club, and supporting militant candidates. By June 1971, serious ideological splits within the league had crippled its effectiveness. With the resignation of key members and amid various charges and countercharges, the league was on the decline (Geschwender, 1977). But during its short life, the league had raised the expectations and demands of a new generation of black workers. It had also forced the white-dominated union bureaucracy to change some of its racist policies. In short, it strengthened the position of black workers within a major mode of interracial cooperation, the black community-labor alliance, which in turn forced the white labor leadership to make some key concessions.

The black community-labor alliance experienced another challenge when, in September 1972, 1,200 black trade unionists met in Chicago to organize the Coalition of Black Trade Unionists (CBTU), stimulated in part by the McGovern campaign and the AFL-CIO neutrality on the 1972 elections. Led by black labor leader William Lucy, secretary-treasurer of the American Federation of State, County, and Municipal Employees (AFSCME), the organization did not perceive itself as simply another protest or black nationalist group, nor did it see itself as a black rival organization to the traditional union structure. In contrast to the League of Black Revolutionary Workers, which was well outside of the traditional union structure and by extension outside of the black community-labor alliance, CBTU saw itself as "an organic part of the union movement" and planned to operate within the union framework (Plastrik, 1973, p. 12).

The workers in CBTU retained faith in the American trade union movement and felt that it was still the most vital force for social change in America. Their faith in the interracial working class struggle was far in advance of their white counterparts within the black community-labor alliance, who not only had failed repeatedly to extend a coopera-tive hand to the poorer sectors of the American working class but had become an "aristocracy of labor" interested only in maintaining their own intraclass racial interests.

The goals of the CBTU were as follows:

> To conduct campaigns to organize nonunion blacks [who numbered about 8 million in organizations of the poor in black communities]; to support actions in opposition to the Vietnam War; to back legislation favorable to Federal revenue-sharing programs that will bolster social service in black communities; to provide a forum for blacks concerning their special prob-lems within unions; and to act as a bridge between the organized labor movement and the black communities where hostility to unions is high. (Plastrik, 1973, p. 12)

The CBTU provided a much needed boost to the battle-weary black community-labor alliance. Its willingness to work within the labor move-ment and, more important, "to act as a bridge between the organized labor movement and the black communities where hostility to unions is high" suggested that the CBTU still had faith in the role of the black community-labor alliance as a major mode of interracial cooperation.

CONCLUSION

The combined efforts of many interracial movements for racial justice and the advancement of African Americans made major contributions to the economic, political, and social advancement of African Americans. For decades, these interracial movements reinforced the efforts of the African American community in its protracted struggle to survive and progress in a country that was all too ready to give free rein to racial oppression. The interracial movements, particularly the dominant modes such as the more progressive segments of the labor movements and the Democratic party, provided African Americans with valuable allies in countless struggles against racism. In fact, the progressive elements of the labor movements and the Democratic party provided most of the white allies in the antiracism struggle. Yet they were plagued with tensions and conflicts as many whites dragged their feet on racial equality and many blacks fought to speed up the pace of change. Black expectations and demands grew as blacks perceived that they were getting closer to full equality.

As early as 1940, black expectations and demands were creating tensions and conflicts within the black-white coalition in the Democratic party. A. Philip Randolph symbolized blacks' rising expectations and demands when, in testimony before Congress, he stated that he would urge young black men to refuse to serve in the armed services unless racial segregation was abolished. No doubt, Truman's pro-civil rights stand was influenced in part by the rising expectations and demands of African Americans within the liberal bloc of the Democratic party.

Blacks and their allies in the Democratic party would continue to push for racial equality against reactionary whites in the same party who were resisting any changes in the racial status quo. The Kennedy administration represented the best example of how the rising tide of black expectations and demands influenced the political coalition of whites and blacks within the Democratic party. The civil rights movement, at the time embodying the core of the rising expectations and demands of African Americans, forced the Kennedy administration to challenge key aspects of the racial status quo. Black leaders, such as Roy Wilkins and Martin Luther King, Jr., prodded Kennedy. Here is a clear example of a liberal president operating within one of the most dominant modes of interracial cooperation, who moved forward only when he was prodded by black expectations and demands.

Black expectations and demands continued to rise during the Johnson administration, complicated by the emergence of black militancy within the civil rights movement. Notwithstanding the Voting Rights Act and the Great Society programs, rising black expectations and demands created a grassroots firestorm that erupted in urban disorder around the country.

Although blacks would continue to support the Democratic party, they were clearly not satisfied with what the party could deliver. Throughout the Carter years and into the Clinton years, the Democratic party, as one of the most dominant forms of interracial cooperation, has fallen far short of meeting the expectations and demands of the African American community.

The black community-labor alliance is the other most dominant mode of interracial cooperation. During the 1930s, this alliance contributed to the struggle for racial equality in the workplace. In the following decades, it continued to play a leading role in that struggle and in other areas. It proved invaluable to the Democratic party's victory in the 1948 national elections. But it too has a long history of rising black expectations and demands, which has generated much tension and conflict.

Between 1939 and 1962, expectation and demand for a black representative on the International Executive Board became a major bone of contention in the UAW. The UAW was by far one of the most progressive unions on racial issues in the country, but it could not keep pace with legitimate black expectations and demands. White board members interpreted such expectations and demands as hypocritical and reverse discrimination. Black union members were also frustrated over the slow pace of movement against racial discrimination in the plants. They wanted the union to move faster. Black workers remained in interracial unions, such as the UAW, but formed other black labor organizations to address expectations and demands that interracial organizations were either unwilling or unable to perform. Here is a classic example of what happens when a mode of interracial cooperation cannot accommodate the rising expectations and demands of a member group.

These problems became even more complicated during and after the AFL-CIO merger. Given the slow pace of racial change within the AFL-CIO and the rising tide of black expectations and demands within the black community-alliance—stimulated in part by the civil rights and black power movements—conflicts and tensions were inevitable. More tensions and conflicts arose as African Americans and Jewish trade unionists began to fight over how best to address racial issues within the labor movement.

As black expectations and demands increased, so did the number of black worker organizations. The NNLC, TULC, and NALC were all founded in the 1950s. The most radical black worker organization, which posed the biggest threat to the black community-labor alliance, was the League of Revolutionary Workers, founded in the late 1960s. The radicalism of the league was probably the reason why more moderate black labor leaders were elected as presidents and vice presidents of previously white-dominated unions.

In 1972, the black community-labor alliance faced another challenge when a group of black workers organized the Coalition of Black Trade Unionists. Once again, black workers felt that their concerns were not being addressed by the AFL-CIO and the Democratic party. Although they still had faith in the American trade union movement and felt that it was still the most vital force for social change in America, they realized that it had to be prodded constantly to be relevant to their needs.

Without constant prodding of black expectations and demands, these dominant modes of interracial cooperation would have fallen far short of any reasonable goals of racial equality. At best, many whites tended to view interracial cooperation as a means to their ends—even if those ends maintained the racial status quo. Black expectations and demands kept whites' eyes on the prize of the true goal of interracial cooperation—racial justice.

NOTES

1. For an excellent history of this alliance, see Meier and Rudwick (1979, chap. 4).

2. For an analysis of the role of the 1941 Ford organizing committee in the development of the black community-UAW alliance in Detroit, see Meier and Rudwick (1979, chap. 20).

5

The White Role in the Struggle for Racial Equality in the 19th Century

HISTORICAL SIGNIFICANCE OF THE ROLE OF WHITES

Any study of the history of interracial cooperation in the United States must take into consideration the role of certain white individuals in interracial movements for racial justice and interracial unity, cooperation, and fellowship. It has not always been clear why whites would risk losing their racial privileges to side with racial minorities. History is filled with stories of brave and courageous members of the ruling elite who fought on the side of the downtrodden; students of race relations in the United States, however, have tended to ignore the role of certain whites in establishing racial justice and creating environments in which interracial unity can flourish.

Students of race relations should pay more attention to this area of race relations. An understanding of the historical role of whites in interracial movements is needed in today's critical stage of racial polarization. We need to draw lessons from the lives of whites who devoted their lives and resources to transforming race relations in the United States. Few contemporary whites know much about the role of whites in the antislavery, antilynching, labor, and civil rights struggles. Few blacks are aware of the long, often lonely, caravan of whites who shared the black struggle for racial justice. This should not be misconstrued as an attempt to overemphasize white sacrifices over black sacrifices or even to equate them within this struggle. Rather, the aim here is to gain a fuller understanding of the role of whites in these struggles. This knowledge can contribute to the building of interracial trust, on which present efforts for racial justice and interracial unity, cooperation, and fellowship can be sustained and future movements and efforts can be encouraged.

For the sake of brevity, the focus will be on a few white persons per movement and/or period who made a major contribution to the interracial struggle for racial justice and the advancement of African Americans.

These women and men were among the most devoted whites in the movement for racial justice during the antislavery and Reconstruction periods. The Grimké sisters, especially Angelina, personified the highest level of devotion to racial justice in the abolitionist movement. John Brown gave the most that any white person could give: his life. And according to W. E. B. Du Bois (1935/1964), Thaddeus Stevens was the "greatest and most uncompromising of abolitionist democrats. . . . No man demanded more for Negroes . . . or was more thoroughly an advocate of complete democracy" (p. 296). These people went far beyond the traditional call of duty for an abolitionist, which often stopped short of socializing with blacks on an equal basis and interacting as fellow human beings. In this sensitive area of interracial unity, cooperation, and fellowship, these people elevated the interracial struggle for racial justice to a higher spiritual level.

THE GRIMKÉ SISTERS

Sarah and Angelina Grimké could have easily become a part of the racially oppressive culture of the plantation South. Like other sensitive young white children on the plantations, they found themselves questioning and wondering about the treatment of black slaves. As a young girl, Sarah was a constant witness to the inhumanity that whites imposed on slaves. On one such occasion, she saw the head of a slave "stuck high on a pole." It was the head of a slave who had attempted to run away from one of the plantations "and whose punishment was to serve as a deterrent to other slaves" (Lerner, 1967, p. 35). Sarah also recounted other less severe but no less dehumanizing punishments devised by members of the first families of Charleston. One particularly horrible punishment (invented by an acquaintance who was quite proud of her ingenuity), "dreaded more by the slave than whipping, unless it [was] unusually severe, . . . [was] standing on one foot and holding the other in the hand." As if this were not sufficiently painful for the slave, other "improvements" were introduced:

> [A] strap was contrived to fasten around the ankle and pass around the neck, so that the least weight of the foot resting on the strap would choke the person. The pain occasioned by this unnatural position was great; and when continued, as it sometimes was, for an hour or more, produced intense agony. (Lerner, 1967, p. 35)

The same woman who invented this macabre torture told Sarah that " 'she had the ears of her waiting maid slit for some petty theft. This she told me in the presence of the girl' " (Lerner, 1967, p. 35). According to some slaveowners, these harsh forms of punishment were necessary because of " 'the peculiar characteristics of the Negro which made him lazy, unwilling, deceitful and slovenly' " (p. 35).

Sarah and her younger sister, Angelina, repeatedly witnessed the inhumanity of slavery and its effect on blacks. Both sisters soon realized the terrible contradictions inherent in the slave culture. One such contradiction was the behavior of a pious member of Sarah's church, well-known for her charitable work, who presented daily readings from the Bible. Yet this same Christian woman had no problem sending a female slave who repeatedly ran away to the workhouse to be whipped. Even worse, the slave woman then had "a heavy iron collar, with three long prongs projecting from it . . . placed around [her neck], and one of her sound front teeth was extracted to serve as a mark to describe her in case of escape" (p. 37). Sarah described this woman's condition:

> "She could lie in no position but on her back, which was sore from scourging, as I can testify from personal inspection, and her only place of rest was the floor, on a blanket. . . . This slave, who was the seamstress of the family was continually in her mistress' presence, sitting in her chamber to sew, or engaged in other household work, with her lacerated and bleeding back, her mutilated mouth, and heavy iron collar, without, so far as appeared, exciting any feeling of compassion." (Lerner, 1967, p. 37)

Sarah could not protect her younger sister from similar horrors of slavery. Angelina came face to face with such a horror when a slave boy was called into her classroom to open a window. As he turned his back to the class to open the window, Angelina could see the recent whip-marks on his legs and back " 'still encrusted with blood and scabs' "

(Lerner, 1967, p. 38). Angelina cried as she told her story to her older sister. At this stage of her life, however, Sarah could give little comfort to her younger sister, who " 'asked for moral judgment, a clear-cut condemnation of slavery as an evil—the same moral judgment Sarah, as a child, had expected from those she loved' " (p. 38).

The children of slaveowners had to be taught to overcome their sensitivity toward slaves. Such sensitivity was considered out of place, an immature sentiment that white children would soon outgrow. Sarah often prayed that slaves about to be punished would be spared. "Sometimes her prayers were answered in unexpected ways, but she recalled later in life that she often cried over the chastisement of slaves" (Lerner, 1967, p. 20). Her feelings for the humanity of slaves caused her and her parents much concern. Given a slave girl as her "constant companion, to wait on her, to serve her needs," Sarah saw her as a little friend, a playmate, and "treated her as an equal." A few years later, this playmate died after being sick. Sarah was heartbroken, which puzzled her parents, who in their learned insensitivity to the humanity of slaves considered the loss a mere temporary inconvenience. From their perspective, slave girls were easily replaceable. Sarah could simply select another "companion" from among the group of idle slave children in the Grimké household. Sarah, however, refused to pick another slave girl to replace her dead companion (p. 20).

The sisters taught Bible classes every Sunday afternoon to slave children. This situation posed a problem for Sarah, because she tended to ask too many questions and refused to accept the traditional answers. For example, because the slave children had such hunger for the message of the Gospel, why not just teach them to read the Bible for themselves? Sarah was dutifully told that reading was bad for slaves because it made them " 'restless and rebellious.' " The minds of slaves were not suited for learning to read. Reading would " 'make them unfit for the labor they must do. Besides, it was against the law' " (Lerner, 1967, p. 22). Sarah found these answers unacceptable.

Not only did she reject these answers, she went so far as to violate a cardinal law of the slaveholding South. As she explained,

"My great desire in this matter would not be totally suppressed, and I took an almost malicious satisfaction in teaching my little waiting-maid at night, when she was supposed to be occupied in combing and brushing my long locks. The light was put out, the keyhole screened, and flat on our stomachs, before the fire, with the spelling book under our eyes, we defied the laws of South Carolina." (Lerner, 1967, p. 23)

The conspirators were caught, and Sarah's act of defiance almost earned the slave girl a whipping. Sarah's father gave her a serious lecture on the gravity of her "offense." The sense of sisterhood with black women, which later characterized both sisters' relationships with free black women in the antislavery movement, was first expressed in this act.

Returning home from the North, where she had accompanied her father in 1819, Sarah met a group of Quakers from Philadelphia who gave her a copy of John Woolman's works. This meeting and Woolman's work would change her life. She read and thought deeply on many passages in his works, including the following passage from "Some Consideration on the Keeping of Negroes," written in 1762:

"Suppose that our ancestors and we had been exposed to constant servitude, in the more servile and inferior employments of life; that we had been destitute of the help of reading and good company; that amongst ourselves we had few wise and pious instructions; . . . that while others, in ease, have plentifully heaped up the fruit of our labour, we had received barely enough to relieve nature; and being wholly at the command of others, had generally been treated as a contemptible, ignorant part of mankind; should we, in that case, be less abject than they now are?" (Lerner, 1967, p. 52)

As Sarah read Woolman's experiences of how uneasy he felt drinking and lodging " 'free-cost with people who lived in ease on the hard labour of their slaves' " (Lerner, 1967, p. 52), she was deeply moved, because he reflected her own experiences of how slavery dehumanized slaves and desensitized white slaveowners. After much soul searching and some difficult discussions with family members, Sarah took the plunge. She not only became a Quaker but soon left the South. She returned for brief visits, but by 1821 Sarah Grimké's destiny as a champion of the slave was beginning to unfold.

Angelina would soon follow her older sister. But before she left the South, she stirred up much trouble within her family and her community by her insistent attacks on slavery. She started daily prayer meetings with the family slaves, a practice that her mother first disapproved of but later accepted. These meetings became the first religious instruction that these slaves had; years later, they wrote moving letters of thanks to

Angelina. But she could not be content with conducting prayer meetings with slaves while professing Christians held slaves. Angelina felt so strongly about the inherent contradiction of professing Christianity while holding slaves that she "appeared at a meeting of the elders of the Presbyterian church, all slaveholders, offering them the fantastic suggestion that they, as a body, should speak out against slavery." They gave her a polite ear but dismissed her concerns without condemnation or threat. Disappointed, she appealed to individual church members, to no avail. Although some church members privately agreed with her, "they would not act on her suggestion" (Lerner, 1967, pp. 70-71).

The horrors of slavery continually filled Angelina's mind as she went about her daily activities. She was particularly shocked by the torturous punishments applied to slaves at the workhouse, where masters " 'too dainty to perform the office themselves' " sent slaves for punishment. " 'Whippings were administered in orderly fashion upon the naked bodies of women as well as men.' " The most horrendous of the punishments administered in the workhouse was the treadmill:

"The most dreaded punishment was the treadmill, a drum with broad steps which revolved rapidly. The slaves' arms were fastened to a handrail above it. Only the strongest and most agile could move their feet in time with the movement of the drum, the others were soon helplessly suspended by their arms, the edge of the steps hitting their legs, knees and bodies at every turn. Several 'drivers' attempted to make the prisoners move by flogging them with a 'cat o' nine tails.' Fifteen minutes on this instrument of torture would cripple a slave for days afterwards." (Lerner, 1967, pp. 77-78)

Angelina's sensitive nature revolted at such treatment. The workhouse left a powerful impression on her. She could not bear to walk down the street where the workhouse was located:

"These are not things I have heard; no, my own eyes have looked upon them and wept over them. . . . No one can imagine my feelings walking down that street. It seemed as though I was walking on the very confines of hell. . . . I suffered so much that I could not get over it for days and wondered how any real Christian could live near such a place." (Lerner, 1967, p. 78)

No wonder Angelina felt guilty when a slave being dragged to the horrible workhouse cried out for help. But Angelina could not do anything to help. In her diary, she cried out feelings: "How long, oh

Lord, wilt thou suffer the foot of the oppressor to stand on the neck of the slaves!" Unlike many whites of her time, including members of her family, who numbed themselves to all the cruelty and unkindness heaped on slaves, Angelina chose to sensitize herself to the pain of slaves:

> "It seemed to me that all the cruelty and unkindness which I had from infancy seen practiced toward them came back to my mind. . . . Night and day they were before me and yet my hands were bound as with chains of iron. . . . If only I could be the means of exposing the cruelty and injustice . . . of bringing to light the hidden things of darkness, of revealing the secrets of iniquity and abolishing its present regulations." (Lerner, 1967, p. 79)

Angelina set out on a course to do just that: to be "the means of exposing the cruelty and injustice . . . [of slavery], of bringing to light the hidden things of darkness, of revealing the secrets of iniquity and abolishing its present regulations." Once she determined that she could and would be the means of "exposing the cruelty and injustice" of slavery, she spared no one, neither family members nor friends of the family. To a group of visitors in her home engaged in their favorite subject of the "depravity of their servants," Angelina retorted that the depravity of slaves was the fault of whites and proceeded to give them a lecture. Each day became the occasion for a struggle over the issue of the oppression of slaves. Why was it necessary, she asked her mother, to call on the slaves to do such things as move a chair or open a window? Why must slaves wait for hours in cold hallways just in case they might be needed or sleep " 'on the bare floor with only a blanket and be awakened at any time their mistress wanted a service performed? Why must they eat their meals at irregular hours?' " (Lerner, 1967, pp. 79-80). Here again, Angelina saw and felt deeply the blatant contradiction between the treatment of slaves and Christian principles.

For more than a year, Angelina fought a valiant but vain struggle against slavery among family and friends to little avail. She became a Quaker like her sister Sarah and went North, where she would leave her indelible mark on the antislavery movement. But she would do much more: She would bring to the antislavery movement a deep and profound understanding of the nature and complexity of white racism and a longing for genuine interracial unity, love, and fellowship.

Angelina was soon disappointed as she saw the shortcomings of the North in the area of race relations. Antiblack riots in New York and

Philadelphia shocked her. In her dismay, she wrote an inspiring letter to William L. Garrison:

"I can hardly express to thee the deep and solemn interest with which I have viewed the violent proceedings of the last few weeks. Although I expected opposition, I was not prepared for it so soon—and I greatly feared abolitionists would be driven back in the first outset, and thrown into confusion." (Lerner, 1967, p. 123)

Angelina told Garrison that " 'the ground upon which you stand is holy ground: never—never surrender it. If you surrender it, the hope of the slave is extinguished' " (Lerner, 1967, p. 123). Without getting her permission, Garrison published her letter in *The Liberator,* which greatly upset both Angelina's Quaker friends, who viewed Garrison as a raving fanatic, and her sister Sarah.

This was only the beginning of Angelina's tremendous influence on race relations in the North. Her genuine love and concern for blacks as fellow human beings increased as she and her sister became close friends with black women in the antislavery movement. Their bonds of friendship with such women as Sarah Douglass would last a lifetime and increase Angelina's and Sarah's sensitivity to racial prejudice (see Barnes & Dumond, 1934). The more sensitive they became to Northern racism, the more they attacked it. They were particularly sensitive to the effect of racial prejudice on blacks in the free states. " 'Northern prejudice against color is grinding the colored man to the dust in our free states, and this is strengthening the hands of the oppressor continually' " (Lerner, 1967, p. 157). As Lerner points out, "The sisters' Southern life experience had brought them in close personal contact with Negroes; their sensitivity to manifestations of race prejudice was unusually keen" (p. 157).

The sisters' commitment to antislavery and interracial fellowship was strengthened by their association with, and Angelina's eventual marriage to, Theodore Weld, the well-known abolitionist. Weld had been involved in the antislavery movement for years before meeting the sisters. He had that rare quality, often missing among white abolitionists, of seeing blacks as fellow human beings, not just as objects in a struggle. He worked on their behalf, and he socialized with them. It was this fellowship with blacks that placed Weld above so many other white abolitionists. Weld had conducted a study of blacks in Cincinnati and discovered much about their struggles to survive. He made it a habit to socialize with blacks at every opportunity:

"If I ate in the city, it was at their tables. If I slept in the city, it was in their homes. If I attended parties, it was theirs—weddings—theirs—funerals—theirs—Sabbath schools—Bible classes—theirs. . . . I was with the colored people in their meetings by day and by night." (Thomas, 1973, pp. 73-74)

When Theodore and Angelina were married on May 14, 1838, it was a bold and courageous statement of their belief in racial unity and harmony. They insisted "on making their wedding an interracial affair" (Lerner, 1967, p. 237), even if it ruffled the feathers of some family members, such as the Grimké's sister Ann in whose house the wedding was to take place. Few white abolitionists would have been willing to go so far in breaching family social values. But Angelina Grimké and Theodore Weld were uncompromising on the issue of racial equality and fellowship. They were prepared to find an alternative place if sister Ann had balked at the idea of an interracial wedding celebration. In the end, Ann consented (Lerner, 1967).

The blacks at this interracial wedding celebration included Sarah Douglass and her mother, longtime friends of the Grimké sisters; Betty Dawson and her daughter, former slaves of the sisters' father, freed by sister Ann; six black groomsmen and bridesmaids, joined by six white groomsmen and bridesmaids; and a black minister who prayed and was followed by a white minister who also prayed. A black confectioner, using only " ' "free sugar" in the baking, suppl[ied] the wedding cake' " (Lerner, 1967, p. 238). An honor roll of well-known white abolitionists attended the wedding, including Garrison, the Chapmans, the Westons, the Tappans, and Gerrit Smith. There were people from all classes. There could be no question that this interracial wedding celebration "was a deliberate demonstration on the part of the hosts" (p. 242). As Angelina explained it, " 'They were our invited guests, and we thus had an opportunity to bear our testimony against the horrible prejudice which prevails against colored persons, and equally awful prejudice against the poor' " (p. 242).

The Grimké sisters never wavered in their constant struggle against slavery and racial prejudice. They did not allow their antislavery associates to rest on their laurels. For the Grimké sisters, to be against slavery was not sufficient. One had to be against racial prejudice. At the Antislavery Convention of American Women, held in Philadelphia in the fall of 1838, one of several resolutions presented by Sarah and "one of the few not adopted unanimously at the convention" (Lerner, 1967, p. 251), dealt with the sensitive issue of racial prejudice, which Sarah saw as the essence of slavery. Sarah held firm to the belief that

"[it was] the duty of abolitionists to identify themselves with these oppressed Americans by sitting with them in places of worship, by appearing
with them in our streets, by giving them our countenance in steamboats
and stages, by visiting them and encouraging them to visit us, receiving
them as we do our white fellow citizens." (p. 251)

Lerner explains the significance of the Grimké sisters' contribution to
the struggle against racism:

The antislavery women showed generally greater awareness of race prejudice and all its implications than did their contemporaries. Their meetings
were integrated and their Negro members were given a chance to take
leadership positions. Still, this call for a conscious policy of demonstra-
tions against segregation in public places was considered controversial
even by abolitionists. In advocating it year after year, and personally
carrying it into practice, Sarah and Angelina made one of their most
significant contributions to the ideology of the antislavery cause. It was an
issue on which they consistently were in advance of most white abolitionists. (p. 251)

The sisters did not let their concerns for family unity prevent them
from constantly pleading with their mother to free her slaves. When
their mother died and left her slaves to the sisters, they freed the slaves
and took care of those they invited to come North. The sisters, as well
as Weld, also extended their love and care to their black nephews, the
sons of Henry Grimké by a slave woman. In 1868, Angelina saw a notice
in the *Anti-Slavery Standard* about an event at Lincoln University in
Pennsylvania, a school for black men, where a young black man named
Archibald Grimké had given an excellent talk. She wrote and introduced
herself. The young man and his brother, Francis, were indeed her
nephews. She expressed in letters how she regretted that during the Civil
War no Grimkés had fought on the side of freedom:

"You my young friends now bear this once-honored name—I charge you
most solemnly by your upright conduct, and your life-long devotion to the
eternal principles of justice and humanity and religion, to lift this name out
of the dust, where it now lies, and set it once more among the princes of
our land." (Lerner, 1967, p. 361)

What could have been merely a brief and kind acknowledgment of a
kinship born out of the horrors of slavery was transformed in the hands

and hearts of the Grimké sisters into the highest expression of interracial love and fellowship. Lerner (1967) says it best:

> Thus began an extended relationship, which is certainly remarkable and probably unique among the complexities of race relations in this country. The discovery of these young colored men was the acid test of the sisters' convictions. Many a good abolitionist would, in a similar situation, have been satisfied to engage in a friendly exchange of letters and let the matter rest at that. But Sarah and Angelina accepted these newly discovered nephews as members of the family and offered more than dutiful recognition and support—they offered their love. (pp. 361-362)

The love that the Grimké sisters offered was expressed through countless deeds of sacrifice on behalf of their nephews. No sooner had they discovered them than they began regular contributions to their expenses. The sisters and Weld also contributed to the education of their nephews' younger brother. The young men visited the sisters' home. Enduring much sacrifice, the sisters and Weld "supported the nephews throughout their years of college. At times Angelina turned all her earnings over to them, whereas Sarah, now retired, deprived herself of all kinds of small pleasures in order to help them" (Lerner, 1967, p. 364). In one of her last letters, Sarah expressed the profound love, respect, and admiration she had for her black nephews, comparing their talents to her white nephews:

> "Is it not remarkable that these young men should far exceed in talent any of the Grimké nephews, even their half brothers bear no comparison with them and my brother Thomas' sons, distinguished as he was, are far inferior to them in intellectual power." (p. 364)

Both Francis James Grimké and Archibald Henry Grimké would become great black leaders; they became two of the greatest monuments to their aunts and uncle.

JOHN BROWN

Compared with the lives of the Grimké sisters, John Brown's life was much more revolutionary. He forced the struggle for interracial justice and the advancement of African Americans to the very limits, which was revolutionary violence as a means to an end. Few white or black abolitionists were willing to go as far as Brown in this struggle. At a time when the antislavery movement needed an infusion of revolutionary spirit, something that could match the arrogance of the proslavery powers, both in the North and the South, Brown came thundering onto the scene on behalf of racial justice.

John Brown gave all that any person could have given in the antislavery struggle: He gave his life and the lives of several of his sons. Brown and the Grimké sisters were motivated by their religious beliefs in the humanity of all people. They viewed blacks, both slave and free, as equal to whites. Both the Grimké sisters and Brown went far beyond the racial views of most white abolitionists, who tended to see blacks in abstract terms but not as breathing, feeling human beings entitled to equal treatment as whites. Commenting on Brown's extraordinary commitment to the racial struggle for blacks, Stephen Oates (1984) explains:

> All his life he would treat America's "poor, despised Africans" as his equals and detest the way white people oppressed them. He would challenge racial discrimination in Ohio, hide fugitive slaves on the underground railroad, and feel an almost paralyzing bitterness toward bondage itself—that "sum of villainies," that "great sin against God"—and toward all in the United States who sought to preserve and perpetuate it. . . . He would become so enraged at his "slave-cursed" land that he could advocate plunging it into a holocaust. (p. viii)

It is always difficult to unravel the complex motives of whites who devoted themselves to the antislavery movement. But as Oates (1984) makes clear,

> We will never comprehend what Brown was about unless we take his religion seriously. . . . From "earliest childhood," he had learned to oppose slavery and to fear an all-wise, just, and all-powerful God, a God who demanded the most exacting obedience from the most frail, wretched sinner He placed on trial in this world. (p. ix)

Brown would be driven by his deep devotion to Calvinism, a belief grounded in "foreordination and providential signs, in the wrathful Jehovah of the Old Testament who intervened in human affairs and directed them to suit His own purpose" (Oates, 1984, p. ix).

John Brown's father also contributed to the making of this man who would sacrifice several of his sons' lives and his own life to the struggle against slavery. His father taught John and his siblings to fear God and obey His commandments "and not to hate Negroes but to be kind to them and oppose their enslavement as a sin against God" (Oates, 1984, p. 8). Perhaps his father's early experience with a black slave influenced him in this direction. After the death of his own father during the Revolutionary War, Brown's father, then 5 years old, "fell in love" with a black slave who had been sent over by a neighbor to plow for his mother and her 11 children. When the slave became sick and died, it obviously affected John's father, who attended the funeral with his mother. Brown's father was also influenced as a youth when he heard a preacher attacking slavery as "a great sin against God" (Oates, 1984, pp. 4-5).

To whatever degree his father's experiences and religious beliefs "might have influenced" John Brown, his own experiences with the inhumanity of slavery influenced him even more. One such experience stands out. After completing a cattle drive during the War of 1812, John found lodging with a landlord who owned a slave about John's own age. He noticed that the slave was "badly clothed" and "poorly fed." In light of what his father had told him about the "evils of slavery" and being kind to blacks and not hating them, John could not help but feel sorry for this young black slave. "But contrition turned to horror when the master, right in front of John, beat the Negro boy with an iron fire shovel." This left a lasting impression on young John Brown. He returned home "with an unrelenting anguish for the 'wretched, hopeless condition' of that 'Fatherless and Motherless' slave boy." Later in life, Brown pointed to this brutal beating of a slave boy as the incident that made him " 'a most determined foe of slavery from then on' " (Oates, 1984, p. 12).

As a young adult, Brown's opposition to slavery steadily increased, encouraged by his father and their antislavery business and religious friends. Brown felt that as a Christian it was his sworn duty to assist slaves in escaping from the South to Canada. He did not hesitate to inform all who would listen to him that he would provide shelter for any runaways from Kentucky or Virginia who came knocking at his door. After he married, had several children, and moved to Pennsylvania, he built a two-room log house and a large barn with a secret room for hiding runaway slaves. His children were taught to " 'remember them that are in bonds as bound with them' " (Oates, 1984, p. 15). Brown and his father were "conductors" on the underground railroad on "a line that crossed the Akron and Hudson" (p. 23). Brown's dedication prompted a contemporary, Charles S. S. Griffing, to say, " 'No one would brave greater perils or incur more risks to lead a black man from slavery to freedom than he' " (p. 53). According to Griffing, Brown would " 'come in at night with a gang of five or six blacks that he had piloted all the way from the river, hide them away in the stables maybe, or the garret' " (p. 53). Brown made it clear that he was ready to give his life for these black fugitives.

Writing to his brother in November 1834, Brown laid out several plans that he felt would assist "poor fellowmen who are in bondage." These plans included adopting a black boy and providing him with a good education, teaching him world history, business, "and general subjects, and above all, try[ing] to teach him the fear of God." Part of the plan involved his hope that some Christian slaveholder would provide him a black for his experiment. If not, then Brown and his family were prepared "to submit to considerable privation in order to get one" (Oates, 1984, p. 32). No doubt influenced by similar educational projects on behalf of blacks, he may well have been inspired by the efforts of Prudence Crandall, who opened a school for black girls in 1833 in Canterbury, Connecticut. The school's opening triggered a white racist backlash that ultimately destroyed the project (Oates, 1984, p. 32). Brown wanted to set up a school for young blacks also.

Brown not only hid fugitive slaves in open defiance of the law but also pleaded with his neighbors to allow fugitive slaves to hide in their homes. But Brown did not stop at criticizing slavery in the open and hiding fugitive slaves. Here again, he went far beyond the traditional call of duty among white abolitionists and assisted blacks living in freedom, in spite of his own countless hardships. And similar to the Grimké sisters, he refused to compromise with any form of racism. For example, in Franklin Mills, Ohio, where he moved his family in 1838, Brown protested the racist practice at a revival that required blacks to sit in the back of the church by the door. "Such discrimination in the House of God made Brown blazing mad." Brown decided he had to do something. The following night, "in a packed meeting house, he defiantly escorted some of the Negroes down to the Brown family pew. The act struck the audience—and the church deacons—like 'a bomb shell.' " Predictably, the next day the deacons visited Brown to "admonish him and labor with him for what he had done. But Brown defied them all; that night, with the bold audacity of a man who knows he is right, Brown took his black brothers straight to his pew." Later the church expelled him and his family ostensibly for "being absent a year without reporting him- or herself to the church." His son, John Brown, Jr., commented that " 'this was my first taste of the proslavery diabolism that had entrenched itself in the church' " (Oates, 1984, pp. 42-43).

It should be noted here that the Grimké sisters protested in much the same way against the racist seating arrangements of the Quakers. Both the Grimké sisters and Brown found slavery and racism totally incompatible with the tenets of Christianity at a time when the vast majority of white Christians had long reconciled themselves to racism within the Christian faith (Wood, 1990).

Brown constantly agonized over the plight of free blacks. Northern discrimination against the free black community deeply troubled him. This included antiblack laws such as the infamous Ohio "black laws," which required a black to show proof that he or she was free before obtaining employment and, if free, to give a bond underwritten by two persons good for security, testifying that the person would be on good behavior and laws that required blacks to pay public school taxes and yet banned them from public schools. Brown joined other abolitionists, mostly from Oberlin College, to fight against such racial discrimination. In January 1837, Brown attended a mass meeting of black and white abolitionists in Cleveland gathered to discuss petitioning the state legislature for repeal of the black laws. "Brown stood before that gathering and gave blacks a rousing address. It spurred them to action, too, for they not only sent an agent out to gather signatures but appointed a committee of correspondence, of which Brown was a member" (Oates, 1984, pp. 40-41). Unfortunately, it would be 12 years before the state of Ohio repealed its infamous black laws.

In 1848, while living in North Elba, New York, Brown became concerned about the living conditions of a black farming community in the Andirondack mountains. They were struggling to survive amid many problems. Their land needed surveying so they could determine if they were located on the correct lots; they did not have good land for cultivation, and some of the farmers were very poor and desperate. Brown not only assisted them in surveying their boundary lines and helped obtain titles to some of their farms, he also sent them 10 barrels of pork and flour. He did this while struggling to take care of his own farming needs. As if he could not do enough for his black neighbors, Brown also hired black workers, including a runaway slave (Oates, 1984, pp. 40-41).

Brown's dedication to racial justice and equality for blacks knew no social bounds. Here again, similarities between the Grimké sisters and Brown are instructive. By taking uncompromising stands on social equality for blacks, both the Grimkés and Brown went far beyond the racial views of most white abolitionists. They demonstrated this principle in their personal lives. No wonder Richard Henry Dana, author of *Two Years Before the Mast,* as a guest in Brown's home, became uncomfortable with and then recorded his disapproval of the respect Brown showed his black friends in Dana's presence. Brown not only referred to his black workers as "Mister," he allowed them to eat at the same table with his family. Such strong convictions on racial justice and social equality explain why Brown " 'boiled with indignation' " when he thought of " 'slavecatchers, reinforced by constables and federal marshals marching into Springfield and North Elba . . . [and other Northern communities] to carry his Negro friends back into bondage.' " He did not hesitate to advise his black friends to organize themselves into guerrilla bands and " 'fight this wicked law with the sword' " (Oates, 1984, pp. 72-73).

In 1847, Brown moved his family to Springfield, Massachusetts, where he befriended blacks, including some runaways. He informed them of Garrison's *The Liberator* and questioned them about racial discrimination in the North and their views on various racial stereotypes, such as those that argued that blacks were "sambos." Apparently, Brown did not like some of the responses to his questions; he later wrote a satirical essay entitled, "Sambo's Mistakes." He did meet and consult with several prominent and more radical blacks, however, who impressed him and whom he also impressed. Among these were Rev. J. W. Loguen, Rev. Henry Highland Garnet, Harriet Tubman, and Martin R. Delany (Oates, 1984, pp. 241-242).

As time went on, Brown became increasingly committed to the freeing of slaves by violence. In December 1855, Brown and his antislavery followers rescued 11 slaves from slaveholders in Missouri, in a raid that provoked President James Buchanan to offer a $250 reward for his capture. In a letter to his son Jason, Brown expressed his willingness to die for the cause of freedom for slaves:

> "I have only a short time to live—only one death to die—and I will die fighting for this cause. There will be no more peace in this land until slavery is done for. I will give them something else to do than extend slave territory. I will carry this war into Africa." (Oates, 1984, p. 171)

In 1858, Brown told some friends that only a massive uprising could end slavery. He believed that unrepentant Southerners had to be punished for their sins and it was God's will that he should lead this uprising. Brown "believed he could raise a veritable army of Negroes" (Oates, 1984, p. 240). As the time grew near for his abortive attack on Harper's Ferry, Brown held conferences with several black leaders. Among these were Henry Highland Garnet, Frederick Douglass, Martin R. Delany, and Harriet Tubman. Brown even came up with a constitution for the new state that would be established after the insurrection. Many of the blacks who signed the constitution approved of the principles in the preamble and shared Brown's hatred of slavery but "were not so sure about joining his force of liberation. The thought of going back to the South must have terrified them. And the plan of invasion itself sounded fantastic—almost mad" (p. 247). Yet Brown was convinced that "God had created him to be the deliverer of the slaves the same as Moses had delivered the children of Israel" (p. 222).

Brown tried in vain to recruit Douglass to join his small band of followers in their attack on Harper's Ferry but Douglass refused. He had little faith in his good friend's plan. Brown pleaded with Douglass, " 'Come with me, Douglass! I will defend you with my life. I want you for a special purpose. When I strike, the bees will begin to swarm and I shall want you to help me hive them' " (Foner, 1981, p. 90). But Douglass again refused.

On the eve of Brown's attack on Harper's Ferry, he told his men, " 'We have here only one life to live and once to die. And if we lose our lives it will perhaps do more for the cause than our lives would be worth in any other way' " (Oates, 1984, p. 289). After the failure of the attack in October 1859 and the death of several of his men, including his two sons, a reporter asked the captured and wounded Brown, " 'Upon what principles do you justify your acts?' " Brown replied,

> "Upon the Golden Rule. I pity the poor in bondage that have none to help them; that is why I am here; not to gratify any personal animosity, revenge, or vindictive spirit. It is my sympathy with the oppressed and the wronged, that are as good as you and as precious in the sight of God." (p. 305)

Later, in response to other questions, Brown once again made it clear why he raided Harper's Ferry: " 'I claim to be here in carrying out a measure I believe perfectly justifiable, . . . to aid those suffering great wrong.' " He then warned his listeners:

> "You had better—all you people of the South—prepare yourselves for a settlement of this question, that must come up for settlement sooner than

you are prepared for it. . . . You may dispose of me very easily . . . but this question is still to be settled—this Negro question I mean; the end of that is not yet." (p. 306)

To whatever extent people might have disagreed with the violent means Brown chose to express his deep concerns for his enslaved black brethren, they had to acknowledge that he lived and would die for his belief in racial justice for blacks. At his trial, Brown gave a moving speech that would go down in history as one of the greatest testimonies of one of the greatest white freedom fighters for black freedom:

> "I see a book kissed which I suppose to be the Bible, or at least the New Testament, which teaches me that all things whatsoever I would that men should do to me, I should do to them. It teaches me further to remember them that are in bonds, as bound with them. I endeavored to live up to that instruction. . . . I believe that to have interfered as I have done in behalf of His despised poor, is not wrong, but right. Now, if it is deemed necessary that I should forfeit my life for the furtherance of the ends of justice, and mingle my blood with the blood of millions in this slave country whose rights are disregarded by wicked, cruel, and unjust enactments, let it be done." (Oates, 1984, p. 327)

Brown left a legacy of white devotion to racial justice and sacrifice on behalf of black people that few whites had equaled in the past or would equal in the future. His life and death became the standard for whites who would join the struggle for racial justice; for blacks, John Brown's sacrifice would become the symbol of how far their truly devoted white friends were willing to travel down the long road toward racial justice.

THADDEUS STEVENS

Although Thaddeus Stevens did not sacrifice his life on the gallows for black freedom, he spent most of it fighting against slavery and the racial oppression of free blacks. Although he initially disagreed with the actions of John Brown at Harper's Ferry and thought he should be hanged for his action, Stevens soon joined many antislavery people who admired Brown for his faith and courage in attempting to overthrow slavery by violence. Born clubfooted and poor on a Vermont farm on April 4, 1792, Thaddeus Stevens would become known as one of the best friends and supporters of the struggling black community. His efforts on behalf of blacks were part of his larger concern for humanity. As Meltzer (1967) explains, "He fought to establish free public schools. He defended fugitive slaves in the courts. He championed the rights of free speech for dissenters. He spoke up for unpopular minorities: Indians, Mormons, Jews, and Negroes" (p. xi). His greatest contribution, however, was to the struggle for racial justice for blacks. "He led the political struggle to free the slaves and to protect their rights through the passage of the Thirteenth, Fourteenth, and Fifteenth Amendments to the Constitution. And he tried to reconstruct the defeated South on a foundation of justice for all and a democracy of true equality" (p. 3).

Some credit must be given to the fact that Stevens was born and raised in Vermont, the constitution of which contained a clause forbidding human slavery. Because Vermont was the first state to take this stand (in 1877), no Vermonter forgot the milestone. Stevens was more influenced by John Mattocks, the leading lawyer and citizen in Peacham, Vermont. Stevens studied law under Mattocks after graduating from Dartmouth and no doubt was influenced by his mentor's antislavery views. Yet in 1821, having practiced law for 5 years in Gettysburg, Pennsylvania, Stevens defended a Maryland slaveholder's right to take his slave back to Maryland. Using the Pennsylvania law that stated that any slave who had resided in the state for 6 months was free, the slave had sued for her freedom. Stevens took the case to the state supreme court, arguing that the "lawmakers intended continuous residence and the court agreed. The slave was sent back to bondage in Maryland" (Meltzer, 1967, pp. 43-44).

Within 2 years, Stevens had moved to the other side of the slavery issue. He would never defend slavery again. At a Fourth of July celebration, he took a public stand against slavery with a toast: " 'The next President. May he be a freeman, who never riveted fetters on a human slave' " (Meltzer, 1967, pp. 43-44). Yet although he did not defend slavery again and was defending fugitive slaves and free blacks in the courts, he was not a member of any antislavery society; "as late as 1835 he was helping a Gettysburg committee raise funds 'in aid of the cause' of [African] colonization" (pp. 48-49). A few months later, he gave a talk at a local antislavery gathering; soon after, he left the colonization committee. Stevens was moving closer to the heart of the struggle for racial justice for blacks.

One can only speculate as to what events or series of events triggered Stevens's desire to cease defending slavery and supporting colonization. He was touched more than once by personal encounters with black victims of slavery; these encounters must have exerted tremendous influence on his decision to dedicate most of his life to the struggle for racial justice for blacks. According to one story, Stevens was on his way to Baltimore with $300 to buy some much needed law books for his library when he ran into a black woman who was crying because her husband was about to be sold. "Thad took out his $300.00, paid for the slave, freed him, and turned back home without his books" (p. 45).

It was not long before Stevens became known as the "runaways' lawyer." At this point in his professional life, Stevens began making choices that took a lot of moral courage. He was living just a short distance from the Mason-Dixon line and was among the few lawyers in the area who would defend fugitive slaves:

> Few lawyers wanted such cases. The slave master was backed by law and the Constitution. Public opinion tended to support enforcement of law, no matter how unjust. Only the most devoted abolitionists flouted the claim of the master. But they had no political influence, so what lawyer cared to ally himself with them? Yet Stevens did. (Meltzer, 1967, p. 45)

He waged a courageous battle against a resolution banning the free discussion of slavery. As a Pennsylvania state legislator, Stevens defeated several efforts to ban free and slave blacks from entering the state. He was not able to "defeat the attack on Blacks' right to vote" (p. 45) however. In July 1837, the Pennsylvania Supreme Court ruled that blacks did not have a legal right to vote. During the 1837 constitutional convention convened to extend the vote to every man over 25, "whether he paid taxes or not," the "delegates voted 77-45 to restrict the vote to white men" (p. 53). Once again Stevens stood his ground. When the delegates were asked to sign the constitutional amendments, Stevens refused "to put his name to this 'white only brand' of Democracy" (p. 57).

Stevens soon developed "a reputation as one of the state's leading antislavery persons" (Meltzer, 1967, p. 53). In the 1848 fall election campaign for Congress, Stevens told voters that he would " 'encircle the slave states of the Union with Free States as a cordon of fire, [so] that slavery, like a scorpion, would sting itself to death' " (p. 81). This uncompromising attack on the slave South so upset the Democratic press that it called him " 'the sworn foe of the South who would ferment internal discord and so widen the breach which every patriot should seek to heal' " (p. 81). During this election, the Democrats pulled out all the stops in their vicious attacks on Stevens's club foot and his black housekeeper. He won the election and 2 years later voted against the fugitive slave bill. He and others lost this fight but it was a new beginning for Stevens, as he embarked on the next stage in his protracted struggle against racial injustice and the advancement of African Americans.

The Fugitive Slave Law did not discourage Stevens from his continual war against slavery. In 1851, he was the chief strategist among several lawyers defending a group of blacks—some of them fugitives—and their white abolitionist allies on trial for their participation in the bloody Christiana battle in which a Maryland slaveowner was killed and his son badly wounded in their attempt to capture a former slave. Southern editors blamed Stevens for the Christiana affair; however, he was not concerned. He made his views on slavery clear in his first speech before Congress, in response to Southern congressmen who threatened to leave the Union if Congress did not abandon its attacks on slavery. Stevens had not been in Congress 2 months before he was recognized as "one of the strongest forces in the antislavery camp" (Meltzer, 1967).

The *Dred Scott* decision, in which Chief Justice Roger B. Taney made his infamous racist statement that still echoes down the corridors of American history that blacks "had no rights which the white man was bound to respect," prompted Stevens to accuse Taney of writing "a false chapter in American history in order to sustain his partisan views." That decision, Stevens said, "dammed Chief Justice Taney to everlasting fame and, I think, to everlasting fire." This decision remained the final word on the rights of blacks until "Stevens himself piloted the Fourteenth Amendment through Congress, overthrowing Taney's reading of the Constitution" (Meltzer, 1967, pp. 111-112).

Stevens's struggle on behalf of blacks expanded during the Civil War and Reconstruction. Stevens in the House and Charles Sumner in the Senate, along with a core of radical abolitionists, kept the pressure on Lincoln to move forward on a number of fronts related to racial justice for blacks. Emancipation was the major concern of both these men. In fact, they "led the struggle against widespread apathy and fear, pushing through Congress the limited emancipation measures that prepared the nation for general emancipation and the Thirteenth Amendment" (Brodie, 1959).

Whenever and wherever he could, Stevens chipped away at slavery and racism. In July 1861, he pushed through an act that seized the property, including slaves, of certain rebels who were using slaves "for war purposes, such as digging entrenchments and driving teams" (Meltzer, 1967, p. 155). In November 1861, he introduced a bill that provided for total emancipation of slaves; however, it failed to pass. In December of that year, he introduced a "resolution asking Lincoln to free every slave who aided in the rebellion, with compensation for loyal masters" (p. 155). That same week, "much behind Stevens," Lincoln "delicately suggested in his Message to Congress that the border states agree to abolish slavery by 1900, selling their slaves to the government, which would then provide for their emancipation and colonization" (p. 155). Stevens was successful in getting a bill through Congress that prohibited "any member of the armed services to return fugitive slaves, which Lincoln approved 'without question' on March 13, 1862" (p. 157).

Convinced that the president had the required power to free all slaves, Stevens never stopped hounding Lincoln on this issue. Stevens's quest for racial justice for blacks took him into two of the most controversial issues of the Civil War: the arming of blacks and equal pay for black soldiers. He began agitating for the enlistment of black soldiers as early as January 1862, when he introduced a bill "calling for the enlistment of 150,000 Negro troops" (Brodie, 1959, p. 160). The bill made it through the House but was killed in the Senate. Still Stevens persisted; when blacks were finally allowed to bear arms in the Civil War, he "led the fight to equalize the pay between white and colored soldiers, which had originally been fixed at $13 per month for white and $10 for colored troops" (p. 161). Commenting on his reasons for fighting for equal pay for black troops, Stevens once again revealed his deep commitment to racial justice for blacks:

"I despise the principle that would make a difference between them in the hour of battle and of death. . . . The black man knows when he goes there that his dangers are greater than the white man's. He runs not only the risk of being killed in battle, but the certainty, if taken prisoner, of being slaughtered instead of being treated as a prisoner of war." (p. 161)

Stevens continued his struggle on behalf of blacks during the Reconstruction period. Always the practical politician, he linked black suffrage to the political security of his party. This was not an easy task at a time when most white Americans believed that only whites should vote. Stevens's plan for "Negro suffrage ran headlong into a political principle already hallowed in the Democratic Party and believed sacred by many of his own, the principle that only white men should vote" (Brodie, 1959, p. 250). In response to this popular belief, Stevens replied,

"Demagogues of all parties, even some high in authority, gravely shout, 'This is the white man's Government.' What is implied by this? That one race of men are to have the exclusive right forever to rule this nation, and to exercise all acts of sovereignty, while all other races and nations and colors are to be their subjects, and have no voice in making the laws and choosing the rulers by whom they are to be governed. Wherein does this differ from slavery except in degrees? . . . If we have not yet been sufficiently scourged for our national sin to teach us to do justice to all God's creatures, without distinction of race and color, we must expect the still more heavy vengeance of an offended Father." (p. 251)

Due in large part to Stevens's efforts and political genius, black (men) received the vote. As Bennett (1969) puts it, "Thaddeus Stevens was the greatest parliamentary leader in American history. Even today, after Kennedy and Lyndon Johnson, it is difficult to grasp the meaning of this strange, brilliant man who was the best friend black people have ever had in power" (p. 49). According to Stevens's plans for racial justice and black advancement, obtaining the vote was insufficient. Stevens realized that blacks needed much more.

In his 70s, tired and bent from age and illnesses, this old white warrior for racial justice wanted freed blacks to have the means to provide for themselves. "Far in advance of his time Stevens argued that economic emancipation was a precondition of political and social emancipation. He had the vision to see that black liberation could not be made real unless it was grounded on economic independence" (Bennett, 1969, p. 53). Stevens differed from Charles Sumner on this point. Sumner believed that "the ballot was 'the essence—the great essential.' " In contrast, Stevens, although valuing the vote for blacks, "placed primary stress on economic reform." Forty acres and a hut would be of more benefit to the freedmen "than the immediate right to vote." Failure to give freedmen land and a hut "would invite the censure of mankind and the curse of heaven." A provision in the Freedmen's Bureau Bill that was "especially dear to his heart" authorized providing the freedmen with 40-acre tracts from unoccupied lands owned by the state. Unfortunately, all of Stevens's efforts to empower blacks economically by providing them with land were defeated (Brodie, 1959, pp. 248-249).

Notwithstanding these failures, Stevens's other efforts on behalf of blacks contributed to their political empowerment. His long life of dedication to racial justice and black political empowerment endeared him to future generations of blacks and provided a model for future generations of whites. Even in death, Stevens continued his struggle for racial justice. He ordered the inscription on his tombstone to read as follows:

"I repose in this quiet and secluded spot, Not from any natural preference for solitude But, finding other Cemeteries limited as to Race by Charter Rules, I have chosen this that I might illustrate in my death The principles which I advocated Through a long life: EQUALITY OF MAN BEFORE HIS CREATOR." (Brodie, 1959, p. 366)

CONCLUSION

Throughout the protracted struggle for racial justice and African American social advancement, there have always been courageous whites willing to sacrifice social status and even their lives for their African American brothers and sisters. The vast majority believed in the social equality of all people. They tended to be as concerned about the humanity of the slaves as about slavery. They were not satisfied with simply mentioning the wrongs of slavery and segregation; they wanted to participate in the struggle to elevate black men and women. They spent most of their lives working on the behalf of African Americans. The first significant generation of these white leaders emerged from among the abolitionists. The Grimké sisters, John Brown, and Thaddeus Stevens were among the greatest of these dedicated whites.

The lives of the Grimké sisters demonstrated that whites born in the midst of the horrors of slavery could transform their lives into instruments of racial justice. Both sisters renounced the privileges of Southern wealth and status to become abolitionists. Unlike many white abolitionists who fought against slavery but held on to many aspects of the racial status quo, the Grimké sisters attacked the racial status quo. They had seen firsthand the demeaning humiliation of African Americans. They knew how racism affected both blacks and whites; they would not compromise with any aspect of the racial status quo.

The Grimké sisters were pioneers in the antiracism struggle. They fought racial prejudice among white abolitionists at the same time that they fought against slavery. They believed so much in the social equality of blacks and whites that they invited blacks to their most cherished social functions, such as Angelina's wedding. This was a bold and courageous act! Angelina knew that she was straining both social and family relations, but she was committed to the principle of social equality. Both sisters acknowledged their black nephews born out-of-wedlock and they provided for their schooling. The Grimké sisters remained true to their principles to the very end of their lives.

The lives of the Grimké sisters offer a model to whites of how far one can go in a commitment not only to social justice but also to spiritual bonding across racial lines. Both sisters were deeply spiritual. No doubt it was this deep spiritual commitment that motivated them to rise above the racial status quo and embrace the humanity of African Americans.

John Brown made the ultimate sacrifice on behalf of African Americans: his life and those of his sons. Brown was a white revolutionary. His commitment to the freedom and equality of African Americans was total. He too believed in the social equality of blacks and whites. Like the Grimké sisters, he did not accept any aspect of the racial status quo. If fact, he openly broke with such white racist customs as not eating at the same table with African Americans. Brown shared his table and his food with his black workers. He cared equally for the slave and the free person of color, and he too was deeply spiritual.

Brown provides the picture of a white person who was willing to sacrifice all he had to his passion for freedom for African Americans. In this sense, his life holds more meaning for African Americans than any of the so-called founding fathers and even the Great Emancipator Abraham Lincoln. John Brown's life, for all its unfortunate violence, demonstrates how far one white man was willing to go in his devotion to the cause of racial justice.

Although Thaddeus Stevens did not give his life for his belief in the antislavery cause, he did spend most of it fighting against slavery and the racial oppression of blacks. He initially disagreed with John Brown's actions at Harper's Ferry but soon came to admire Brown. Once he became committed to the struggle for racial justice, he never wavered. Stevens was one of a few moral giants among the political leaders of his time. He began taking a moral stand against slavery and defending runaways.

With his defense of the Christiana defendants, Stevens crossed the line into the camp of whites who sided with black rights over white oppression even if white lives were lost. Stevens continued to protest white oppression of blacks at all levels. At a time when most Americans shared Chief Justice Taney's belief that African Americans had no rights that the white man was "bound to respect," Stevens criticized the *Dred Scott* decision. This stand took a lot of courage; what took even more courage was his effort to steer the Fourteenth Amendment through Congress, "overthrowing Taney's reading of the Constitution" (Brodie, 1959, pp. 111-112).

Stevens played a key role in keeping the pressure on Lincoln to protect the rights of newly emancipated slaves. During and after the Civil War, Stevens hounded Lincoln on behalf of African American rights. Stevens was not satisfied with simply freeing slaves. He wanted more for them. He played a leading role in the political empowerment of African Americans by working ceaselessly to obtain for them the vote. This great white warrior wanted blacks to have more than just the right to vote. He realized that they also needed economic independence.

These four courageous whites demonstrated that there were whites who were willing to make great personal sacrifices on behalf of African Americans. Their lives and the lives of other white abolitionists provided the spiritual foundation for a future generation of whites and blacks to believe that, in the midst of every struggle for racial justice, there are always brave and courageous people willing to carry their share of the burden.

6

The White Role in the Struggle for
Racial Equality in the 20th Century

BUILDING ON THE LEGACY

The Grimké sisters, John Brown, and Thaddeus Stevens, among other self-sacrificing whites during the antislavery and postslavery struggles, not only left a proud legacy for future generations of whites to follow but also established high ideals regarding the rightful role of whites in sharing the burden of racism. Whites studying the lives of these four white warriors against racism, who were also devoted to the social uplifting of African Americans, can see the sacrifices their predecessors had to make to stay true to their ideals regarding the common humanity of all people. In their uncompromising struggle for racial justice and the social uplifting of African Americans, these four whites became true spiritual brethren. Their commitment to the struggle for racial justice was more spiritual than social, economic, or political. It was this deep spiritual commitment to racial justice and the social uplifting of African Americans that was the greatest legacy any white reformer could leave to future generations of white Americans, who had few such people to emulate.

Throughout the 20th century, several generations of whites have been involved in the protracted struggle for racial justice and the social uplifting of African Americans; they have viewed themselves as the spiritual descendants of the abolitionists. Some of the earlier white reformers and founders of the NAACP, such as Oscar Villard and Mary

White Ovington, had blood ties to distant relatives who had been abolitionists. But the spiritual legacy of white involvement in this persistent social movement went much deeper than blood and spread much wider than mere family tradition. The courage and devotion of the Grimké sisters, John Brown, and Thaddeus Stevens, among other dedicated whites, became the proud legacy of countless known and unknown whites throughout the 20th century who wanted to see the United States live up to its most cherished ideals. They knew this could be realized only through their participation in the struggle for racial justice and in the lifting of the burden of racism from the shoulders of African Americans.

Although one cannot recount all the varied roles that so many dedicated whites played during this century in the struggle for racial justice and black social uplifting, certain whites at crucial stages in the history of American race relations did play key roles in challenging and knocking down racial barriers to black social, economic, and political advancement.

At a time when the vast majority of whites firmly believed that blacks should be kept "in their place" by whatever means necessary, a small group of dedicated whites from a range of social backgrounds and professions decided that they would side with the most despised race in the United States. This group included social workers, lawyers, judges, labor leaders, religious leaders, housewives, common workers, philanthropists, and scholars. The members were bonded together by a common belief—that they, as whites, had to share the burden of racism. Foremost were those who founded the NAACP and devoted much of their lives to its long struggle for racial justice and the advancement of African Americans. Because the NAACP is the oldest civil rights organization in the United States, with the longest history of interracial struggle for racial justice and the advancement of African Americans, it provides the best examples of the range of roles played by whites both within and without the organization in this struggle.

MARY WHITE OVINGTON
AND JOEL E. SPINGARN

Since the beginning of this century, the NAACP has provided America and the world with sterling examples of whites dedicated to the struggle for racial justice and the social uplifting of African Americans. As Chapter 2 points out, other organizations, institutions, and movements have also provided their share of dedicated whites. But during the era of legal segregation, the NAACP produced more white soldiers in the struggle for racial justice than any other organization. Although the contributions of these whites were of uneven quality, as were their levels of dedication to the struggle, many were notable for their great dedication and self-sacrifice. Mary White Ovington was one of the most dedicated whites, not only in the NAACP but also within the larger interracial movement. Walter White, a black official in the NAACP who helped shape its history and a close associate of Ovington, wrote this in the foreword of Ovington's (1947) book, *The Walls Came Tumbling Down:*

> Although I have searched diligently for the most descriptive phrase to cause you to know Mary White Ovington as we have worked with her many years, I can think of none more precise than "Fighting Saint." Born of a family of culture and means, she might have been secure in conforming to the prejudices and conditions of her society. Instead she threw herself into the most difficult social problem in America—the Negro Question. She did so with full awareness, despite her modest disclaimers to the contrary, of the scorn, insult, and even physical danger her espousal of ex-slaves and their descendants would bring down on her. She has marched serenely ahead armed with the assurance that the fight she was making was as much, in the words of the late James Weldon Johnson, to save white America's soul as it was to save black America's body. . . . Unlike most pioneers, however, she has lived to see enormous changes as a direct result of her own efforts. But being the perfectionist she is, she will never be content until she sees the complete attainment of her goal—the abolition of the color line in Democracy. (White, 1947, pp. vii-viii)

In his introduction to *Half a Man,* Ovington's study of the conditions of blacks in New York, published in 1911, Charles Flint Kellogg (1969) had this to say about Mary White Ovington:

> No white woman in America has done more in behalf of full equality for the Negro American than has Mary White Ovington. Her life exemplifies the greatest participation of women of the progressive era in public affairs and social problems. Like many of the progressives, she came from the upper middle class—professional people and intellectuals. Like them she emphasized change, not through force and violence but through disclosure of social wrong, alteration of popular attitudes through education and redress by orderly legal and democratic processes. The publication in 1911 of *Half a Man* was the fruition of her mature experience, study, and thinking on the Negro problem in New York. (p. xi)

What made Ovington "unique among women in the progressive movement [was] her wholehearted espousal of the cause of the Negro, which during the age of reform was divorced from other humanitarian movements" (Kellogg, 1969, p. xi). Although white women reformers, such as "Jane Addams, Lillian Wald, Florence Kelly, and Inez Milholland also supported emancipation of the Negro . . . their chief interest lay in other reforms of the day—settlement house work, maternal health, child care, consumers' leagues, and women's suffrage" (Kellogg, 1969, p. xi). This "wholehearted espousal of the cause of the Negro," which made Ovington so unique among white women reformers of her day and among the vast majority of male reformers, enabled her to develop rare insights into the best role for whites to play in the interracial struggle for racial justice and African American social and economic advancement.

Like several of the whites who were destined to play a key role in the NAACP, Ovington was from a well-to-do family. Born on April 11, 1865, in Brooklyn Heights, New York, into a radical abolitionist family, Ovington was exposed early to the struggle for racial justice. Her father left Plymouth Church in Brooklyn "because he felt the pastor, Henry Ward Beecher, was not radical enough on the slavery question, and he joined the small Unitarian church of which his wife was a member" (Kellogg, 1969, p. xii). Her maternal grandmother was an ardent abolitionist and a friend of William Lloyd Garrison. This grandmother, who lived with the family, related stories of abolitionist "meetings and of mobs she had encountered. They heard, too, the story of Prudence Crandall, who had lived in a neighboring town and was imprisoned for admitting Negro girls to her school for young ladies" (Kellogg, 1969, p. xii). As Kellogg explains, "No wonder that in childhood Mary White Ovington's imagination was stirred by tales of the underground railway and her heroes were the fugitive slaves making their dangerous way to the safety of far-off Canada" (p. xii).

Her father's decision to leave the Plymouth church, Ovington (1947) wrote later in life, might have been "an obscure issue now but a real one then," and it added to the many other experiences that accounted for her "intensity of sympathy for a race that I felt had been diabolically brought in slave ships to this country, and after arrival systematically wronged by enslavement" (p. 6). Although she was exposed to the good and bold examples of her abolitionist parents and grandmother and to the works of white authors, such as Thomas Nelson Page, who wrote of "the faithful uncle or mammy who settle wisely important problems in the lives of the whites," in her youth she lived and moved within a sheltered white world. Gradually, however, Mary White Ovington's interest in the blacks and in racism began to transform her world.

Several dramatic experiences contributed to Mary White Ovington's lifetime dedication to the struggle for racial justice on behalf of African Americans. The following two experiences were perhaps the most formative in preparing her for her later role as a founder of the NAACP. The first experience occurred when she was a settlement worker at the Greenpoint settlement in New York City between 1896 and 1903:

> During my first two years as a settlement worker, the Negro was non-existent. Then one afternoon we had a dramatic meeting. I took fifteen boys, representing eight nationalities, for an outing to Prospect Park. We went in an open trolley, and the boys were more than ordinarily noisy. I may say that I soon learned at Greenpoint to discount national traits. Whether his parents were born in Ireland, Germany, Denmark, Italy, or the Russian Ghetto, every mother's son became an American, earmarked by the public schools and the street life. They were active, destructive, likable children. As we neared the park, . . . we began to pass a line of unimproved wooden houses on whose steps, for it was a hot day, colored women sat and talked to one another. Suddenly, as at a signal, every boy jumped on his feet and yelled, "Nigger, Nigger, Nigger!" The colored women looked unconcerned, taking it as part of life, but I was hot with anger. The performance was not repeated on the return trip, not because my speech at the Park on brotherhood had made an impression, but because I was the boss. Yet the boys had no race prejudice. Their yelling was a ritual that they had learned. When the Astral employed a colored janitor, the same boys seriously interfered with his work, so anxious were they to talk with him. He never seemed to me especially amusing, nor did he say anything remarkable, but he had a fascination for the children. (Ovington, 1947, p. 11)

The other experience took place in the winter of 1903, during Ovington's last year at the settlement. It was not until this year that, "the Negro and his problems came into my life, where they will remain until my death. It happened accidentally, as important things often happen" (Ovington, 1947, p. 11). As a member of the Social Reform Club, Ovington worked on a committee assigned to give a dinner for Booker T. Washington and his wife. The president of the club told the committee not to limit the program to the conditions of Southern blacks but to encompass "conditions at our own door" (Ovington, 1947, p. 12). Although Booker T. Washington and his work at Tuskegee occupied center stage during the dinner, the conditions of blacks in New York were not forgotten, and this was the point at which "the Negro and his problems" came into the life of Ovington. As she explains it,

> We learned of our dark neighbors living around the corner. It was a picture of ramshackle tenements, high infant mortality, and discrimination in employment that made it almost impossible for a Negro to secure work that paid a decent wage. A colored physician testified to this, and assured us that conditions grew worse, not better, as immigrants, in great numbers, entered the city port. We left the meeting, as [the president] intended we should, with a realization that not only in Alabama but in New York we had a Negro problem. The next year I left Greenpoint Settlement and became a fellow of Greenwich House, engaged in a study of the Negro in New York City. (Ovington, 1947, p. 12)

Ovington's commitment of her life "to the cause of the Negro" moved her to study systematically the social and economic causes of African American poverty in New York. This study would greatly expand and deepen her understanding of how the structure of white racial oppression prevented blacks from developing their full potential. But more important, it demonstrated the need for whites who elected to devote their lives to the struggle for racial justice and the advancement of blacks to take the time to study the conditions under which blacks lived and then to become involved in changing those conditions. In this regard, Ovington represents an excellent role model for whites engaged in the struggle for racial justice and the advancement of blacks.

Ovington's study of blacks in New York was not her only book on blacks. Kellogg (1969) points out that, "all of Miss Ovington's published works reflect her interest in Negroes" (p. xxi). For example, as a result of her experiences with black children in the black tenement districts of Manhattan and Brooklyn, Ovington realized "the paucity of literature suitable for Negro children, and she wrote three books which were pioneer works in meeting the longing of Negro children for stories of their own people and instilling a sense of worth and pride in their race" (p. xxi). During the 1920s, Ovington wrote two other books on race and the black experience. *The Shadow* (1920) is a novel that revolves around a theme of race within the labor movement. It was serialized in Ireland and England and in the African American press. In 1927, Ovington wrote *Portraits in Color,* in which "she sketched the life and work of twenty distinguished Negroes, men and women, presenting them as human beings of value and dignity" (Kellogg, 1969, p. xxi). Twenty years later, she wrote an autobiographical account of the NAACP titled *The Walls Came Tumbling Down* (Ovington, 1947). Although the first step in any meaningful and purposeful role for whites in the struggle for racial justice and black advancement is to obtain accurate information regarding the conditions that produce and maintain racial oppression, a second step is to try to step out of the role of the white observer into the role of fellow-traveler with the victims. This is exactly what Ovington did. She moved deeper and deeper into the social, psychological, and spiritual worlds of African Americans. She deliberately cultivated close friendships and did not shy away from the conflicts and tensions that are the inevitable growing pains of such interracial friendships.

One of the first significant steps in Ovington's role in the struggle occurred during the winter of 1907-1908, when she lived in a black tenement working on a survey for a book on blacks in New York. The tenement, The Tuskegee, was a model tenement built by Henry Phipps "as the result of the combined efforts of Miss Ovington and John E. Milholland to interest [Phipps] in an experiment in model housing for Negroes" (Kellogg, 1969, p. xviii). This was a major breakthrough for black housing because until then Phipps had been interested in improving only the housing conditions of whites living in slums. That Ovington had been involved in improving the conditions of blacks so early in her career speaks volumes for how she saw her expanding role in the advancement of African Americans.

Unfortunately, Phipps did not allow Ovington to set up her settlement work in the black tenement, so she had to give up that idea. But she continued her work for black advancement by teaming up with Verina Morton-Jones, one of the first African American physicians in the country. They established the Lincoln Settlement for African Americans. Ovington recruited a board of directors for the Lincoln Settlement, became its chairperson, and did the fund raising to support the venture; Morton-Jones functioned as the "headworker" (Kellogg, 1969, p. xviii).

Soon after, Ovington learned a cruel lesson concerning the price whites are often forced to pay when they give up their role in an exclusively white world for a role in the interracial movement for racial justice. In the spring of 1908, the Cosmopolitan Club, an interracial organization founded in 1906 for the purpose of "correcting misinformation about the Negro and bridging the gulf between Negroes and whites . . . [which] met from time to time in the homes of Brooklyn's well-to-do Negro families," accepted Ovington's suggestion to have an interracial dinner at a restaurant (Kellogg, 1969, p. xviii). Almost 100 professional persons attended, including clergy, social workers, and editors, among them many distinguished white and black professionals. When the news of this first interracial dinner in New York became public, it caused a furor. The dinner was labeled a "sordid event" and an "orgy," and Ovington bore the brunt of the media's attacks:

> Their principal target was Miss Ovington. When the Brooklyn papers took up the matter, the outcry against her was so great, the threats of withdrawal of support from the Lincoln Settlement were so many, that she and the Board had to give assurances against any repetition in order to insure the continuance of the Settlement. (Kellogg, 1969, p. xix)

Ovington's own report of the white racist reaction to this interracial event demonstrates how well she was beginning to understand the social consequences of her role in the vulnerable interracial movement:

> The storm broke the next morning and poured down anathema, not on the Negroes this time—they were only tools—but on the degenerate whites. The New York papers were deeply displeased, and their editors said so in dignified language. They read us all a lesson and showed especial indignation at the two publicists, Holt and Villard. No paper gave any idea of what the meeting was about or of the almost religious character of the speeches. This had no news value. What was news was that colored and white had sat down together at a public restaurant. (Ovington, 1947, p. 45)

The Southern newspapers were ruthless in their denunciation of Ovington. The *Savannah News* printed an account of the interracial dinner that read as follows:

> "Worst of all was the high priestess, Miss Ovington, whose father is rich, and who affiliates five days every week with Negro men and dines with them at her home in Brooklyn, Sundays. She could have had a hundred thousand Negroes at the Bacchanal feast had she waved the bread-tray. But the horror of it is she could take white girls into that den. That is the feature that should arouse and alarm Northern society." (Ovington, 1947, p. 46)

The newspapers did not stop at slander and insult; they printed Ovington's mailing address, which resulted in her receiving "unspeakable" mail. Yet she survived. "I went to another dinner about this time that clinched my determination to devote such ability as I had to the cause of the Negro." The dinner was given by the Intercollegiate Socialist Society, who presented Lucien Sanial, "an old man who had stood with the workers at the Paris Commune." He told the diners that they had to be willing to repudiate their class and that even then most of them would be useless. Ovington went home "profoundly disturbed." She knew that she was not a member of the working class. "I was only cheering and throwing a few pennies." What could be her role in changing society? "Very well then, I would cease to work for socialism and give what strength and ability I had to the problems of securing for the Negro American those rights and privileges into which every white American was born" (Ovington, 1947, p. 48).

Ovington's role in the protracted struggle for racial justice and the advancement of African Americans had been steadily evolving. She was slowly beginning to realize the price she would have to pay; she realized she would lose many privileges by accepting the role of white fellow traveler in this movement. But she was not alone. After the establishment of the NAACP, she found herself in the proud and grand company of other whites who had decided to play key roles in the struggle.

From the founding of the NAACP in 1909 until her retirement in 1947, "Miss Ovington was a moving spirit within the NAACP" (Kellogg, 1969, p. xix). As she and other whites became more involved in the development of the NAACP, the needs of the organization in relation to the various racial problems facing African Americans and the lack of trained blacks with time to spare determined the roles of whites. This created a necessary racial division of labor, as Ovington (1947) explains:

We used to pride ourselves on never knowing how many white members we had and how many colored—we do still. It would be correct, however, to say that more board work was done at this time by white than by colored. In the field, the situation was the reverse. But in New York we still had only one executive who was not white, Du Bois. Our secretary in 1917, Roy Nash . . . was white; so was Seligmann, director of publicity. So were Martha Gruening, assistant secretary, and Mary Childs Nerney, secretary for three years before Nash. Legal work that emanated from New York was in the hands of white men.

As our program was directed primarily against segregation, this almost exclusive employment of whites may sound out of place, but it was the result of circumstances. Few colored people were trained to take such executive positions as we had to offer, and also few had the leisure of our volunteer white workers. I had taken the work of the secretary for a year, between Frances Blascoer's regime and Mary Nerney's. We were very poor and I could give my services. Others gave many hours each week. (p. 111)

Many of these whites, including Ovington, made a conscious choice to turn their backs on white middle- and upper-class comfort and to assume roles that the vast majority of whites looked on with contempt. Ovington performed any role that the NAACP needed. She served as secretary and chairperson of its board of directors twice and during one period was director of branches. When she retired in 1947, she was treasurer. She performed many other roles as well.

When the racist film *Birth of a Nation,* with its gross distortion of the Second Reconstruction, filled with antiblack propaganda, came to the screen in 1915, the NAACP sent Ovington to Boston to attend a hearing before the mayor. Because she had seen the film, her role was to point out to the mayor why the film should not be shown in the city. "I had decided," she says, "to speak only of that part that treated the Negro as a dangerous, half-insane brute" (Ovington, 1947, p. 128) She felt that the entire movie was false. She had read thousands of pages in the Report of the Congressional Committee on the Ku Klux Klan and was familiar with the KKK's treatment of blacks. "I knew of the aspiring Negroes the Klan had beaten and lynched, of the homes and school-houses burned, of women treated with brutality. But the picture, the *Birth of a Nation,* was the South's side of the story" (p. 128). Ovington's role, however, was not to ask the mayor to censor Southern history. Rather, it was to "show . . . that the method of presentation might injure the Negro in the city where it was shown; if it was so bestial as to create antagonism, even violence, then it should not be produced" (p. 128). Ovington made her plea using a scene in the movie that showed a black man pursuing a white girl to her death: "His great clutching hands, repeatedly pictured, were enough to make a Bostonian on Beacon Hill double-lock the door at night" (p. 128). When the film finally appeared on the screens in Boston, only the beginning and the end of that scene were shown, leaving the audience wondering about the cause of the girl's death (pp. 128-129).

Moorfield Storey, the first president of the NAACP and for many years its foremost lawyer, also attended the hearing. When David Wark Griffith, the producer, held out his hand to greet the famous Boston lawyer, Storey refused to shake it, saying, "I do not see why I should shake hands with you, Mr. Griffith." Ovington (1947), seeing historical significance in Storey's gesture, interpreted it as a sign of the times. "It was the first time, and it might be the last time that . . . I would ever see a Northern gentleman refuse to shake hands with a Southern gentleman because he had given the country a malicious picture of the Negro" (p. 129).

Ovington's role in this situation should not be underestimated. *Birth of a Nation* was very popular among many whites and, as Ovington (1947) puts it, "It must have been a decade before it ceased to educate our children on the Southern conception of the Negro" (p. 127). Progressive whites, such as Ovington and Storey, needed to be seen taking a stand against such a popular film because it reinforced so many racist beliefs about African Americans. Another white NAACP official, Oswald Garrison Villard, was among the first to attack the film by refusing to accept an advertisement for it in his newspaper, the *Evening Post* (Ovington, 1947, p. 127).

Whites who demonstrated their willingness to share the burden of racism by taking public stands against it helped educate the white majority and break up and challenge the white consensus on racism. Performed by blacks alone, such actions could easily have been ignored as pleading and protest by an aggrieved racial minority. As additional whites performed these vital roles, they encouraged more timid whites to join them in the struggle.

Ovington's work in the field exposed her to experiences that enlarged and clarified her role as a white person in the struggle. "As the work at the office grew more technical and was carried on by salaried executives, I found that I could be of best service as a field worker" (Ovington, 1947, p. 221). She visited branch offices around the country, discussed race relations with black and white scholars, and had the honor of meeting Mary McLeod Bethune, one of the foremost African American educators. Ovington's travels exposed her to more of the distressing social and economic conditions of African Americans. On one visit to the South, she became "discouraged at the small effect the [white] Northerner seemed to exert in the South" (p. 228). She noticed how Northern tourists attended Mary Bethune's Sunday afternoon meetings, "listened to a good talk, heard the singing of the spirituals, and were regaled with excellent tea. . . . But the white Northerner seemed impotent when faced with the injustice of race lines" (p. 228). Ovington could not help but notice that Rollins College in Winter Park, Florida, "known for its progressive ideas in education, and for its Democracy," was in the same city where African Americans "lived across the tracks. Their street was unpaved. They had only a grammar school. To earn their livelihood, they crossed the tracks and entered the well-kept, attractive white neighborhood, where they performed household tasks for others" (p. 228). She writes,

> Everything that I enjoyed was closed to them. They could not enter the library or the motion picture theater. They could not go to the plays given at the college theater, or to the lectures. They must not bathe in any one of the city's twenty-eight lakes, not even in the summer. Unless they were working for the whites, they must be on the other side of the railroad track by half-past eight at night. Their section was not properly lighted, and no recreation was provided. I heard disparaging talk about their immorality, but the white people, returning from the movies or concerts or drives over the lovely roads (for whites only) were in no position to cast any stones. (pp. 228-229)

Although Rollins College was "progressive," "a large majority of the students" and some professors were liberal minded, and many of the visitors were "quiet elderly people who, for the most part, were charitably inclined," Ovington (1947) reports, the College was part of a city that was as "prejudiced and unjust in its treatment of Negro citizens as any town in the South" (p. 228). Clearly, this so-called progressive white educational institution and its so-called liberal-minded white students and professors fell far short of what Ovington saw as the best role as a concerned white in the struggle for racial justice.

Ovington's trips in the field provided countless opportunities to understand the broader framework of the interracial struggle for racial justice and the role of other progressive whites in that struggle. During one trip in 1933 to Mississippi and Alabama, she met several progressive Southern white women interested in the race issue. One encouraged Ovington to attend the Scottsboro trial of nine young black men accused of raping two white young women who were hoboing on the same train. This trial exposed Ovington not only to the racist legal system of the South but also to the courageous stand of whites who challenged it, such as Samuel Liebowitz, the New York lawyer for the black defendants, and Judge Horton, whose "conduct of the trial had made him hated by many [whites]" (Ovington, 1947, p. 234).

For whites to be truly effective in the interracial struggle for racial justice and black advancement, they had to monitor their relationships with their black coworkers constantly. Given the NAACP's racial division of labor that in turn determined roles by race, whites had to be very sensitive to racial paternalism. Ovington understood the danger of this when she confessed to Oswald Villard, another white NAACP official, that she " 'still occasionally [forgot] that the Negroes were not poor people for whom I must kindly do something . . . they were men with most forceful opinions of their own' " (Lewis, 1993, p. 469). Because Villard and Du Bois, the only black official of the New York NAACP, often clashed over various issues, Ovington tried to help Villard to understand Du Bois's world. " 'He does do dangerous things,' " she said of Du Bois. " 'He strikes out at people with a harshness and directness that appalls me, but the blow is often deserved and it is never below the belt' " (Lewis, 1993, p. 483). In 1913, when Villard resigned his position over one of many conflicts with Du Bois, the situation so affected Ovington that she told Villard she was

> "sick at heart over it. . . . It means a confession that we cannot work with colored people unless they are our subordinates. And anyone who believes in segregation will become a little more firmly convinced that he is right. And when we demand that some colored man be put in office and given a place in which he will be the equal of a white man, we shall be told, 'You can't give a nigger a big job. Haven't you found it out yourselves.' It puts us back five years." (Broderick, 1969, pp. 167-168)

To her credit, Ovington had the historical foresight to understand what Villard, as a key white officer and benefactor during the formative years of the NAACP, never quite understood—that "in order to build mass support, the NAACP had to be seen as a crusading force increasingly guided by African Americans themselves. If Villard ever grasped this, he was incapable of conveying any urgent commitment to such a goal" (Lewis, 1993, p. 485).

Notwithstanding Ovington's defense of Du Bois, she did not allow herself to play the role of the ingratiating white liberal impervious to the mistakes and foibles of black colleagues, no matter how brilliant they were. When Du Bois challenged certain organizational policies, Ovington wasted little time in standing up to him.[1] Ovington's ability to accept the goal of an interracial struggle "increasingly guided by African Americans themselves," which by its very nature demanded her willingness to change her own role in the struggle to accommodate the goal, enabled her to survive the many changes in the roles of liberal whites within the NAACP during her long tenure. By the time Ovington retired in 1947, the roles of blacks and whites in the NAACP had undergone significant changes, yet whites were still playing critical roles in the unfolding interracial struggle for racial justice.

Joel E. Spingarn was yet another dedicated white during the formative years of the NAACP who, after he joined the ranks of this struggling organization, spent the rest of his life in the interracial struggle for racial justice and the advancement of African Americans. Unlike Ovington and Villard, who were linked by family to the abolitionists, Joel E. Spingarn and his brother Arthur could boast of no such tradition. Yet both brothers, despite their lack of an abolitionist family tradition, spent long years in the trenches in the interracial struggle for racial justice. From the fateful moment in 1910 when his attention was drawn to a newspaper piece about the treatment of a black sharecropper in Arkansas, to his death in 1939, Joel E. Spingarn contributed more than his share to the struggle.

Spingarn was born in May 1875 into a family of Jewish immigrants who had settled in the United States several decades earlier. His brother Arthur was born 3 years later. His colleagues in the NAACP were influenced by their abolitionist lineage, but Spingarn had no such influence. His father saw little of worth in Abraham Lincoln and "remained a staunch Democrat throughout the post-Civil War period" (Ross, 1972, p. 3). There is no evidence that Spingarn's father had any "active interest in the race problem" (p. 4). Spingarn's idealism and talent for practical struggle, which he developed while challenging the status quo as a professor at Columbia University, influenced his role as a white in the NAACP more than the tradition of abolitionism influenced the role of his white colleagues. It was this idealism and inclination for practical struggle that saved the NAACP more than once.

Spingarn's role as a white in the interracial struggle for racial justice and the advancement of African Americans has to be understood in the context of his earlier career as a latter-day Renaissance man. Before he joined the NAACP in 1910, "he was already nationally known as a 'foremost scholar in the field of literary criticism' " (Ross, 1972, p. 3). According to Ross,

> J. E. Spingarn immersed himself in an endless variety of pursuits, both intellectual and practical. Enamored by the concept of the scholar as a man of action, he encompassed within his lifetime the careers of teacher, writer, poet, publisher, horticulturist, progressive politician, soldier, and humanitarian reformer. (p. 3)

He was not by any means a mere dabbler or jack-of-all-trades. Ross (1972) attests that "Spingarn undertook so many pursuits was perhaps neither uncommon nor phenomenal. But that he excelled in all of them would have made him an extraordinary man in any age" (p. 3). After joining the NAACP in 1910, Spingarn used most of these talents and a considerable part of his wealth on behalf of the NAACP.

Spingarn's first efforts on behalf of African Americans occurred in 1910, when he bought the Heart of Hope Club in Amenia, New York, for the purpose of providing free hot meals and recreational facilities for poor blacks. In this case, however, "his compassion had far outstripped his practical knowledge," for he was forced to seek advice from Du Bois on how to run the club (Ross, 1972, p. 12). But his heart was in the right place. He was touched even more deeply when he read a newspaper report concerning a black tenant farmer in Arkansas who had murdered his former white landlord in self-defense and escaped to Chicago. The Chicago authorities caught the man and forced a confession out of him. When the Southern sheriff arrived in Chicago to transport the black tenant farmer back to Arkansas, "he boasted that a mob was waiting to burn" the black farmer (p. 20). Years later, Spingarn recounted how much this affected him, explaining that one can never know "by what strange current of emotion he is moved . . . why one injustice appeals to him more than another, but I know that at that moment I said, 'I don't care what happens, Steve Green[sic] will never be extradited to Arkansas' " (p. 20). Being a man of action, Spingarn found out that the NAACP and a black Chicago group, the Negro Fellowship League, were working to block the extradition of the black farmer; he joined in the struggle by sending money and obtaining more information. Spingarn was well on his way to long-term involvement in the interracial struggle for racial justice and the advancement of African Americans.

In the fall of 1910, Villard invited Spingarn to join the NAACP. Spingarn accepted, and another dynamic and committed white was a part of the struggle. It was not long before Spingarn had flung himself wholeheartedly into the work of the NAACP by becoming an officer and activist on the NAACP's New York Vigilance Committee. Vigilance committees were forerunners of what would evolve into branches of the NAACP. Their purpose was "to keep a close watch on race relations in a given locality, combating discrimination and segregation whenever possible, at the same time serving as the local eyes and ears of the New York-based parent organization" (Ross, 1972, p. 21). Spingarn's role as a white activist within the NAACP rapidly developed with his involvement in the campaigns of the New York committee. On a visit to a theater with several of his black friends, the group was refused tickets. With Spingarn's testimony in court, the committee won a suit against the theater's management. During this early period, Spingarn also used his influence to keep the son of a black member of the NAACP from being excluded from New York's Central Preparatory School because of race. Soon he had recruited Arthur, his younger brother and a lawyer, to join what was to be a long struggle for racial justice (Ross, 1972, pp. 21-22).

Perhaps the best way to comprehend Spingarn's involvement in the NAACP's struggle for racial justice and African American advancement is to understand the critical role he played during the organization's formative period. By the time Spingarn joined the NAACP, it was the most influential radical interracial organization struggling on behalf of African Americans' civil rights. Yet some serious organizational and ideological problems were hampering its development. Its radical program alienated certain segments of the black community and key "wealthy white potential donors who found Washington's accommodationism more appealing than the Association's demands for immediate and total racial equality" (Ross, 1972, p. 26). In addition, NAACP branches were struggling with internal problems, ranging from male-female conflicts to member-leader conflicts, compounded by the complications of the decision-making chain of authority from the local level to the national level. "In short, by 1914 the Association had barely begun to cope with the problems which confronted it" (p. 26). This was the point at which Spingarn played his most vital role:

> It was in the midst of this, the darkest period in the Association's history, that Spingarn reached back in time to resurrect the spirit of nineteenth-century Abolitionism, the only major movement in American history that approximated the NAACP's ideal of equal rights and fair treatment for black Americans. (p. 26)

Spingarn saw his role and the role of other white liberals in the NAACP as that of "new abolitionists." He, more than any of the white liberals in the NAACP, embraced the abolitionist tradition with gusto. He introduced the term *new abolition* in December 1912, in part because he was disappointed in the failure of Progressivism to address racial issues. The incident that pushed him into embracing the new abolitionist approach was the rejection by the Progressive Party's platform committee of a civil rights plank that he and Du Bois "had drafted and which Spingarn had personally presented to the committee" (Ross, 1972, p. 26). Furthermore, the Progressive convention refused black delegates seats, and Theodore Roosevelt, for whom Spingarn had the greatest respect, advised him to be aware of that "dangerous" Du Bois. These events confirmed his belief in the need for a movement modeled on the principles of the Abolitionist movement. "Beginning with the New Abolitionist campaign in 1913, Spingarn embraced the courage and determination of the nineteenth-century abolitionists with a fervor which rivaled that of Garrison and Phillips" (p. 26).

More than any other role that he was destined to play during his more than three decades working on behalf of racial justice and the advancement of black Americans, Spingarn's role as a new abolitionist during several years of rousing and indignant speeches, lectures, and protests planted an indelible image in the minds of a generation of blacks and whites involved in the interracial struggle for racial justice and served as a thorn in the side of racists and lukewarm liberals. Spingarn firmly believed that white America had little or no concern for the problems of African Americans. He decided his role would be to increase the awareness of whites and the aspirations of African Americans.

He accomplished this in a number of ways. He encouraged black bloc voting, pointing out that the balance of power that blacks had in "seven critical states could be utilized both to elect sympathetic white candidates and to place blacks in important political offices" (Ross, 1972, p. 28). He differed from Du Bois in that he never embraced the concept of an African American third party. Instead, he firmly believed that blacks should participate in both parties. He believed in and strongly supported cultural nationalism among African Americans as a way of fostering unity. In 1913, Spingarn made an offer of a gold medal worth $100 "to be rewarded annually to the man or woman of African descent who had attained the highest achievement in any field of elevated or honorable endeavor during the preceding year" (p. 28). This offer reflected Spingarn's belief that African Americans had special talents in the arts. Spingarn insisted that African Americans should think of themselves as "rich, rich by inheritance and by temperament, but willing to share your great gifts with your poor, cold, uninspired brothers of white blood" (p. 28). This belief in the preservation of the African American cultural heritage "remained one of Spingarn's concerns throughout his life" (p. 28). He was one of only a few whites in the struggle for interracial justice and the advancement of African Americans who truly understood and supported the belief "that a greater emphasis upon black cultural nationalism must be a vital aspect of any new direction taken by the Negro" (p. 29).

The more Spingarn got into his role as a new abolitionist, the more radical he became, sometimes to the chagrin of other white members of the NAACP. For example, in 1913 he aroused the anger of Villard, who had recruited him into the NAACP 3 years earlier, when he told a group of African Americans in Baltimore not to restrict themselves to nonviolence to secure their rights. In New Jersey, he related a story of a black man with a shotgun standing at the door of his cabin to protect his rights. A newspaper in Quincy, Illinois, compared Spingarn to John Brown: " 'He wishes to seize the U.S. Arsenal and be a John Brown the second' " (Ross, 1972, p. 29). Spingarn did not help dispel the concerns of his more timid white liberal associates by his delight in telling how his speeches had made his white audiences melt away before he had finished. Newspaper reporters waited for him with a "handshake or a hammer" (p. 29).

Spingarn's militant stand grew out of his increasing disillusionment with white social uplift programs and the accommodationist approach of Booker T. Washington. He refused to compromise with white audiences and told an Omaha audience that the black problem would continue as long as segregation and discrimination took the place of justice. He told the audience that all he wanted "is absolutely fair treatment among men regardless of color." He told whites in Detroit that slavery had brought blacks to America and now "we must pay the price of slavery." His favorite point during these new abolitionist tours was linking the struggle for the advancement of blacks to the well-being of the entire nation. The African American must be guaranteed rights "for our own sake, as well as for his—perhaps even more for our sake than for his" (Ross, 1972, p. 33).

Spingarn's visits stimulated the work of the NAACP in the cities on his tour. Blacks and whites joined the local branches of the NAACP. After his lecture in Detroit, close to 25 influential whites "expressed interest in the branch's work" (Ross, 1972, p. 29). During this tour, Spingarn's work resulted in the establishment of "the first NAACP college chapter at predominantly black Howard University" (p. 29). It is difficult to obtain an accurate measure of the full effect of Spingarn's dynamic new abolitionist tours. One estimate is that about 70,000 people heard Spingarn's message during the three tours (Ross, 1972). Regardless of the numbers, Spingarn's message infused a new spirit not only in the NAACP but also in the entire interracial movement for racial justice and the advancement of the African American.

Spingarn's new abolitionist tours established his role in the struggle as a radical white with two major tasks: (a) to educate whites about the nature of racial discrimination and the role they should play in eliminating it and (b) to encourage African Americans to be relentless in their struggle for full equality. In the summer of 1914, Spingarn, Du Bois, and William Picken (black dean of Morgan State College and an active member of the Baltimore branch of the NAACP) went to Louisville, Kentucky, to lead the black community in protest against a residential segregation ordinance that had just been enacted. Spingarn gave a speech at a black church before a predominantly black audience of more than 800 people. This speech was one of his most eloquent pronouncements on the question of segregation. He told them, " 'In the name of all right thinking people, I come here to protest the wrong being done . . . to let you know that there are men who do not approve of such injustice.' " He said that African Americans had helped build Louisville as much as whites, that blocking off any minority group from the larger society could result only in developing " 'a permanently inferior civilization in our midst which must serve forever as a corrupting force in the movement of the larger civilization of which it must continue to remain a part.' " He then reminded Louisville whites that " 'there is no such thing as a "Negro problem": it is an American problem, for, while injustice exists, the whole country is in danger.' " To African Americans, he posed a revolutionary challenge: " 'Rather die now than live 100 years in a ghetto' " (Ross, 1972, pp. 34-35).

Like many of his radical white heroes of the abolitionist era, Spingarn was becoming a hero to the generation of African Americans of his day. "By 1917 the name of Spingarn had become synonymous in the minds of countless blacks with the uncompromising stand against inequality and segregation which had formed the keystone of the fiery new abolitionism of a day not long past" (Ross, 1972, p. 85). African Americans knew that he would not compromise on the issue of segregation: "There is no recorded instance in which Spingarn hinted that the Negro should bow to expediency, even when temporary segregation promised the only avenue to advancement of the race" (p. 85).

Spingarn's challenge to "rather die now than live 100 years in a ghetto" would not be the last time that he would hint the use of violence on behalf of racial justice. He gave a talk at the NAACP annual conference in 1919 in which he denounced the crude white Southerners who had been put in charge of African American troops. He then suggested that armed struggle might be needed to obtain rights for African Americans. Probably realizing how his statement shocked the delegates, he quickly retracted it (Ross, 1972, p. 133). Perhaps Spingarn saw himself in the role of John Brown, believing that only bloodshed could ultimately cleanse the land from racial justice and secure full equality for African Americans.

As an educator, Spingarn could not resist playing the role of teacher-scholar in the struggle for racial justice. He believed that solid facts could help change people's racial attitudes and behavior, which explains why he spent time attempting to educate influential Southern whites. He had a "virtual passion for sending pro-Negro literature, especially the *Crisis,* to influential white Southerners" (Ross, 1972, p. 43). When he discovered that the Peabody College for Teachers (a white institution) in Nashville, Tennessee, was planning to buy books on African Americans for its library, he made an offer to supply books. "Throughout his career in the NAACP," writes Ross (1972), "Spingarn's faith in appeals to the white conscience through the medium of the written word was unabated; he rarely missed an opportunity to forward pro-Negro literature not only to white Southerners but also to white Northerners and even to acquaintances abroad" (p. 43).

One cannot ignore the role that wealth has often played in the participation of whites in the interracial struggle for racial justice and the advancement of African Americans. Although at times whites have used their wealth to control the nature and pace of the struggle, Spingarn was very careful not to use his wealth to determine his role within the NAACP. Instead, he used his money on behalf of the struggle. For example, in 1912 he contributed $50 to the Nashville Urban League. In 1917, after attending the Southern Sociological Congress, he donated $200 "toward the Congress' work in fostering amicable race relations in the South" (Ross, 1972, p. 43). At times, Spingarn used his wealth, as did other wealthy whites in the organization, to help their less wealthy black colleagues. For example, Spingarn and his wife often loaned Du Bois money to supplement his small salary. During the 1920s, the Spingarns made substantial financial contributions to several major fund drives of the NAACP. In addition, the Spingarns also "supplied a list of wealthy whites in the New York area who might be induced to contribute to the drive" (p. 117). Without white wealth and the leisure that it provided for several talented and devoted whites to work full-time in the NAACP, both the NAACP and the broader interracial struggle would have been much less successful.

Spingarn also played a key role as treasurer for the NAACP. His experiences as a director for two mills and as a business partner in the Harcourt and Brace publishing company provided him with valuable financial skills sorely needed by the NAACP during the 1920s. As the NAACP began collecting more funds than ever, Spingarn became one of its "most astute and professionally minded financial advisers." His greatest single contribution was his insistence "upon careful, long-term investment of the NAACP's surplus fund." There was another benefit from having Spingarn—or, for that matter, any white liberal—in the role of treasurer of the NAACP: the "belief—whether real or imagined—that the organization's enemies would be less likely to level charges of mismanagement of funds" (Ross, 1972, pp. 117-120).

As the NAACP matured, even someone as committed as Spingarn became concerned about the changing roles of whites in an organization drawing increasingly on African Americans to fill its leadership positions. Twice in his career with the NAACP, Spingarn had to confront the question of the changing role of whites in the interracial struggle for racial justice and the advancement of African Americans. In 1915 and in 1933, he resigned his offices in part because he felt that the board refused to accept his views because he was white. Both times he suggested that an African American take his place. His deep concern about his and other white liberals' role in the struggle peaked in 1933 at the second Amenia Conference, when he asked young African Americans gathered at the conference what role "white liberals like himself were to have in the continuing struggle for black advancement" (Ross, 1972, p. 110).

Conflicts between Du Bois and Spingarn over the independence of the *Crisis,* which Du Bois edited, and over Du Bois's developing philosophy of black economic separatism as opposed to the Spingarn philosophy of noneconomic liberalism and his uncompromising stand against segregation for any reason, complicated even further the question of the changing roles of the liberal whites in the organization.[2] Du Bois and Spingarn had a long friendship in the NAACP. Although they had their ups and downs, they were always frank and honest, often at the expense of each other's feelings. It was Du Bois who first acknowledged the significant role that Spingarn played in the advancement of African Americans. At a time when the people engaged in the interracial struggle for racial justice needed to take stock of the needs of the black community, according to Du Bois (1970),

Joel Spingarn was among the first to realize this and he proposed to call in August a conference of persons interested in the race problems at his beautiful home, Troutbeck, in the peace and quiet of Amenia. . . . Here colored and white men of all shades of opinion might sit down, and rest and talk, and find agreement so far as possible with regard to the Negro problem. (p. 243)

For over three decades, these two warriors, one African American and the other Jewish American, stood shoulder to shoulder against the worst forms of racial oppression. In 1934, some of their long-standing ideo-logical differences, only partially associated with the changing roles of whites in the NAACP, contributed to the growing conflicts over Du Bois's position on self-segregation. After a long and bitter fight with major NAACP officers over philosophy and policies, Du Bois left the NAACP. Spingarn, along with his brother Arthur and Mary White Ovington, the three remaining members of the old guard, gave ground to a group of younger black militants, such as Ralph Bunche and John P. Davis, who rejected the philosophy of noneconomic liberalism. When he died in 1939, Spingarn was president of the NAACP, but the powerful board chairmanship was in the hands of an African American (Ross, 1972). To the end, Spingarn devoted his life to the interracial struggle for racial justice and the advancement of African Americans. Du Bois dedicated his 1970 book, *Dusk of Dawn,* to Spingarn, with these words: "To Keep the Memory of Scholar and Knight." In the same book, Du Bois expressed with great devotion his respect for his old comrade:

The recent death of Joel Spingarn brings vividly to my mind the influence which he had at that time upon my thought and action. I do not think that any other white man ever touched me emotionally so closely as Joel Spingarn. He was one of those vivid, enthusiastic but clear-thinking ideal-ists which from age to age the Jewish race has given the world. He had learned of the National Association for the Advancement of Colored People just after a crisis in his life and he joined us eagerly, ready for a new fight, a new thrill and allegiances. I was both fascinated by his character and antagonized by some of his quick and positive judgments. We fought each other continually in the councils of the Association, but always our admi-ration and basic faith in each other kept us going hand in hand. We disagreed over the editorial power which I should have in the conduct of the *Crisis,* and yet the *Crisis* had no firmer friend than Spingarn. Of greatest influence on me undoubtedly was Spingarn's attitude toward the war. He was fired with consuming patriotism. He believed in America. . . . He

wanted me and my people, not merely as a matter of policy. . . . It was
due to his advice and influence that I became, during the World War,
nearer to feeling myself a real and full American than ever before or
since. (pp. 255-256)

Although Mary White Ovington and Joel E. Spingarn are two of the
most outstanding white liberals who worked full time for the NAACP,
other white liberals in the organization made major contributions to the
interracial struggle for racial justice and the advancement of African
Americans. These were the white lawyers who played key roles in the
NAACP's major legal battles during the formative period of the NAACP
before the rise of the great African American civil rights lawyers
Charles Houston and Thurgood Marshall.

WHITE LAWYERS:
MOORFIELD STOREY, ARTHUR B. SPINGARN,
NATHAN R. MARGOLD, AND JACK GREENBERG

Moorfield Storey was the first and the most distinguished of the white
lawyers who worked for the NAACP between 1911 and 1929. He was
a brilliant Boston constitutional lawyer and was once president of the
American Bar Association. He had been a secretary for the great radical
abolitionist Senator Charles Sumner. He was the main link between the
old and the new abolitionist traditions. His father, Charles Storey,
became a "Sumner Republican" in 1850 due to his indignation over
Webster's support of the Fugitive Slave Law. That same year, Charles
Storey introduced his son to Senator Charles Sumner, who was recuper-
ating after a savage beating from a Southern zealot (Hixson, 1972).

From 1867 to 1869, Moorfield Storey worked as Sumner's personal
secretary; at this time, Sumner was "the staunchest advocate of civil
rights for the freedman among American statesmen of his time" (Hixson,
1972, p. 11). This exposed Storey not only to the radical influence of
Sumner but also to major events that shaped his attitudes toward race
relations for the rest of his life. During his tenure as Sumner's secretary,
Storey wrote his father complaining of President Johnson's persistent
references to the "Africanization" that would result if civil rights were
granted to African Americans. To Storey, such references were "an abomi-
nable appeal to prejudice" (p. 188). As a result, he "developed a lifelong
admiration for the ideals and the career of Charles Sumner" (p. 120).

Building on the solid tradition of the abolitionists and such current heroes as Garrison and Sumner, Storey "wanted to bring back the moral fervor of the abolitionists" (Hixson, 1972, p. 43). As his legal career unfolded in the wake of growing racial discrimination against blacks, he found inspiration in reflecting on a similar period in America's history:

"Ah, what a time it was to live in, when 'the frozen apathy' which Garrison deplored when he founded *The Liberator* was gradually yielding, and the tide of freedom was consistently rising; when the annexation of Texas with a slave constitution, the Fugitive Slave Law, the repeal of the Missouri Compromise, the expulsion of Samuel Hoar from Charleston, the return of Anthony Burns, the assault on Sumter, the outrages in Kansas, and the growing insolence of the slave lords taught the North . . . what slavery meant to free men as well as slaves, until secession and the attack on Sumter brought the smoldering fires into fierce life and the conflagration began in which slavery finally perished." (Hixson, 1972, p. 43)

Storey grounded his struggles against American imperialism abroad and racial discrimination at home on his views of the abolitionists. He could see America drifting away from the abolitionist tradition that had culminated in the end of slavery and the granting of citizenship to African Americans. Already white America had grown tired of protecting the rights of African Americans. He said,

"We are passing through a reaction against the great principles of freedom and equal rights to advance which Garrison devoted his life, and we need assured faith. We need to be reminded how much can be accomplished in a good cause by courage, persistence, and unwavering devotion against odds which seem to be overwhelming—how certain is the triumph of right." (Hixson, 1972, p. 43)

In 1907, Storey spoke at the third annual meeting of the Niagara Movement in Boston. Storey's public appearance at this meeting represented "the first support it had won from whites of real eminence." Several years later, he became the first president of the NAACP. As president, he explained the major objective of the NAACP:

"The object of the National Association is to create an organization which will endeavor to smooth the path of the Negro race upward, and create a public opinion which will frown upon discrimination against their property rights, which will endeavor to see that they get in the courts the same justice that is given to their white neighbors, and that they are not discriminated against as they are now all over the country. We want to make race prejudice as unfashionable as it is now fashionable." (Sitkoff, 1978, p. 17)

Storey was concerned about all oppressed peoples but focused on the plight of the African American because he realized that they were the most oppressed people in the country. He rarely missed an opportunity to fight racial discrimination against African Americans. In 1910, when the American Bar Association expelled a Harvard Law School graduate because he was African American, Storey threatened to resign from the ABA. As a result of his pressure, the ABA backed down. Several years later, Storey protested the exclusion of African American alumni from the social functions of the Harvard Club of Philadelphia and refused to join the Boston Club because of a similar practice. He struck several major blows against the rising tide of white supremacy. He opposed the views of Harvard president Charles W. Eliot, who believed in racial purity as the key force in the advancement of civilization and waged his own intellectual Holy War against historians who were distorting the writing of Reconstruction history. He played a key role in the NAACP's opposition to the showing of the racist anti-Negro film *Birth of a Nation* and caused a stir when he refused to shake hands with the producer. He took a position against President Woodrow Wilson's policy of racial discrimination. In the early 1920s, he fought against a policy of racial discrimination in college dormitories and won (Sitkoff, 1978).

Notwithstanding all of his protests against racism, Storey's major contribution to the interracial struggle against racial injustice and the advancement of African Americans occurred in the legal area. As explained by Howard Sitkoff (1978),

> any organization devoted to securing equality before the law, as the NAACP has been devoted, is particularly dependent upon the processes of litigation for the realization of its goals; and here someone with Storey's legal skills and professional prestige was invaluable. Relying on the careful investigations conducted by the Association's branches and the preliminary presentations of the cases by local lawyers, Storey appears to have determined the constitutional basis for the NAACP argument. In several notable cases, he was thus able to halt the judicial trends of 3 decades toward racial proscription. (p. 45)

Storey's work defending the rights of African Americans helped make racial prejudice much more unfashionable than it would have been had he not decided to join the struggle for racial justice. From the time he joined the NAACP until his death in 1929, he represented the NAACP in all its appearances before the U.S. Supreme Court (Hughes, 1962; Kluger, 1977).

The Supreme Court battles that Storey won for the NAACP had far-reaching social and political ramifications for millions of African Americans and for the broader interracial struggles for racial justice. As Mary White Ovington (1947) explains, "Moorfield Storey won this case, our first case, 'the Grandfather Clause' . . . and his presence before The Supreme Court set the highest standard for our growing organization" (p. 116). There can be no doubt that Storey's role as president of the NAACP gave it tremendous credibility among the legal community and contributed in no small way to attracting top white lawyers to assist the organization.

Storey realized that African Americans would have to play a key legal role in the interracial struggle against racial injustice. The time was fast approaching when African Americans would no longer be satisfied with having their white friends, no matter how devoted to the struggle, fighting their legal battles. By 1926, just 3 years before his death, Storey headed a team of NAACP lawyers that included two African Americans for the first time. The team lost the Restrictive Covenant case but it presented to the High Court and the American public an interracial team of lawyers fighting for American racial justice (Kluger, 1977). Ovington (1947) describes this interracial team: "The legal committee, headed by William H. Hastie, is made up of many eminent lawyers of both races" (p. 271). Storey represented the NAACP for the last time in 1927. He was then 82 years old and still fighting on behalf of the rights of African Americans.

Storey was a vital link between the old and the new abolitionists. He fought a long and good fight against all forms of racism and paved the way for the great victories against racial injustices that future lawyers would fight. Hixson (1972) reminds us that "the NAACP's eventual success in achieving the total destruction of 'white supremacy' was launched with the victories won by Moorfield Storey" (p. 145). Many people have said that the NAACP was the beginning of a "new abolitionism, a second commitment of some white Americans to join in the fight for the freedom of their black countrymen" (p. 145). In the case of Moorfield Storey, it would no doubt be more accurate to say that the NAACP represented the culmination of the abolitionist commitment of Senator Charles Sumner and his idea of equality before the law.

Arthur B. Spingarn was one of the pioneer white lawyers who helped shape the role of white lawyers in the interracial struggle for racial justice and the advancement of African Americans. "Many of America's most significant gains in integration have been achieved through court rulings obtained by the National Association for the Advancement of Colored People whose president from 1940 through 1965 was Arthur B. Spingarn" ("Arthur B. Spingarn," 1965, p. 398). His roles involved directing the legal defense work of the NAACP for many years; he was also vice president from 1911 to 1940. His early exposure to the indecent and unjust manner in which African Americans were treated in a civil rights case he was trying "filled him with an indignation that he . . . felt repeatedly in his almost sixty years of service in the cause of the American Negro" (p. 398).

Because the NAACP had very little money to pay employees, particularly lawyers, Spingarn volunteered his services as the NAACP's counsel without pay. In winning the first case he tried before the Supreme Court, Spingarn won for African Americans the right to vote in primary elections in Texas. From 1911 to 1940, he chaired the national legal committee of the NAACP; from 1940 to 1957, he was president of the NAACP Legal Defense and Educational Fund, Inc. His work resulted in many Supreme Court victories in civil rights cases that "made legal history and contributed significantly to establishing racial equality" ("Arthur B. Spingarn," 1965, p. 398). As a result of his affiliation with the NAACP and his legal defense of African Americans, the young lawyer lost many clients. But as the NAACP became acceptable to more whites, Spingarn's clientele increased. People began seeking him out for his legal work. At this stage of his life, people looked on him as "a celebrity and a pioneer in a new and noble cause" (p. 398).

Arthur Spingarn played a key role in the NAACP's long but abortive struggle to obtain an antilynching law. In 1922, while engaged in this struggle, he turned to the Garland Fund for financial support "for an immediate publicity campaign that would move the great mass of Americans to write hesitant senators on the Bill's behalf" (Zangrando, 1980, p. 4). The fund responded with a grant of $3,365 to purchase advertisements as part of the NAACP's anti-lynching campaign (Tushnet, 1987). After the death of Moorfield Storey in 1929, Spingarn inherited the NAACP's legal burdens. As the chief volunteer lawyer, he recruited an impressive list "of eminent civil-libertarians" (Kluger, 1977, p. 131) in the long and difficult struggle for racial justice.

In addition to being the chief volunteer lawyer, from 1911 to 1940 Arthur Spingarn was also vice president of the NAACP. After the death of his brother, Joel, the NAACP board elected him president. In his acceptance speech, Spingarn committed himself to yet another role in the interracial struggle for racial justice:

> "I trust that as long as I shall be its president, the National Association for the Advancement of Colored People will never in the slightest degree swerve from its courageous, militant and intelligent struggle to obtain for the Negroes of the country their full manhood and each and every privilege awarded to all Americans by the Constitution of the United States." (Kluger, 1977, p. 399)

Arthur Spingarn lived long enough to witness radical, and often painful, challenges to the roles of aging liberal white leaders in the interracial struggle for racial justice and the advancement of African Americans. In a 1961 interview, he made the following comment on the "new developments" in this struggle: "A lot of these people . . . think they lit the torch. We lit the torch and they're carrying it now" ("Arthur B. Spingarn," 1965, p. 399). Spingarn did not think that the freedom riders accomplished much by staying in jail. Segregation, he believed, could be stopped only by legal action. Although he wished they were better organized, he could not blame them. "After all, we've been waiting for almost one hundred years for what we're legally entitled to" (pp. 398-399). His use of "we" indicates that his long struggle alongside his black colleagues had made them of one blood in the interracial struggle. He probably could see the handwriting on the wall, however. Young militant African Americans within the NAACP began challenging his leadership. They wanted an African American as leader of the NAACP. Understanding the nature of the changing roles of whites in the NAACP, Arthur Spingarn agreed to remain in office only to the end of 1965.

This did not mean that whites no longer had a role to play in the NAACP or, for that matter, in the broader interracial struggle for racial justice. Rather, it meant that the traditional roles of whites as leaders in this struggle were changing as African Americans became more skilled and confident in taking on leadership roles.

Nathan R. Margold was another white lawyer who contributed to the interracial struggle for racial justice. Although he did not devote long years of his life to the struggle, as did Storey and Spingarn, he did make a major contribution to the work of the NAACP.

Margold was a European-born Jew who attended Harvard Law School and worked with the future black dean of Howard Law School, Charles

Houston, on the *Harvard Law Review*. In 1930, he became a special counsel to the Pueblo Indian Tribes in their struggle to obtain their land title claim. This was also the year that the NAACP retained him "to frame the legal drives financed by the Garland grant" (Kluger, 1977, p. 133). He was needed to develop a strategy for improving the legal rights of African Americans in the area of education. From 1930 to 1933, Margold functioned as a special counsel and prepared a "detailed book-length study that called for an attack on school segregation and the separate-but-equal clause" (Lowery & Marszalek, 1992, p. 345). The Margold Report pushed for an attack on racial segregation "based on the fact that underfunded southern schools were not equal" (p. 345). This report became the Bible for black and white NAACP lawyers engaged in legal campaigns against racial discrimination in education. More specifically, the Margold Report became the "premier document of [the] Legal Defense and Educational Fund" (p. 345).

Others such as Jack Greenberg would also carry on the tradition of white lawyers within the interracial struggle for racial justice. By 1949, when this young Jewish lawyer joined the NAACP Legal Defense Fund, the roles of white lawyers had changed in relationship to the roles of black lawyers (Greenberg, 1994). Unlike the days of Moorfield Storey and Arthur Spingarn, when there were few skilled African American lawyers to lead the legal charge against racial discrimination, by the time Greenberg was hired by Thurgood Marshall, African American lawyers such as Charles H. Houston and William Hastie were legends. Greenberg became part of an interracial team that would make legal history. The team included Thurgood Marshall, Constance Motley, Robert Carter—Marshall's deputy—and Franklin Williams. Greenberg and Carter played key roles in preparing the way for the 1954 landmark decision in *Brown v. Topeka Board of Education* (Greenberg, 1994; Kaufman, 1993; Kluger, 1977).

As he traveled throughout the country as a Legal Defense Fund lawyer, Greenberg discovered the real world of racial discrimination that dogged the lives of African Americans. This exposure to racism angered him. His greatest opportunity as a white warrior in the interracial struggle for racial justice came during the civil rights movement. Although he had contributed much to the legal struggle against discrimination in education, his legal contribution to the civil rights movement would be far greater. In the fall of 1961, Marshall asked Greenberg to succeed him as head of the Legal Defense Fund because he was being nominated by President John F. Kennedy to the Second Circuit of the

U.S. Court of Appeals. Greenberg's appointment caused much concern among some staffers, such as his longtime colleague Robert Carter, who wanted the job and who felt that if he could not have it, some other African American lawyer should have gotten it. The *Amsterdam News* voiced the same concern (Kaufman, 1993).

Thurgood Marshall's long years of working with Greenberg on tough civil rights cases had convinced him that Greenberg needed to head up the fund. Greenberg's appointment came when African Americans were struggling with sometimes contradictory goals, wanting to strengthen the interracial struggle against racism using all the best resources at hand, which included talented and devoted whites, while attempting to build an African American leadership within interracial organizations.

Marshall's appointment of Greenberg rather than Robert Carter was motivated by his concern for having the most capable person head the fund so that the struggle against racism could be effectively fought and won. Unfortunately, some African Americans had problems with a white in that role. Considering the successes of Greenberg in obtaining financial support and legal personnel for the fund in its support of civil rights protesters, he performed his role well. Perhaps his success was due to the way Greenberg framed the struggle. As he explained to a journalist, " 'Civil rights is not a Negro cause; it is a human cause, a serious problem in world society. True, our organization is designed primarily to aid Negroes in the push for equality, but the cause is human, not Negro' " (Kaufman, 1993, p. 98).

In 2 years as head of the fund, Greenberg increased the budget from $10,000 to $1.5 million annually. He recruited top Ivy League-educated lawyers, many with prestigious law review credentials. But his most impressive achievement as head of the fund was in the field working on behalf of African American rights in the South, as Kaufman (1993) notes,

> Working with 102 cooperating lawyers throughout the South, the Legal Defense Fund in 1963 defended 10,467 civil rights demonstrators, fought 168 groups of legal action in 15 states, and brought 30 cases to the Supreme Court. . . . Other lawyers . . . enlisted in the movement in the South and won important, path-breaking cases, but for consistency in civil rights work and the changes he wrought in the law, none could match Greenberg or the Legal Defense Fund. His pursuit of top legal talent to enlist in the cause was relentless. (p. 98)

Greenberg had his faults, and some blacks and whites felt that he and the fund were too conservative, but during a critical period in the history of the civil rights movement, he did his best to carry on a long tradition of white lawyers who devoted major portions of their lives to the interracial struggle for racial justice.

ESTHER BROWN:
A HOUSEWIFE INVOLVED IN THE STRUGGLE

Let me round out the profile of whites who threw in their lots with African Americans with the story of a remarkable Jewish housewife who played a key role in the struggle for equal educational opportunities in Kansas and contributed to the broader struggle that led to *Brown v. Board of Education.*

In 1948, Esther Brown was living a comfortable suburban life with her husband and family in Merriam, Kansas, southwest of Kansas City, Missouri. Brown had grown up in Kansas City, where segregation was the law. But she had no idea of the terrible educational system that law created for African American children. According to Kluger (1977),

> Certainly she did not know that the South Park school district, which sent its Negro children to a broken-down wooden grade school without plumbing, proper heating, or anything more than a tiny basement room for a cafeteria, was in violation of the Kansas state law that permitted segregation only in cities of more than 15,000. (p. 388)

Brown was "shocked by the sight of the school" and the poor living conditions of her black maid. When her maid asked her what blacks should do about the bond issues that the white community was voting for to build a new white school, Brown told her blacks should oppose the bond until their poor school was fixed up. Taking her advice, some blacks went to the school board, but all they received for their trouble was a stop sign in front of the black school. "That really got me angry for the first time," Brown remembered (Kluger, 1977, p. 388). She then went before the white school board to make an appeal. All that they offered were new light bulbs for the black school and used desks from the old white school as soon as the new white school was built. Such rabid racism sickened Brown (Kluger, 1977, p. 388).

Many whites would not have gone this far. After seeing the poor living conditions of their black help, they would have felt sorry but left it at that. The white board's response to Brown's appeal would have turned back many well-meaning whites, but not Brown. Esther Brown was beginning to assume her role as a white warrior in the struggle for racial justice and the advancement of African Americans. When the bond issue passed, over black opposition, Brown began rallying the black community. She was asked to attend a community meeting of whites to discuss the condition of the black school. During the meeting she was yelled at and insulted. She left that meeting a changed person. "She went on a one-woman crusade. The blacks did not know what to make of her. No white person had ever taken their side with such vehemence before" (Kluger, 1977, p. 389). She hired a black lawyer to file a suit against the school system, helped organize a boycott of the run-down black school, set up a private school with certified teachers in homes and churches, and went on a fund-raising campaign to support the schools and the suit. She contacted NAACP branches around the state informing them she had a story to tell (Kluger, 1977, pp. 389-390).

Brown did everything she could to raise money for the private schools and the lawsuit. One Sunday she raised only $6.21 at a church. She raised $400 "making a pitch at midnight, with thirty black children in tow, on-stage at a Billie Holiday concert in Kansas City" (Kluger, 1977, p. 390). She had to borrow "money for the gasoline that carried her to all her one-night stands, and when she wasn't on the road she got up early to fire the furnaces at the protest schools she had organized" (p. 390). People threatened and insulted her; someone burned a cross on her lawn; her husband was fired from his job; she had a miscarriage. On top of all this, her "father-in-law called her a Communist behind her back" (p. 390). But she continued her fight for racial justice. She contacted Thurgood Marshall's office at the Legal Defense Fund for assistance, which sent Franklin Williams to work with a local black lawyer. "They won the case and the black children of South Park were ordered admitted to the white school" (p. 390).

Esther Brown had won her first battle. She had grown up oblivious to the effects of racial segregation on the lives of African Americans in her city. But once she became aware, she became a white warrior for racial justice and rallied many blacks who had been worn down by their struggle to survive each day. Before the black children went to the white school for the first time, Esther Brown did something very special for each of them:

Mrs. Brown bought a new dress for every little girl and a new shirt for every little boy. And she brought seven children from an especially destitute family to her home and bathed them and took them to Kansas City University Health Center for emergency dental care "which frightened the hell out of them." (Kluger, 1977, p. 390)

Brown did not stop with her victory of getting black children into the white school. She went to Wichita, the largest city in Kansas, and prodded the NAACP there to start a lawsuit against segregation. Unfortunately, the harsh realities of racial dependency undermined her efforts. Many African American teachers who were dependent on the segregated school system failed to support Brown's efforts. But that did not stop Brown; she went next to Topeka, where she joined hands with the local NAACP in what turned out to be the legal victory of the century for all those involved in the interracial struggle for racial justice: *Brown v. Board of Education.*[3] When the Legal Defense Fund sent Jack Greenberg and Robert Carter to Topeka, Esther Brown welcomed them and found them accommodations. She enlisted the assistance of the Jewish Community Relations Bureau of Kansas City in finding expert witnesses who could support the NAACP's position that segregated education was harmful to African American children. A former secretary of the Topeka branch of the NAACP said of Esther Brown, " 'I don't know if we could have done it without her' " (Kluger, 1977, p. 390).

CONCLUSION

A new generation of whites carried on the proud tradition of white participation in the interracial struggle for racial justice and the advancement of African Americans. Some, like Mary White Ovington and Moorfield Storey, had family ties to the abolitionist generation, whereas others, such as the Spingarn brothers, followed their own sense of justice and spent major portions of their lives working for racial justice. They came from a variety of professional backgrounds. Ovington was a social worker; Joel Spingarn was an accomplished man of letters; Arthur Spingarn and Moorfield Story were lawyers. All of these whites were associated with the NAACP.

These whites paved the way for another generation of whites. They also provided models for the larger society, demonstrating that some bold and courageous whites were still willing to stand beside African Americans in their struggle for racial justice. This point cannot be overemphasized. Considering the tragic state of race relations at the time of the founding of the NAACP, many whites were more than willing to turn their backs on the plight of African Americans. What was needed was a strong interracial offensive against all forms of racism.

Ovington, the Spingarn brothers, and Storey played major roles in positioning the NAACP as the foremost interracial organization fighting racism. But they also exhibited in their personal lives age-old qualities that made them stand out. Once they had committed to the struggle, all four persisted to the end of their lives. Although Storey did not spend as much time as the others on certain aspects of the NAACP's work, he was a steady warrior for the cause. Because he had worked for Charles Sumner during the Reconstruction period, he was the link between the old and new generations of whites in the interracial struggle for racial justice and African American advancement. Ovington took the time to research and publish works on the social conditions of African Americans; this in itself proved invaluable in educating the larger society about the causes of African American poverty.

Joel Spingarn's new abolitionist tour raised the consciousness of blacks and whites; he demonstrated how committed whites must be to the struggle for racial justice. In addition, he established an award for African American artists and writers. Here was a white who went beyond the traditional concerns for racial justice—important though those concerns were. Spingarn was sensitive to the need for African Americans to feel proud of themselves. Being Jewish, he understood how the prejudices of the larger white society excluded and ignored the cultural achievements of African Americans.

Arthur Spingarn worked as a lawyer for the NAACP for years without pay. His work resulted in several critical Supreme Court civil rights cases that made legal history and contributed to the expansion of legal rights for African Americans. He too demonstrated how committed a white could be to the struggle for racial justice. There were other white lawyers as well, such as Nathan R. Margold and Jack Greenberg, who made major contributions to the struggle for racial justice. In the early 1930s, as a special counsel to the NAACP, Margold prepared a major study that called for an attack on school segregation and the separate-but-equal clause. This report became the Bible for black and white lawyers in their struggles to desegregate the Southern school system. Jack Greenberg spent a lifetime in the struggle for racial justice. Hired by Thurgood Marshall, Greenberg joined the NAACP Legal Defense Fund and traveled throughout the South with African American lawyers fighting segregation.

Esther Brown, a Jewish housewife living a comfortable life in a suburban community in Kansas, decided to take a stand for racial justice when she discovered that legal segregation created horrible educational conditions for African American children. At great sacrifice to herself and her family, she joined in the struggle to dismantle racial segregation in education. She encouraged African Americans to protest, engaged in fund-raising campaigns, worked with the NAACP, and assisted in setting up a network to support desegregation. Brown was a model of what can happen when whites are exposed to the realities of racial oppression and make a moral choice.

The whites discussed in this chapter represent the tip of the iceberg in a great saga of whites who, over the centuries, have joined in the interracial struggle for racial justice and the advancement of African Americans. There are many more whose lives I could have profiled. This chapter should be seen as confirmation that there are whites who want to become part of "the other tradition"; we should find and embrace them, so we can get back to making a living reality of Dr. Martin Luther King, Jr.'s dream of the "beloved community."

NOTES

1. Like other staff members, Ovington also had some problems with Du Bois over his management of the *Crisis* (see Aptheker, 1973, pp. 430-431).

2. Du Bois and Spingarn had some bitter exchanges on this issue before Du Bois retired (see Du Bois, 1934a, 1934b; Spingarn, 1934).

3. The plaintiff in this case was the black family made famous by the lawsuit. See Kluger, 1977, pp. 408-410.

7

Building on the Legacy:
An Opportunity

CONNECTING THE PAST TO THE PRESENT

The preceding chapters are not meant to be exhaustive historical analyses of interracial unity and cooperation. Rather, they are meant to be brief historical snapshots of the "other tradition" of race relations in the United States, to motivate concerned individuals, groups, and organizations to continue the tradition of unifying a racially polarized and fragmented society.

It should be clear at this point that the tradition of interracial unity and cooperation has exerted a powerful influence on the history of race relations in the United States. Notwithstanding the influence of white racial oppression, this history offers solid proof that race relations in the United States can be improved when sufficient will and vision exist to do so. African Americans and white Americans, the two largest racial groups with the longest and most persistent history of racial tension and conflict, are also the two racial groups with the longest and most persistent history of interracial unity and cooperation. This latter historical tradition will empower blacks and whites with the will and vision to break out of the cycle of racial polarization and fragmentation into the cycle of racial unity and harmony.

Each chapter focused on particular aspects of the history of interracial unity and cooperation to help the reader gain an appreciation of how those aspects relate to the broader history of race relations in the United

States. For example, Chapter 2, "Interracial Unity From Colonial Times to the Present," although far from an exhaustive treatment of the subject, attempts to expose readers to the little-known history of cooperation between blacks and whites over the centuries. Interracial unity and cooperation are shown to be not just an historical aberration but a consistent pattern of race relations that have run a parallel path alongside racial oppression. The knowledge of this pattern of interracial unity and cooperation can give readers hope for its continuation. Lessons can be drawn from the various interracial movements, from the antislavery movement to the civil rights movement, that are useful in building new interracial movements for racial justice and interracial unity and harmony.

Given the degree of racial polarization and fragmentation in present-day society, especially among blacks and whites, both races need to know about the interracial movements described in Chapter 2. Rather than engaging in the endless ritual of racial blaming and counterblaming that presently exists in so many racially polarized and fragmented communities, blacks and whites can choose to join in building a powerful interracial movement for racial justice and interracial unity and harmony. Exposing blacks and whites, in college classes or in race relations workshops, to past interracial movements encourages them to work for the promotion of interracial justice, unity, and harmony in their communities. The historical picture of black and white abolitionists working together against all odds, despite ideological differences, is a valuable lesson for present-day interracial organizations struggling to overcome internal racial conflicts and tensions.

Chapter 3, "Maintaining the Racial Status Quo," contains key lessons for minorities and majorities working in interracial movements for racial justice and the advancement of particular minority groups. Perhaps the most valuable lesson is that interracial cooperation does not guarantee that the racial majority will relinquish its privileges. As Chapter 3 points out, many whites with the best of intentions will hold on to certain aspects of the racial status quo. This tends to be a developmental stage in many models of interracial cooperation. One could hardly expect that whites would not bring racial cultural baggage when they join interracial movements. For example, in the antislavery movement, several white abolitionists—including William Lloyd Garrison and Maria Westin Chapman—found it difficult to refrain from dictating decisions to their black coworkers. The best approach is to see this tendency, common among whites, as part of the developmental process of building an interracial movement.

As we work on building and sustaining an interracial movement today, we must be prepared to address this tendency of whites to maintain certain aspects of the racial status quo; we must develop effective methods and strategies to address it without destroying the movement in the process. We have only to review the most recent history of interracial cooperation to realize that the failure to address this issue in present-day interracial efforts will result in serious setbacks in building and sustaining an interracial movement. Studying the history of how blacks and whites succeeded or failed in addressing this issue will help us avoid their mistakes and replicate their successes.

The lesson to be learned from Chapter 4, "Black Expectations and Demands," is that black expectations and demands are inevitable in the dominant modes of interracial cooperation. If the modes are functioning well, rising black expectations and demands can be healthy signs of well-balanced interracial cooperation, a part of the organic growth of the mode. In dysfunctional cases, whites, as the dominant group in the mode, will attempt to control blacks as the less dominant group; blacks, in turn, will react with expectations and demands that will not further the organic growth and development of the mode. Several of the examples in Chapter 3 show how interracial cooperation worked well up to a point, then began to break down when blacks and whites were unable or unwilling to come to terms with different perspectives and agendas. They did not share a unified vision of interracial cooperation that addressed the needs of both blacks and whites in these coalitions.

We have not advanced very far from the interracial stalemate that crippled several very promising modes of interracial cooperation. For years the United Auto Workers (UAW) and black trade unionists could not agree on the need to elect a black to the International Executive Board. This was due in large part to the lack of a unified vision that could embrace the perspectives of both parties. These issues can still be found in interracial settings today, where the rising expectations and demands of blacks are creating tensions and conflicts because of the lack of a unified vision that works for both blacks and whites. Present-day interracial organizations must work on developing a unified vision that can accommodate the rising expectations and demands of blacks— or any other minority—in a way that furthers the organic growth and development of all parties in the organization.

Chapters 5 and 6, which focus on the role of whites in the struggle for racial equality in the 19th and 20th centuries, have profound applications for the present state of race relations. Whites and blacks alike need to know about the historical role of whites in the interracial struggle for racial justice and the advancement of African Americans. We must educate an entire generation of whites to reclaim the best of their interracial history. White youth need to know this history so that they can become part of the continual interracial struggle for racial justice. Black youth need to know this history so they can join hands with white youth in bridging the growing racial gap. I have seen the effects that this history can have on both black and white youth in university classes.

These chapters offer other lessons that can be applied to the present state of race relations. By studying the profiles of whites who dedicated their lives to the interracial struggle for racial justice and the advancement of African Americans, we gain valuable insight into the kind of whites needed to build and sustain present-day interracial movements. We must learn to recognize and recruit these kinds of whites for the long struggle ahead; if we cannot find enough of them, then we must train other whites to emulate them. We must also study the values and visions of whites such as the Grimké sisters, John Brown, Mary White Ovington, the Spingarn brothers, and countless others so we can better understand what drove them to side with blacks at a time when interracial cooperation was unpopular among the majority of white Americans. Many whites today hold similar values and visions and are looking for an interracial movement that will not blame them for past and present wrongs but will welcome them in love and fellowship to join in building and sustaining interracial movements.

THE NEED FOR A NEW PARADIGM IN U.S. RACE RELATIONS

The history of interracial unity and cooperation has been very useful in my work as a professor of history and urban affairs teaching graduate courses in race and poverty, as well as in training clients in race relations workshops conducted by New World Associates, Inc. (NWA). In both settings, participants are exposed to selected historical examples of racism and interracial unity and cooperation. The latter examples expose people to the interracial struggle for racial justice. These examples can encourage people to have faith in this struggle, in the hope that they will join in it to improve the state of race relations in the United States and the world.

The history of interracial unity and cooperation confirms the possibility that concerned people can improve the present state of race relations in the United States. This can occur, however, only after we have educated a critical mass of people from all racial groups to accept the principle of the organic oneness of the human race. This process can begin in the classroom and in race relations workshops geared to the public. Graduate students participating in my seminar in race and poverty learn about the negative effects of racism and positive effects of interracial unity and cooperation. They learn about the persistence of poverty due to housing segregation, which creates and maintains racial polarization and fragmentation in metropolitan areas. This is the *cycle of racial polarization and fragmentation.* This cycle begins with a belief in white racial superiority, which sets in motion a series of negative historical consequences. Students are then introduced to the *cycle of racial unity and harmony,* which begins with a belief in the organic oneness of the human race and sets in motion a series of positive historical consequences.

New World Associates's race relations workshops also use these cycles in training clients. In fact, the cycles were developed to help clients in NWA's race relations workshops to better visualize both the present state of race relations, as characterized by the cycle of racial polarization and fragmentation, and the potential for improvement in the present state of race relations, as characterized by the cycle of racial unity and harmony. This approach is but a crude first step in efforts to develop a more useful paradigm in race relations intervention.

THE CYCLE OF RACIAL POLARIZATION AND FRAGMENTATION

If we hope and expect to improve contemporary race relations in the United States, we must radically change our thinking about the causes of and solutions to current racial problems. A useful way to view contemporary racial problems is to view them as sequences of a cycle of racial polarization and fragmentation in which we are trapped, because we do not know the point in the cycle where we can break out and move into the cycle of racial unity and harmony.

The cycle of racial polarization and fragmentation is based on a series of historical causes and consequences that began with a belief in white racial superiority. This racial belief produced a counter racial belief among many blacks that viewed whites as historical enemies-oppressors (see Figure 7.1). Sequence 1 in Figure 7.1 is the starting point for the rest of the cycle. This is the point where we begin to understand how and why we have remained trapped in this cycle. In contrast, Figure 7.2 shows the cycle of racial unity and harmony, a process enabling us to break out of the cycle of racial polarization and fragmentation.

The belief in white racial superiority—that some races (mainly whites) are better than others—leads in turn to a counterbelief among many racial minorities that whites cannot be trusted, that they are, in effect, the historical enemy-oppressor. These two racial views tend to reinforce each other throughout the cycle of racial polarization and fragmentation. Because whites have historically held the reins of power, they have been able to reinforce, maintain, and perpetuate their racial beliefs through various means of socialization. This is where Sequence 1 of the cycle advances to Sequence 2. Education and socialization have been used to socialize both the majority and minority in the values, myths, and theories of white racial superiority. Sequence 3 in the cycle is the application of values and theories of racial superiority to specific racial groups. The various racial theories concerning blacks developed during and after slavery are an example of such an application.

At Sequence 4 in the cycle of racial polarization and fragmentation, we see examples of the effects of Sequence 3, as the application of values and theories of racial inferiority to specific racial groups leads to racial discrimination in housing and jobs and the racial isolation of inner-city blacks and suburban whites.

Sequence 4 leads to Sequence 5, the increased poverty of racial minorities, social pathology, family and community breakdown, and crime and violence. The cycle continues through Sequence 6, in which whites begin to fear what they have, in fact, created by their racist beliefs and their applications of those beliefs. By Sequence 7 in the cycle, whites and blacks are rapidly moving apart. Many whites are in flight to the suburbs to escape increasingly black and poor central cities, and, when possible, many blacks are avoiding whites. Social isolation of blacks and whites is rapidly reaching a critical stage of irreversible social isolation. The cycle continues to Sequence 8, in which white flight and black avoidance fuels the cycle even further as expressed in race riots. At this point, we arrive back at Sequence 1, where many whites are unable or unwilling to accept the historical consequences of their belief in white racial superiority, which sets the entire cycle in motion. Whites rationalize Sequences 5 through 8 by reverting back to Sequence 1. Thus, the cycle continues.

This cycle is an oversimplification of a complex historical sequence of events. But it can assist us in visualizing how we are trapped in such a cycle and how we can move into a cycle of racial unity and harmony. We already know that racial unity and harmony is possible; we have seen convincing historical examples. But how can we expand a tradition of racial unity and cooperation to the point that it can reverse the very strong tradition of racial polarization and fragmentation? What is needed to lead larger numbers of blacks and whites from a cycle of racial polarization and fragmentation into a cycle of interracial unity and harmony?

THE CYCLE OF
RACIAL UNITY AND HARMONY

As difficult as it might seem to break out of the cycle of racial polarization and fragmentation, it can be as simple and profound as a spiritual conversion. It involves a radical shift in how blacks and whites view their most fundamental relationship as fellow human beings. In short, it is nothing more or less than the recognition of the organic unity of the human race, as applied to all aspects of black-white interaction. This is the first sequence in the cycle of racial unity and harmony (see Figure 7.2). This recognition cannot occur unless a person is deeply committed to a core set of spiritual values and principles.

Once a critical mass of blacks and whites reaches this stage of spiritual commitment to a belief in their organic unity, they will be able to break free of the cycle of racial polarization and fragmentation and move into the cycle of racial unity and harmony. One can scarcely visualize the tremendous social, economic, cultural, and spiritual advancements the United States, as well as other multiracial societies, would be able to achieve once they have taken this vital first step. Reflect back on the influences of the interracial struggles for racial justice and the advancement of African Americans in the transformation of key segments of American society to catch a small glimpse of the vast potential for the transformation of the present state of race relations in the United States. All that is needed is a critical mass of blacks and whites to recognize their organic unity and begin relating to each other on the basis of that recognition.

It is vitally important to increase the number of blacks and whites who believe in the oneness of the human race so as to speed up the transforming

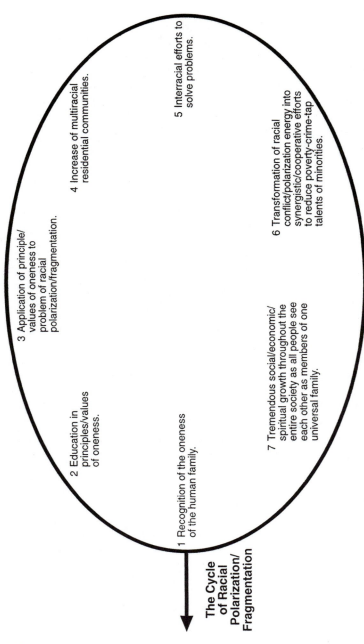

Figure 7.1. The Cycle of Racial Polarization and Fragmentation
SOURCE: New World Associates, Inc.

1 Recognition of the oneness of the human family.

2 Education in principles/values of oneness.

3 Application of principle/values of oneness to problem of racial polarization/fragmentation.

4 Increase of multiracial residential communities.

5 Interracial efforts to solve problems.

6 Transformation of racial conflict/polarization energy into synergistic/cooperative efforts to reduce poverty-crime-tap talents of minorities.

7 Tremendous social/economic/spiritual growth throughout the entire society as all people see each other as members of one universal family.

The Cycle of Racial Polarization/ Fragmentation

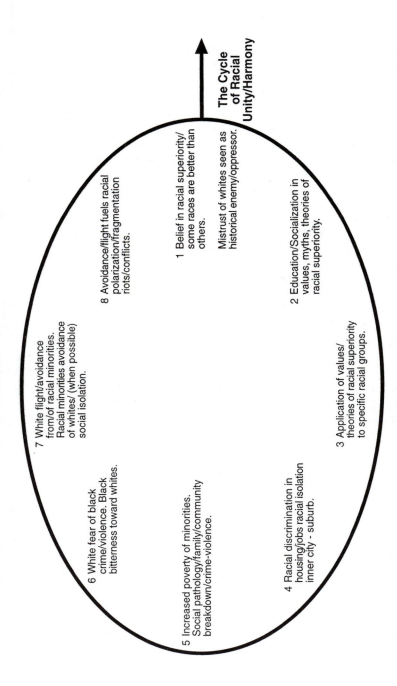

Figure 7.2. The Cycle of Racial Unity and Harmony
SOURCE: New World Associates, Inc.

The Cycle
of Racial
Unity/Harmony

1 Belief in racial superiority/ some races are better than others.

Mistrust of whites seen as historical enemy/oppressor.

2 Education/Socialization in values, myths, theories of racial superiority.

3 Application of values/ theories of racial superiority to specific racial groups.

4 Racial discrimination in housing/jobs racial isolation inner city - suburb.

5 Increased poverty of minorities. Social pathology/family/community breakdown/crime-violence.

6 White fear of black crime/violence. Black bitterness toward whites.

7 White flight/avoidance from/of racial minorities. Racial minorities avoidance of whites/ (when possible) social isolation.

8 Avoidance/flight fuels racial polarization/fragmentation riots/conflicts.

influences of the cycle of racial unity and harmony and diminish the disunifying influences of the cycle of racial polarization and fragmentation. This is a contest for the very soul of America. Once a critical mass of blacks and whites recognizes the organic unity of the human race, we must proceed to Sequence 2 in the cycle: education in the principles and values of oneness. All around us we see the negative effects of the cycle of racial polarization and fragmentation, whether on college campuses between black and white students or in urban centers between central city blacks and suburban whites. We need to develop a powerful interracial movement to educate large numbers of people, particularly blacks and whites, in the principle of the organic oneness of the human race.

This will lead to Sequence 3 in the cycle: the application of the principles and values of oneness to problems of racial polarization and fragmentation. At this stage, the application of the principles and values of oneness to problems of racial polarization and fragmentation will be perfected and will emerge as the most effective approach to racial problems in the United States.

Once a critical mass of blacks and whites begins educating increasing numbers of people about the social, economic, cultural, and spiritual benefits of applying the principles of the organic oneness of the human race to specific racial problems in the United States, we will reach Sequence 4: increase of multiracial residential communities. As blacks and whites recognize their organic unity and the benefits that can occur from applying this principle to all aspects of their lives, they will want to live together so as to increase the many and varied social, economic, cultural, and spiritual benefits of their organic unity.

Sequence 5 involves interracial efforts in solving various social problems. I have already discussed some examples of blacks and whites working together to solve specific racial problems. But these interracial efforts occurred and are occurring within a racially polarized and fragmented society. When society becomes more racially unified as the result of the influences of the cycle of racial unity and harmony, interracial efforts in solving problems will rapidly increase.

By the time we reach Sequence 6 in the cycle, society will be ready for a quantum leap in interracial unity and harmony. Racial unity and harmony will have broken the hold of the cycle of racial polarization and fragmentation. The application of the principle of the organic unity of the human race to the racial problems of society will transform the energy that has gone into racial polarization and fragmentation into synergistic and cooperative efforts to reduce poverty and crime and tap the talents of racial minorities for the benefit of the entire society.

This will lead to Sequence 7, where there will be tremendous social, economic, and spiritual growth through the entire society as increasing numbers of racially and culturally diverse people see each other as members of one universal family. The cycle will complete itself in Sequence 1, the recognition of the oneness of the human family.

APPLYING THE CYCLE
OF RACIAL UNITY AND HARMONY
TO COMMUNITY RACE RELATIONS

Although the cycle of racial unity and harmony is only a visionary tool, I have used it to guide my own thinking and that of my students and NWA's clients onto new paths of improving community race relations. The cycle has been helpful in encouraging students to think of current racial problems in terms of the lack of interracial unity within metropolitan "communities." In NWA race relations workshops, my colleague and I have been training clients, ranging from white corporate executives to black community leaders, to approach community race relations from a systemic, vision-driven model based on the cycle of racial unity and harmony. The main purpose is to educate people to see the great potential for the improvement of race relations. I discuss some aspects of this approach in a paper I wrote for the After Coleman Young: Detroit in Transition Conference (Thomas, 1994). In this paper, I address the issues of the conference by focusing on the need of the city to play a leading role in unifying a racially polarized metropolitan community.

The Role of Detroit

We have reached a critical point in both the history of race relations in metropolitan communities and the history of black leadership in major postindustrial cities. These two historical processes have been converging since the first elections of black mayors in the mid-1960s and the growth and insularity of predominantly white suburbs over the last two decades. Urban scholars and politicians have been aware of these developments for many years. Many have lamented the growing racial polarization between the predominantly black cities and the predominantly white suburbs. Others, however, including some black politicians and a host of white suburban politicians, have accepted this racial polarization as unfortunate but too difficult to solve.

Some black politicians understandably have seen the growth of pre-dominantly black cities as political power bases won after decades of political struggles against resistant whites, who staged long struggles to hold on to the office of the mayor, city councils, police departments, and the like.[1] In fact, the last 25 years have seen a relentless rear-guard struggle among many whites to hold on to key sectors of the very cities they were abandoning in large numbers against an expanding and politicized black population. This highly racialized political struggle has left an ugly legacy of racial polarization that still contaminates race relations in most metro communities.

The ascendancy of black control of some major cities has contributed to the age-old fears and anxieties of whites concerning black political empowerment. A generation of white suburbanites has been fed a steady diet of fears and anxieties about the black inner cities. Many have justified their fears and anxieties by pointing to the tragic increase of crime and violence among inner-city black populations. They see no connection between racism and poverty; few white suburban political and business leaders have risen to the challenge of demythologizing these fears and anxieties with an active campaign of education.

In many white suburbs, an array of racial beliefs has grown up over the decades—beliefs that are remarkable in their similarities to the racial beliefs of the slave- and segregation-era South. Rather than examine the history of racism that has created the present problems of the black central city, many suburban whites blame the black victims of white racism. Far too many white suburbanites have grown comfortable with the image of black crime and poverty as permanent fixtures of the black central cities and have no wish to leave the comfort of their suburbs. They have developed a suburban culture that is inward looking and insular, oblivious to the problems of the black central cities.[2]

In 1985, Robert McCabe, then a relatively new white arrival in Detroit and president of Detroit Renaissance, commented, "It took me one week out here to find out what terrible feelings were expressed by suburbanites for the city. I'd find people who had . . . tremendous sense of pride that they haven't been in downtown Detroit in 15 years and don't intend to go" (McGill, 1985, p. 7a). My own teaching experiences confirm this. White students from metro-Detroit suburbs in my race relations history classes often share the racial fears, anxieties, and myths they have been taught by parents, friends, and educators in these suburbs. In my talks and workshops with white suburban teachers and administrators, I have pointed out that they are not preparing these young suburban whites to live in a more diverse 21st century.

Conversely, a generation of blacks came of age in the Coleman Young years who are as alienated from the white suburbs as the white suburbs are from them. And much like their white suburban counterparts, they have racial beliefs that, unlike many of the white suburban racial beliefs, are based on their experiences of deliberate racial exclusion. They are angry and hopeless and preoccupied with their survival. They see very little relevance in reaching out to whites in distant suburbs who they know fear and distrust them and really don't want them around. Above them are several layers of black professionals and leaders who grew up during the Coleman Young years of black political empowerment during which the white-suburban/black-central-city racial polarization reached its peak. Many of these young black professionals are not emotionally or ideologically prepared for transitioning to a new era of race relations in which a more complex pattern of racial and cultural diversity will soon replace the black-white pattern within the Detroit metropolitan community.

The Detroit Hispanic community has also been in a state of politicalization for many decades. Many Hispanics have felt alienated from the black political process and are understandably pushing for greater involvement in the future of Detroit's political and social life.

In the last decade and a half, conflicts between blacks and Arabs have moved to central stage in many poor, black neighborhoods. Arab store owners and black customers have found themselves embroiled in many conflicts, some leading to injury and death. These conflicts have contributed to the racial polarization of the larger metro community.

Economic and social development in the metropolitan community cannot be separated from the present state of race relations. As long as racial polarization is allowed to grow unchecked throughout the metropolitan community or is addressed in traditional, ineffectual crisis management ways, the metropolitan community will never develop to its fullest potential.

Given the dismal state of race relations in the metropolitan community, what role should the city of Detroit play in preparing this increasingly diverse metro-community for the 21st century? The first role is that of a vision builder for the creation of a racially unified metropolitan community. Detroit has a history of race relations that can enable it to take a leadership role in this process. It has a wealth of interracial experiences dating to World War I, with the cooperation between black and white leaders in the Urban League. It has a long history of alliances between the black community and labor, dating to the 1930s, that have often played a key role in fostering positive race relations. Detroit has shown a remarkable willingness and ability to heal deep racial wounds. One must only examine the efforts of the city to heal itself after the race riots of 1943 and 1967 to feel confident that it has the ability to foster a healing process in the larger metropolitan area (Thomas, 1987). Programs such as FOCUS: HOPE, the Race Relations Division of New Detroit, and the Race Relations Council of Metropolitan Detroit, along with various suburban organizations, have played key roles in the long struggle for racial justice and interracial cooperation between Detroit and its mostly white suburbs.[3]

At this juncture in the history of Detroit and its suburbs, however, there is the need for a more systemic long-term approach to address the racial polarization in the metro community. Traditional crisis management approaches to race relations are not sufficient for the task ahead. I cannot emphasize the critical importance of Detroit's playing the leading role as vision builder in preparing the community for the 21st century. In consultation with progressive elements in the suburbs, Detroit must embrace a credible vision of racial unity to guide the metropolitan community through the present stage of racial polarization to a future stage of racial unity. The city must resist the temptation to relegate race relations to the bottom of its policy agenda or to the institutional and organizational divisions of labor that presently exist within the race relations community. This fragmentation of race relations work has created problems of duplication and redundancy. All of the city's policies should be driven by a vision of metropolitan racial unity. Most race relations efforts, programs, and policies in metro-Detroit do not focus on a racial-unity, vision-driven, systems approach to racial unification.

A vision-driven, long-term, systemic race relations approach based on a racial unity model should be designed in consultation with religious and civic groups, race relations organizations, and community groups. A racial unity model of intervention is based on the principle of the oneness of the human race. Such a principle holds that all social, political, and economic problems in metropolitan communities are by their very nature interconnected—that they cannot be solved independently of each other. They must be approached systematically. Because racial polarization permeates the entire metropolitan community, it cannot be solved through piecemeal, unit-specific approaches. The approach must be systemic and based on the principle of the oneness of the human race. Thus, a new paradigm of race relations is needed: racial unity that is designed for systemic, long-term intervention.

Recommendations

The first step the city should take in this approach is to *adopt a racial-unity model as its major approach to race relations.* The city should consult with organizations, institutions, and communities that are already using some aspect of this model to understand its application to racial problems. One such community is the Detroit Bahá'í community, which was awarded a Community Award in 1993 by the Race Relations Council of Metropolitan Detroit "for establishing a monthly program that brings together people of different races, ethnicities, and faiths in each other's homes to discuss race relations issues." The Detroit Bahá'í community uses a racial unity model that has been developed and refined over many decades by its national body and by local Bahá'í communities throughout the country.[4] FOCUS: HOPE and New Detroit have both used aspects of this model. The city should hold workshops to introduce the model to all concerned people throughout the metropolitan community. Business, educational, civic, and religious leaders should be invited to consider this model in their approaches to their particular racial concerns. They should be encouraged to rethink their specific racial concerns within the context of the racial unity model.

The second step is for the city to *get key people throughout the metropolitan community to commit themselves to a long-term process of community building across racial, cultural, and economic boundaries based on a shared vision of metropolitan racial unity.* The shared-vision component is key. The city must lead the way in articulating the need for a shared vision of racial unity. It must emphasize the relationship between racial unity and social and economic progress throughout the metropolitan community. Detroit must not succumb to the race relations path of least resistance and opt for some short-term, traditional crisis management approach to the present crisis of racial polarization. Only a well-articulated, vision-driven, racial-unity process will succeed in breaking the metropolitan community out of the cycle of racial polarization and fragmentation.

The city should sponsor an envisioning workshop in which key people come together to envision what they would like race relations in the Detroit metropolitan community to look like in the next century. Racial unity based on the principle of the organic unity of the metropolitan community should be the framework in which this envisioning takes place.

The third step is for the city to *articulate race relations concerns and interests and formulate policies regarding race,* primarily within this racial unity framework. Such articulation and policy formulation will ensure increasing degrees of unity among other participants in the systemic, long-term approach throughout the metropolitan community and will decrease the problems of duplication and redundancy so characteristic of traditional race relations approaches.

Once the city is seen as taking the lead in unifying the racially polarized metro community by a clear articulation and support of a systemic, long-term, racial-unity approach that is basic to all of its social and economic programs, people will have more hope for the future of race relations within the metropolitan community. They will be encouraged by the organic relationship to other social and economic developments within the metropolitan community, such as improving the economic and social well-being of minority and poor communities, reducing crime and violence, healing the alienation of minority youth, and bridging the racial gap between suburban whites and inner-city blacks and Hispanics.

A final note of caution: The city must be prepared to face an uphill battle in introducing this new systemic, long-term, racial-unity model. The race relations field has been stuck in the reactive, crisis management mode for decades. Many race relations practitioners might feel threatened by this new race relations paradigm. To many experienced race relations workers, this approach will seem too visionary and ambitious. Many will want to maintain unit-specific, reactive approaches. The city must be prepared to point out that the present state of race relations in the Detroit metro community is too severe, and the extent of racial polarization has gone too far for traditional race relations interventions to work. Racial problems are systemic and deep. There is no shared vision of intervention. There are as many race relations approaches as there are race relations workers. The city must point out that the present state of racial polarization calls for the most ambitious undertaking that the metro community is capable of mobilizing. Nothing less than a racial-unity, systemic, long-term approach will break the metro community out of its cycle of racial polarization and move it into the cycle of racial unity; only within the cycle of racial unity will any metropolitan community be able to grow and prosper without continuous racial fear and anxiety about the future.

NOTES

1. For an example of black political struggles in Detroit, see Darden et al. (1987) and Rich (1989, pp. 61-167).

2. For an interesting analysis of the political ramifications of black-central-city/white-suburb polarization, see Edsall and Edsall (1992, pp. 215-255).

3. New Detroit has been a great model of racial healing for decades (see Fine, 1989, pp. 320-322).

4. For examples of how Bahá'ís have applied this model of racial unity to their community life, see Thomas (1993, chap. 8).

References

'Abdu'l-Bahá. (1982). *The promulgation of universal peace: Talks delivered by 'Abdu'l-Bahá during his visit to the United States and Canada in 1912* (2nd ed., H. MacNutt, Comp.). Wilmette, IL: Bahá'í Publishing Trust.

Allen, R. L. (1969). *Black awakening in capitalist America: An analytic history.* Garden City, NY: Anchor.

Appointment and function of the director of Negro economics, United States Department of Labor. (1918). *Monthly Labor Review, 7,* 37-38.

Aptheker, H. (Ed.). (1967). *A documentary history of the Negro people in the United States: From colonial times through the Civil War.* New York: Citadel.

Aptheker, H. (Ed.). (1973). *The correspondence of W. E. B. Du Bois: Vol. 1. Selections, 1877-1934.* Amherst: University of Massachusetts Press.

Aptheker, H. (1975, January-February). The history of anti-racism in the United States. *The Black Scholar,* pp. 16-22.

Arthur B. Spingarn. (1965). *Current biography yearbook, 26,* 398-399.

Ashmore, H. S. (1982). *Hearts and minds: The anatomy of racism from Roosevelt to Reagan.* New York: McGraw-Hill.

Askew, A. (1979). A friendship: Part two. In R. G. Blumberg & W. J. Roye (Eds.), *Interracial bonds* (pp. 186-190). New York: General Hall.

Bahá'u'lláh. (1976). *The hidden words of Bahá'u'lláh* (Rev. ed., S. Effendi, Trans.). Wilmette, IL: Bahá'í Publishing Trust.

Balyuzi, H. M. (1972). *'Abdu'l-Bahá: The center of the covenant of Bahá'u'lláh.* London: George Ronald.

Barnes, G. H., & Dumond, D. L. (Eds.). (1934). *Letters of Theodore Dwight Weld, Angelina Weld and Sarah Grimké 1822-1844* (Vol. 1). New York: D. Appleton-Century.

Bennett, L., Jr. (1969). *Black power U.S.: The human side of reconstruction, 1867-1877.* Baltimore: Penguin.

Bernstein, I. (1991). *Promises kept: John F. Kennedy's new frontier.* New York: Oxford University Press.

Berry, M. F. (1993). Blacks let Clinton slide on civil rights issues: Lani Guinier isn't the only example. *Emerge, 4*(10), 38-42.

Block, H. (1958). Craft unions and the Negro in historical perspectives. *Journal of Negro History, 42,* 10-33.

Blum, J. M. (1991). *Years of discord: American politics and society: 1961-1974.* New York: Norton.

Bond, J. (1923, February). The inter-racial commission of the South. *Opportunity, 1,* 13-14.

Boskin, J. (1976). The revolt of the urban ghettos. In J. Boskin (Ed.), *Urban racial violence in the twentieth century* (pp. 151-169). Beverly Hills, CA: Collier Macmillan.

Breen, T. H., & Innes, S. (1980). *Myne owne ground: Race and freedom on Virginia's eastern shores, 1640-1676.* New York: Oxford University Press.

Broderick, F. (1969). *W. E. B. Du Bois: A study in minority group leadership.* New York: Atheneum.

Brodie, F. M. (1959). *Thaddeus Stevens: Scourge of the South.* New York: Norton.

Brown, W. O. (1933, September). Interracial cooperation: Some of its problems. *Opportunity, 11,* 272-273, 285.

Bunche, R. J. (1973). *The political status of the Negro in the age of FDR.* Chicago: University of Chicago Press.

Calverton, V. J. (1927, January). The American Inter-Racial Association. *Opportunity, 5,* 23.

Carson, C. (1981). *In struggle: SNCC and the black awakening of the 1960s.* Cambridge, MA: Harvard University Press.

Chafe, W. H. (1989). Postwar American society: Dissent and social reform. In M. J. Lacey (Ed.), *The Truman presidency* (pp. 156-173). Cambridge, UK: Cambridge University Press.

Clayton, C. (1934, September). College interracialism in the South. *Opportunity, 12,* 267-269.

Collins, S. D. (1986). *The rainbow challenge: The Jackson campaign and the future of U.S. politics.* New York: Monthly Review Press.

Conrad, E. (1969). *Harriet Tubman.* New York: Paul S. Eriksson.

Crouthamel, J. L. (1976). The Springfield, Illinois, race riot of 1908. In J. Boskin (Ed.), *Urban racial violence in the twentieth century.* Beverly Hills, CA: Collier Macmillan.

Crowe, C. (1970). Tom Watson, populists, and blacks reconsidered. *Journal of Negro History, 55*(2), 99-116.

Darden, J. T., Hill, R. C., Thomas, J., & Thomas, R. W. (1987). *Detroit: Race and uneven development.* Philadelphia: Temple University Press.

Davis, M. D., & Clark, H. R. (1992). *Thurgood Marshall: Warrior at the bar, rebel on the bench.* New York: Birch Lance Press.

Du Bois, W. E. B. (1934a). Postscript by W. E. B. Du Bois. *Crisis, 41*(2), 52-53.

Du Bois, W. E. B. (1934b). Postscript by W. E. B. Du Bois. *Crisis, 41*(4), 115.

Du Bois, W. E. B. (1962). *John Brown.* New York: International Publishers.

Du Bois, W. E. B. (1964). *Black reconstruction in America: 1860-1880.* Cleveland: World Publishing Company. (Original work published 1935)

Du Bois, W. E. B. (1970). *Dusk of dawn: An essay toward an autobiography of a race concept.* New York: Schocken.

Du Bois, W. E. B. (1988). *The autobiography of W. E. B. Du Bois.* New York: International Publishers.

Editorials. (1935, November). *Opportunity, 13,* 327.

Edsall, T. B., & Edsall, M. D. (1992). *Chain reaction: The impact of race, rights, and taxes on American politics.* New York: Norton.

Fine, S. (1989). *Violence in the model city: The Cavanagh administration, race relations, and the Detroit riot of 1967.* Ann Arbor: University of Michigan Press.

Foner, P. S. (Ed.). (1950). *The life and writings of Fredrick Douglass (Vols. 1 and 2)*. New York: International Publishers.

Foner, P. S. (1981). *Organized labor and the black worker, 1619-1981*. New York: International Publishers.

Foster, A. L. (1929, March). A cooperative adventure in the field of race relations. *Opportunity, 7*, 98-99.

Franklin, J. H. (1993). *The color line: Legacy for the twenty-first century*. Columbia: University of Missouri Press.

Franklin, J. H., & Moss, A. A., Jr. (1988). *From slavery to freedom: A history of Negro Americans* (6th ed.). New York: McGraw-Hill.

Gara, L. (1967). *The liberty line: The legend of the underground railroad*. Lexington: University of Kentucky Press.

Georgakas, D., & Surkin, M. (1975). *Detroit: I do mind dying*. New York: St. Martin's.

Geschwender, J. (1977). *Class, race and worker insurgency: The league of revolutionary black workers*. New York: Cambridge University Press.

Giglio, J. N. (1991). *The presidency of John F. Kennedy*. Lawrence: University Press of Kansas.

Glatthaar, J. T. (1990). *Forged in battle: The Civil War alliance of black soldiers and white officers*. New York: Free Press.

Gordon, L. (1971). Attempts to bridge the racial gap: The religious establishment. In L. Gordon (Ed.), *A city in racial crisis: The case of Detroit—pre and post-the 1967 riot* (pp. 18-19). New York: William C. Brown.

Greenberg, J. (1994). *Crusaders in the courts*. New York: Basic Books.

Hacker, A. (1992). *Two nations: Black and white, separate, hostile, unequal*. Toronto: Scribner.

Harding, W. G. (1923, September). Letter from President Warren G. Harding to Mr. Eugene K. Jones, April 25, 1921. *Opportunity, 1*, 259.

Harlan, L. R. (Ed.). (1972a). *The Booker T. Washington papers* (Vol. 1). Urbana: University of Illinois Press.

Harlan, L. R. (Ed.). (1972b). *The Booker T. Washington papers* (Vol. 2). Urbana: University of Illinois Press.

Haynes, G. E. (1921). *The Negro at work during the war and reconstruction*. Washington, DC: Government Printing Office.

Hill, H. (1961). Racism within organized labor: A report of the five years of the AFL-CIO, 1955-1960. *Journal of Negro Education, 30*, 109-118.

Hill, H. (1969). Black protest and the struggle for union democracy. *Issues in Industrial Society, 1*(1), 19-29, 48.

Hixson, W. B., Jr. (1972). *Moorfield Storey and the abolitionist tradition*. New York: Oxford University Press.

Hughes, C. A. (1985). A new agenda for the South: The role and influence of the Highlander Folk School, 1953-61. *Phylon, 46*(3), 242-250.

Hughes, L. (1962). *Fight for freedom: The story of the NAACP*. New York: Norton.

Ives, H. C. (1976). *Portals to freedom* (Rev. ed.). London: George Ronald.

Jones, E. K. (1926, March). A practical year of interracial cooperation. *Opportunity, 3*, 98-102.

Jordan, W. D. (1969). *White over black: American attitudes towards the Negro, 1550-1812*. Baltimore: Penguin.

Kaufman, B. I. (1993). *The presidency of James E. Carter, Jr.* Lawrence: University Press of Kansas.

Kaufman, J. (1988). *Broken alliance: The turbulent times between blacks and Jews in America.* New York: Mentor.

Kellogg, C. F. (1969). Introduction. In M. W. Ovington, *Half a man: The status of the Negro in New York* (pp. xix-xx). New York: First American Century.

Kessler, S. H. (1952). The organization of Negroes in the Knights of Labor. *Journal of Negro History, 35*(11), 248-276.

Kluger, R. (1977). *Simple justice: The history of* Brown v. Board of Education *and black America's struggle for equality.* New York: Vintage.

Knotts, A. (1988). Race relations in the 1920s: A challenge to southern Methodist women. *Methodist History, 26*(4), 199-212.

Langston, D. (1993). The women of Highlander. In V. Crawford, J. A. Rose, & B. Woods (Eds.), *Women in the civil rights movement* (pp. 145-167). Bloomington: Indiana University Press.

Lasker, B. (1925, April). Some obstacles of race cooperation. *Opportunity, 2,* 101-104.

Lerner, G. (1963). The Grimké sisters and the struggle against race prejudice. *Journal of Negro History, 48*(4), 277-291.

Lerner, G. (1967). *The Grimké sisters from South Carolina: Pioneers for women's rights and abolition.* New York: Schocken.

Lewis, D. L. (1954). *History of Negro employment in Detroit area plants of Ford Motor Company, 1914-1941* [History seminar paper]. University of Michigan, Ann Arbor.

Lewis, D. L. (1993). *W. E. B. Du Bois, biography of a race, 1868-1919.* New York: Henry Holt.

Litwack, L. F. (1965). The emancipation of the Negro abolitionist. In M. Duberman (Ed.), *The antislavery vanguard: New essays on the abolitionists* (pp. 137-142). Princeton, NJ: Princeton University Press.

Lowery, C., & Marszalek, J. F. (1992). *Encyclopedia of African American civil rights: From the emancipation to the present.* New York: Greenwood.

Marshall, R. (1964). Unions and the Negro community. *Industrial and Labor Relations Review, 22,* 179-202.

Massey, D. S., & Denton, N. A. (1993). *American apartheid: Segregation and the making of the underclass.* Cambridge, MA: Harvard University Press.

McAdam, D. (1988). *Freedom summer.* New York: Oxford University Press.

McCoy, D. R. (1984). *The presidency of Harry S. Truman.* Lawrence: University Press of Kansas.

McGill, A. R. (1985, January 8). Race: A troublesome road toward a new era of trust. *Detroit News,* p. 7a.

Mehlinger, L. R. (1916). The attitude of the free Negro toward African colonization. *Journal of Negro History, 1*(3), 276-301.

Meier, A. (1954). Booker T. Washington and the rise of the NAACP. *Crisis, 61,* 69-76.

Meier, A. (1970). *Negro thought in America, 1880-1915.* Ann Arbor: University of Michigan Press.

Meier, A., & Rudwick, E. (1975). *CORE: A study in the civil rights movement.* Urbana: University of Illinois Press.

Meier, A., & Rudwick, E. (1979). *Black Detroit and the rise of the UAW.* New York: Oxford University Press.

Meltzer, M. (1967). *Thaddeus Stevens and the fight for Negro rights.* New York: Thomas Y. Crowell.

Models of unity: Racial, ethnic, and religious. (1992). Chicago: Human Relations Foundation of Chicago and National Spiritual Assembly of the Bahá'ís of the United States.

Morrison, G. (1982). *To move the world: Louis G. Gregory and the advancement of racial unity in America.* Wilmette, IL: Bahá'í Publishing Trust.

Nalty, B. C. (1986). *Strength for the fight: A history of black Americans in the military.* New York: Free Press.

Nash, G. G. (1990). *Race and revolution.* Madison, WI: Madison House.

New Detroit. (1990). *1990 annual report: Focus Hope.* Detroit, MI: Author.

Oates, S. B. (1984). *To purge this land with blood: A biography of John Brown.* Amherst: University of Massachusetts Press.

Orenstein, G. F. (1979). A friendship: Part one. In R. G. Blumberg & W. J. Roye (Eds.), *Interracial bonds* (pp. 175-185). New York: General Hall.

Ovington, M. W. (1927). *Portraits in color.* New York: Viking.

Ovington, M. W. (1947). *The walls came tumbling down.* New York: Harcourt Brace.

Pilkington, C. K. (1985, Spring). The trials of brotherhood: The founding of the Commission on Interracial Cooperation. *Georgia Historical Quarterly, 69,* 55-80.

Plastrik, S. (1973, Winter). Coalition of black trade unionists. *Dissent,* pp. 12-13.

Quarles, B. (1938). The breach between Douglass and Garrison. *Journal of Negro History, 23,* 144-154.

Quarles, B. (1961). *The Negro in the American Revolution.* Chapel Hill: University of North Carolina Press.

Quarles, B. (1968). *Frederick Douglass.* New York: Atheneum.

Quarles, B. (1969). *Black abolitionists.* New York: Oxford University Press.

Record, W. (1971). *The Negro and the communist party.* New York: Atheneum.

Reed, L. (1991). *Simple decency and common sense: The Southern Conference Movement, 1938-1963.* Bloomington: Indiana University Press.

Rich, W. C. (1989). *Coleman Young and Detroit politics.* Detroit, MI: Wayne State University.

Ross, B. J. (1972). *J. E. Spingarn and the rise of the NAACP, 1911-1939.* New York: Atheneum.

Rudwick, E. (1972). *Race riot at East St. Louis July 12, 1917.* New York: Atheneum.

Saunders, R. (1969). Southern populists and the Negro, 1893-1895. *Journal of Negro History, 54,* 250-254.

Schofield, J. W., & McGivern, E. P. (1979). Creating interracial bonds in a desegregated school. In R. G. Blumberg & W. J. Roye (Eds.), *Interracial bonds* (pp. 106-119). New York: General Hall.

Scott, E. J. (1969). *Negro migration during the war.* New York: Arno Press and the New York Times. (Original work published 1920)

Sitkoff, H. (1978). *A new deal for blacks: The emergence of civil rights as a national issue: The depression decade.* New York: Oxford University Press.

Spiller, G. (Ed.). (1970). *Inter-racial problems: Papers from the first universal races congress held in London in 1911* (Rev. ed.). New York: Citadel.

Spingarn, J. E. (1934). Segregation—A symposium. *Crisis, 41*(3), 79-80.

Stampp, K. M. (1967). *The era of reconstruction, 1865-1877.* New York: Vintage.

Stanfield, J. H. (1987, Summer). Northern money and Southern bogus elitism: Rockefeller Foundation and the Commission on Interracial Cooperation Movement, 1919-1929. *Journal of Ethnic Studies, 15,* 1-22.

Steele, C. H. (1979). Bonds between Indians and other racial groups in an urban setting. In R. G. Blumberg & W. J. Roye (Eds.), *Interracial bonds* (pp. 36-51). New York: General Hall.

Steele, J. D. (1929, April). Principles which should govern the relations of white and colored people in the United States. *Opportunity, 7,* 288-290.

Terkel, S. (1992). *Race: How blacks and whites think and feel about the American obsession.* New York: New Press.

Thomas, B. P. (1973). *Theodore Weld: Crusader for freedom.* New York: Octagon.

Thomas, R. (1987). Looking forward: The Detroit experience after the riots of 1943 and 1967. In J. Benyon & J. Solomos (Eds.), *The roots of urban unrest* (pp. 148-151). New York: Pergamon.

Thomas, R. W. (1992). *Life for us is what we make it: Building black community in Detroit, 1915-1945.* Bloomington: Indiana University Press.

Thomas, R. (1993). *Racial unity: An imperative for social progress* (2nd ed.). Ottawa: Association of Bahá'í Studies.

Thomas, R. (1994, March). *The role of the city in unifying a racially polarized metropolitan community.* Paper presented at the After Coleman Young: Detroit in Transition, Urban Policy Conference, East Lansing, MI.

Thurman, H. (1979). *With head and heart.* New York: Harcourt Brace.

Tushnet, M. V. (1987). *The NAACP's legal strategy against segregated education, 1925-1954.* Chapel Hill: University of North Carolina Press.

Tygiel, J. (1984). *Baseball's great experiment: Jackie Robinson and his legacy.* New York: Vintage.

Visions of race unity: Race unity conference. (1992). Atlanta, GA: National Spiritual Assembly of the Bahá'ís of the United States.

Ward, A. L. (1979). *234 days: 'Abdu'l-Bahá'í's journey in America.* Wilmette, IL: Bahá'í Publishing Trust.

Washington, J. M. (Ed.). (1986). *The essential writings and speeches of Martin Luther King, Jr.* New York: HarperCollins.

Weiss, N. J. (1974). *The national Urban League, 1910-1940.* New York: Oxford University Press.

West, C. (1994). *Race matters.* New York: Vintage.

White, W. (1947). Foreword. In M. W. Ovington, *The walls came tumbling down.* New York: Harcourt, Brace, and Company.

Wiebe, R. H. (1979). White attitudes and black rights from Brown to Bakke. In M. V. Namorato (Ed.), *Have we overcome: Race relations since Brown* (pp. 165-171). Jackson: University Press of Mississippi.

Williamson, J. (1986). *A rage for order: Black-white relations in the American South since emancipation.* New York: Oxford University Press.

Wood, F. G. (1990). *The arrogance of faith: Christianity and race in America from the colonial era to the twentieth century.* New York: Knopf.

Woodward, C. V. (1974). *The strange career of Jim Crow.* New York: Oxford University Press.

Zangrando, R. L. (1980). *The NAACP crusade against lynching, 1909-1950.* Philadelphia: Temple University Press.

Index

About the Author

Richard W. Thomas is a Professor of History and Urban Affairs Programs at Michigan State University (MSU) and President and Founder of New World Associates, Inc., a race relations consulting service. He has taught at MSU since 1971 and has lectured and conducted workshops on race relations throughout the United States, as well as in Canada, England, and Switzerland, for more than 20 years. He is author and coauthor of several books on race relations and the African American experience, including *Detroit: Race and Uneven Development* and *Racial Unity: An Imperative for Social Progress.* In 1995, he was awarded the Wesley-Logan Prize by the American Historical Association and the Association for the Study of Afro-American Life and History for his book *Life for Us Is What We Make It: Building the Black Community in Detroit, 1915-1945.*